LINCOLN   FREEDOM

Lincoln
and Black Freedom:

A Study in Presidential Leadership

by LaWanda Cox

University of South Carolina Press

Copyright © University of South Carolina 1981
Published in Columbia, S.C., by the
University of South Carolina Press, 1981
FIRST EDITION
Manufactured in the United States of America

Library of Congress Cataloging in Publication Data

Cox, LaWanda C. Fenlason.
Lincoln and black freedom: etc

1. Lincoln, Abraham, 1809–1865—Relations with Afro-Americans. 2. Afro-Americans—History—To 1863. 3. Afro-Americans—History—1863–1877. I. Title.
E457.2.C84   973.7′092′4   81-3350
ISBN 0-87249-400-4   (AACR2)

To
The memory of
My husband and fellow historian
JOHN H. COX

Contents

Preface

This volume was not deliberately conceived. It has been written in response to a challenge that came in three disparate reactions to a reading of the deleted first section of a documentary manuscript too lengthy for publication in its entirety. The collection had been undertaken at the invitation of Richard B. Morris as general editor of the series, *Documentary History of the United States*. Our goal was a sourcebook centered on the issue of the black man's status that would be useful, comprehensive, and provocative. The published volume, *Reconstruction, the Negro, and the New South*, begins with the conflict between President Andrew Johnson and Congress in early 1866; what remained of the original manuscript opened with the presidential message of March 1862 on gradual compensated emancipation and dealt largely with Lincoln's reconstruction policy. One reader asked for an epilogue in which "the Coxes would ... look back ... and give us their thoughts on the ultimate meaning of these documents, both for their own time and for the future of American race relations." A second had himself discovered an ultimate meaning, an "implicit conclusion ... that the death of Lincoln was a disaster." Unlike Andrew Johnson, his successor, "Lincoln would have joined with the radicals or at least the moderates in seeking to guarantee the basic civil rights of the former slave." The third reader saw as a purpose of the volume "that Lincoln proceeded, logically and irresistibly, to his Emancipation Proclamation out of some deeply rooted principle or belief."

After the death of my husband and collaborator, the idea of a second documentary collection was abandoned, but the challenge of the three readers bedeviled me. In the pages that follow I try to resolve the nagging questions. Was Lincoln, indeed, impelled to emancipation and civil rights for freedmen by the irresistible logic of a deeply rooted belief? As president, had he led or did he lag, as many thought, in respect to black freedom? Of what import was the quality of his presidential leadership? Could Lincoln—could any decision-makers at the nation's capital—have insured substantive freedom and equal citizenship for the ex-slave?

To attempt an answer to such questions may be presumptuous and foolhardy in view of their elusive nature, the wealth of old and new Lincoln scholarship, and the vigorous reexamination now underway of the black experience and the roots of poverty in the postemancipation South. Nevertheless, I have ventured.

My approach to the challenge of this undertaking has been one of reflection rather than research. Yet mine have been reflections not from the quiet contemplation of an armchair but from the clutter of my study, an intermittent dialogue over a number of years with books, notes, manuscripts, papers published and unpublished. Indeed they led beyond my study in pursuit of evidence not previously examined, most importantly to the Salmon P. Chase Papers of the Library of Congress and of the Historical Society of Pennsylvania. In the company of Mr. Lincoln even the rediscovery of the familiar is an intellectual adventure, and to that has been added the excitement of an occasional fresh clue, a different reading, the emergence of a variant "Lincoln image," and the drama of events in Lincoln's Louisiana that might have changed the course of Reconstruction. The results of my inquiry are presented with awareness of the hazard in what I have attempted: to probe the historic boundaries of the possible, and to enlarge our knowledge of Lincoln's role in this nation's yet uncompleted passage from slavery into freedom.

Acknowledgments

How so large an indebtedness could have been incurred in the writing of so small a volume, I cannot explain, only acknowledge.

Librarians and archivists have extended many courtesies, some beyond the call of duty and others which fall within their regular pattern of assistance yet constitute an extraordinary service. I wish to thank in the National Archives both those who searched and found and those who searched in vain, Elaine C. Everly, William D. Grover, James Harwood, and George P. Perros. Members of the Manuscript Division of the Library of Congress have unfailingly provided help to me both in person and by mail; I am particularly indebted to Paul T. Heffron and John C. Broderick. Similarly I have received ready assistance from Rodney G. Dennis and Mrs. Richard B. Currier of the Houghton Library of Harvard University, from James E. Mooney and his staff of the Historical Society of Pennsylvania, from Collin B. Hamer and his associates of the Louisiana Division of the New Orleans Public Library. In addition, my inquiries about specific documents have brought prompt and careful attention from the Library of the Boston Athenaeum, the State Historical Society of Missouri, the Southern Historical Collection of the University of North Carolina Library, the Manuscript Division of the University of Rochester Library, the Connecticut Historical Society, the Huntington Library, and the Louisiana State University Library. Here at home I have profited from the resources of the New York Public Library. Finally, a word of appreciation for the Library of the New York Historical Society, which manages despite the pressures of the present age to maintain not only its traditional standards of excellence in service but also a special graciousness.

Over a number of years, Peyton McCrary and I have corresponded about matters of importance to an understanding of wartime Reconstruction in Louisiana. I have greatly profited from his expert knowledge of the subject and from his generosity in sharing with me several elusive documents he uncovered. His interpretation of events I have found reassuring where we agree and challenging where we differ.

As a "traditional" historian who has welcomed the contribution of the quantifiers but at times felt overwhelmed by their methods and vocabulary, I owe a very personal debt to two who expertly practice the skills, and one who interprets them lucidly without fear or favor— Gavin Wright, Stanley L. Engerman, and Harold D. Woodman. All three have come to my assistance, and our exchange has not been limited to the quantifiable; I have gained from the special insight that each brings to an analysis of the postbellum South.

A number of other scholars have also been generous in sharing with me their expertise in matters of substance and of bibliography: William Cohen on black migration, LeRoy P. Graf and David W. Bowen on Andrew Johnson, Herman Belz on the concept of legitimacy, Harold M. Hyman and John Niven in my fruitless search for two key missing documents of presidential Reconstruction. I have also had the privilege of an extended interview with W. Arthur Lewis, who kindly acceded to my request for a perspective based upon his broad knowledge of the problems of development in areas of poverty. Needless to say, those with whom I consulted have no responsibility for the views at which I have arrived, views with which in a number of instances they will doubtless disagree.

In the footnotes, and not infrequently in the text, I have tried to indicate my debt to the scholarship of others upon whose work this effort must of necessity draw heavily. I have made a special effort to indicate those secondary accounts that have alerted me to specific documents of importance which otherwise would not have come to my attention and to recognize recent work in the field. Since the relevant scholarly literature is vast, and my acquaintance with it extends back many years, it has not been possible to account for all indebtedness.

The Political History Group of the Institute for Research in History, of which I am a member, heard an early version of Chapter Five.

ACKNOWLEDGMENTS

I have benefited from their lively comments, varied special knowledge, and comparative perspectives.

During my "affair with Mr. Lincoln" friends have shown me great tolerance. Their letters have piled up without replies, their invitations have been neglected, their otherwise carefree moments have been encumbered by my struggle with the imponderables of the past. For their forbearance I am grateful. To three such good friends I am doubly indebted. Each has read with close attention to detail my manuscript in its entirety—Catherine Pabst, Madeleine Hooke Rice, and Hans Trefousse. The text is much the better for their red pencils and suggestions.

LaWanda Cox
New York City
October 1980

The Record Reexamined

CHAPTER ONE

" 'Can we *all* do better?' "

In respect to the changing status of southern blacks, emancipation and Reconstruction can be viewed as a single continuing process. Because the subordination of the black man, as slave and as nonslave, had helped shape southern life and institutions in an intimate, pervasive manner, any substantial change in the antebellum relationship between blacks and whites meant a reconstruction of southern society. After Sumter, the North under the leadership of Abraham Lincoln set out to "restore" the South but soon found itself involved in "reconstruction."[1]

War waged on southern soil acted as a corrosive upon the South's peculiar institution. However, to attribute slavery's destruction to war, and the ready response of blacks to the opportunity it afforded,[2] can be misleading. Neither Congress nor president waited passively for slavery's disintegration; action was essential if escape from bondage was to be extended to all and freedom guaranteed by the destruction of the institution itself.

A generation removed by more than a century from a legal order that sanctioned the ownership of human beings, and one keenly aware of the problems remaining once the legal institution was destroyed, is apt to take its destruction for granted and look to history only for the limitations upon black freedom.[3] Such a perspective distorts the historical record. Slavery in the United States had been a tenacious institution protected by the Constitution and aggressively defended by nearly half the states of the Union; it was an institution in effect untouchable by

[3]

legal means in time of peace. The war powers of Congress and president opened it to attack, but the limits of those powers were uncertain and highly controversial. Nor was the questionable authority of the nation over a state institution the only obstacle to slavery's wartime destruction. Slave states loyal to the Union had no intention of surrendering the institution, and further north the Democratic party exploited the resentment of those men of the free states who would preserve the nation but not willingly fight to liberate the slave. A tortuous road led to the great decisions that changed the legal status of all southern bondsmen from slave to free. The end was in sight when Lincoln died, for the Thirteenth Amendment had finally cleared Congress on January 31, 1865, though it was not declared the law of the land until the following December.

Both for those who eagerly would destroy slavery and for those who came reluctantly to accept its end, it was strategic, and comforting as well, to declare slavery a casualty of armed conflict. Despite many such statements, during 1863 and 1864 antislavery men feared the battle against the South's peculiar institution might yet be lost or compromised. However inevitable slavery's end may appear in retrospect, contemporary concern was real, and not without cause. Thus in assessing Lincoln's role, it is essential to keep clearly in mind two facts obscured by the intervening century: the destruction of slavery as an institution was the first essential for equal citizenship and, at least until the fall elections of 1864, there was no assurance that slavery would be totally destroyed.

That the freeing of slaves and the destruction of slavery as an institution carried an implication beyond the elimination of property in human beings was generally recognized. So long as victory over slavery appeared uncertain, however, the question of the ex-slave's status in freedom remained secondary. Both were partisan issues, subject not only to the usual vagaries of politics but also to the exceptional uncertainty of a two-party contention sharply divided on the questions of slavery and race. Democratic victory, with control of Congress and the White House, would have reversed the wartime momentum for emancipation and equal status. The constitutionally binding decisions first for freedom and then for equal citizenship were made by the Republican party for the nation without the support of the northern Democracy or the free consent of the South. A party position as to the status of the freedman was emerging but had not yet found official sanction at the time of Lincoln's death. It was formulated and enacted into law in the face of presidential opposition from his successor.

The presidential leadership of Abraham Lincoln, and of Andrew Johnson, as it affected the effort to change the status of blacks, was critically influenced by each man's attitudes toward slavery and race. Those of Lincoln have been the subject of major historical controversy.[4] On one crucial point, however, most Lincoln scholars agree—Lincoln held a deeply felt conviction that slavery was morally wrong and should be placed on the road to extinction. In championing a moderate program of denying slavery expansion in the territories rather than joining with abolitionists in calling for a more immediate solution, Lincoln did not disguise his immoderate goal. However unrealistic his expectations, he believed that geographic restriction would ultimately result in slavery's destruction. Yet an incongruity existed in the limits of his policy and the sweep of his moral condemnation. He based the latter upon the authority of the Declaration of Independence, upon its principle that all men (not whites alone) are born equal and entitled to inalienable rights. For Lincoln, limited policy and sweeping principle were morally compatible. During one of the debates with Douglas in 1858, he advanced the explanation. In defense of the men who had fought for the revolutionary principles of equality and freedom, and then established a government that recognized slavery, he argued that to the extent "a necessity is imposed upon a man, he must submit to it." Slavery existed, and agreement on the Constitution could not have been had without permitting slavery to remain. But necessity did not invalidate the standard raised in the Declaration of Independence:[5]

> So I say in relation to the principle that all men are created equal, let it be as nearly reached as we can.

Lincoln's succinct admonition can illuminate his antislavery record as president. It captures a drive, a goal, a fundamental attitude toward men—white or black—consistent with his actions and thus

[5]

provides a useful perspective from which to examine his role as leader. When war opened possibilities unapproachable in the 1850s, Lincoln's reach was not found wanting. Indeed, there is something breathtaking in his advance from prewar advocacy of restricting slavery's spread to foremost responsibility for slavery's total, immediate, uncompensated destruction by constitutional amendment. The progression represented a positive exercise of leadership. It has often been viewed as a reluctant accommodation to pressures; it can better be understood as a ready response to opportunity. Willing to settle for what was practicable, provided it pointed in the right direction, Lincoln was alert to the expanding potential created by war. Military needs, foreign policy, Radical agitation did not force him upon an alien course but rather helped clear a path toward a long-desired but intractable objective. Having advanced, Lincoln recognized the danger of a forced retreat, a retreat to be forestalled with certainty only by military victory and constitutional amendment. His disclaimer of credit for "the removal of a great wrong" which he attributed to "God alone," though in a sense accurate, for the process of emancipation did not follow his or any man's design, was nonetheless misleading.

After preservation of the Union, the most pressing of the "necessities" to which Lincoln felt compelled to submit as an antislavery man were those imposed by his respect for the Constitution and for government based upon consent. He shared with his generation, Republicans and Democrats alike, a profound attachment to what J. G. Randall called "the American people's underlying sense of constitutional government." In imposing radical change upon the South, the Republican majority sought to "keep right" with their heritage of self-government under law, never shed a repugnance for revolutionary means. Alfred H. Kelly and Harold M. Hyman have made this unmistakable; even radical Republicans, to use their words, " 'rejected without serious debate the argument for revolutionary legitimacy' " because they were "incurably Constitution-bound."[6] Both Lincoln and his party would bend, if neither would break, allegiance to Constitution and majority consent, but they did not necessarily agree as to what was justifiable.

[6]

The constraints under which Lincoln felt he must labor were not always recognized by antislavery men, and this gave rise to charges of irresolute policy and wavering commitment. In striving for consent, he would tailor an argument to fit his hearer. To develop public support or outflank opposition, he would at times conceal his hand or dissemble. And he kept his options open. While such skills added to his effectiveness, they also sowed mistrust and confusion. Similarly misunderstanding arose from his constitutional scruples, which he applied to congressional action as well as his own. Also diminishing the recognition of his leadership was the vanguard position of the Radicals. That he marched behind them should not obscure the fact that Lincoln was well in advance of northern opinion generally and at times in advance of a consensus within his own party. Viewed against his deference to the processes of persuasion and the limitations set by the Constitution, the persistence and boldness of his actions against slavery are striking.

Lincoln took the initiative against slavery March 6, 1862, when he sent to Congress a special message on gradual, compensated emancipation. This early proposal was so legally conservative in its apparent deference to the rights of states, loyal or disloyal, and so unproductive of any border-state action as to obscure the audacity of the executive initiative and its radical contemporary significance. At the time, Congress had not yet taken any action against slavery as such. The Confiscation Act of August 1861 would affect only slaves used by the South for strictly military purposes; the first legislation to attack slavery in a direct though geographically limited way, the bill to abolish slavery in the District of Columbia, had yet to pass either house. Lincoln's message, on the other hand, officially linked general emancipation with the war effort. He defended his proposal as one of "self-preservation" which would destroy hope in the Confederacy by encouraging a first step against slavery in the loyal border states and thereby "substantially end the rebellion."[7] The offer of federal financial aid was not limited to loyal states.

The message took Congress and the public by surprise. The most important black newspaper of the period "could hardly believe the news" and after close scrutiny, and some delay, enthusiastically pronounced it "half silent evidence of power and will to blast the institution of slavery at any moment." The interpretation was justified, not only in retrospective knowledge of the Emancipation Proclamation but by the implications that can be glimpsed in the wording of the message despite its ambiguity and its "impregnable armor" against constitutional objections. What was asked of Congress would be "merely initiatory" and not "itself a practical measure," but it was Lincoln's express "hope that it would soon lead to important practical results." In "earnestly beg[ging] the attention of Congress and the people," Lincoln rejected the suggestion that he substitute "respectfully" for "earnestly." And Lincoln's earnestness was "in full view of my great responsibility to my God, and to my country." In this first major antislavery document of his presidency the word order of "God" and "country" may be not unworthy of note.[8]

The importance Lincoln attached to his proposal is confirmed by a letter of Wendell Phillips which has only recently come to light. Phillips was lecturing in Washington. Lincoln had his private secretaries attend the lectures, then sent word that he would like to see Phillips at the White House. The meeting lasted more than an hour with Phillips finding it "hard to get a word in edgewise" because the president "talked so fast & constantly." What Lincoln talked about was the March 6 message. He told Phillips that he had worked three months on it "—all by himself, no conference with his cabinet." Phillips spoke well of it, but Lincoln "did not think I valued the message quite enough & as usual told a story." The story was of an Irishman in legally dry Maine who asked for a glass of soda with "a drop of the crathur [put] into it *unbeknown to myself.*" Lincoln made his point explicit: he "meant *it* [slavery] *should die.*" Phillips wrote his wife that he left feeling "*rather encouraged.* He [Lincoln] is better than his Congress fellows." Phillips' confidence in Lincoln was grudgingly given. "He struck me as perfectly honest," Phillips wrote, "but a man of very *slow mind.*"[9] And the confidence did not prove to be long-lived.

The March 6 message brought quick action in Congress but not in the loyal slave states. Lincoln had included the text of a joint resolution which he asked to be adopted "substantially" as worded. On March 11 it passed the House and on April 2 the Senate. No Republican voted against it, and there was even a scattering of Yea votes from northern Democrats and border-state Unionists. The day before the House vote, Lincoln had focused his persuasive powers upon a group of border-state representatives at a White House conference arranged through Postmaster General Montgomery Blair. When no state action followed the Senate's concurrence, Lincoln persisted. On July 12 he read a prepared appeal to another assembled group of border men. Two days later he sent to Congress in a second special message on emancipation a draft bill that would compensate any state abolishing slavery "either immediately, or gradually" with 6 percent interest-bearing bonds of the United States. There was protest in the Senate that the president had no right to introduce a bill in Congress. In the House, a measure limited to loyal states acting within five years was introduced but not brought to a vote before adjournment.[10]

When Congress reassembled in December, Lincoln, undaunted by objections to his drafting a bill, included in his annual message the text of a proposed constitutional amendment of three articles complete except for the rate of interest on bonds and the amount of compensation for each slave. Earlier presidents undeterred by John Quincy Adams' objection to the propriety of such action, had suggested amendments, but usually they had done so in vague general terms. None had been so audacious as to ask passage of a fully drafted proposal.[11]

Arguments available to Lincoln in trying to induce slave-state representatives to initiate gradual, compensated emancipation could not in the nature of things match his earnestness. They were unpersuasive to most border-state Unionists and when reread today appear singularly unconvincing. Lincoln could not argue the moral wrong of slavery, for that would not touch those he would move. He could not press the point that permanent peace would require an end to slavery, for no peace was in sight. His principal contention was that state action would "substantially end" or effectively "shorten the war." The valid counterargument, used by those to whom he appealed, held that emancipation would consolidate the spirit of rebellion.[12] Lincoln's effort to enlist, or at least neutralize, economic interest by portraying compensation for slaves as money saved from the cost of war depended upon his main contention that the war would be shortened and was similarly vulnerable. More cogent in retrospect was his argument that, for slaveholders, compensation in hand was far better than being left with "nothing valuable" as the abrasive impact of war undermined slavery; yet in 1862 slavery's extinction did not appear foreordained, nor in fact was its fate settled.

In his eagerness to persuade, Lincoln gave or implied assurances that skirted the edge of credibility. After the March White House conference, its participants recorded what they understood as a commitment from Lincoln that he would countenance no direct or indirect coercive action by the federal government for emancipation—they also recorded his unwillingness to have his words made public lest they "force a quarrel" with the " 'Greeley faction.' " A few months later, on the eve of his decision to issue an emancipation proclamation, he did not go so far as to forswear federal action, but he did dissemble. He urged the border-state men to act in order to relieve him and the country from pressure for military emancipation. Understandably, his implication that action against slavery in the border states would mute the call for military emancipation did not appear persuasive to his listeners.[13]

Lincoln's extraordinary effort on behalf of gradual, compensated emancipation is often interpreted as reflecting an overriding concern for moderation, an effort to forestall more radical measures. His actions are more consistent with the view that he sought the largest possible degree of legal security and popular acceptance for an initial move against slavery. There was nothing moderate about emancipation by executive proclamation, upon which he decided in mid-July and acted in September. Lincoln may have preferred gradualism, but he certainly did not insist upon it. Both his July and his December messages sanctioned immediate emancipation. The constitutional amendment he offered in December, which looked to state action over a period extending to 1900, was neither so gradualist nor so compensatory as it appeared. Lincoln's text contained a provision of dramatic potential.

Article two would make "forever free" all slaves "who shall enjoy actual freedom by the chances of war, at any time before the end of the rebellion." And only loyal owners would be compensated!

Less dramatic but of far-reaching significance in view of the existing legal structure of state-national authority was Lincoln's turning to *federal* action on slavery by seeking a constitutional amendment. Interestingly, his concern that wartime *de facto* freedom be made irreversible, a concern that often surfaced after he issued the final Emancipation Proclamation, had found official expression in his proposed amendment before he signed the proclamation. This concern, like the weak logic and subterfuge in his appeal to border men, argues that Lincoln did not approach emancipation solely as a device for winning the war. So does his timing. He initiated a proposal for general emancipation in March 1862, at a time when General Grant's victories in the west still cheered Union men, and he persisted in efforts to obtain a constitutional amendment in late 1864 and early 1865 when military victory was in sight.

Lincoln's antislavery impulse is reflected also in the words with which he urged upon Congress his constitutional proposal of December 1862. His appeal for action closed with one of Lincoln's most eloquent passages. He began: "Fellow-citizens, *we* cannot escape history"; he concluded: "The way is plain, peaceful, generous, just—a way which if followed, the world will forever applaud, and God must forever bless." Lincoln's fervor is consonant not with the moderation of the means he proposed but with the virtue of the end in sight, the destruction of slavery. His appeal sought primarily to remove the objections of proslavery men, but it also addressed those who wished more drastic immediate action. He challenged them not on the desirability of more radical measures but on the possibility of obtaining them. His words revealed Lincoln's continuing pragmatic aim and strategy in respect to slavery: "It is not 'can *any* of us *imagine* better?' but 'can we *all* do better?' Object whatsoever is possible, still the question recurs 'can we do better?' "[14]

Lincoln's concern for a firm constitutional base for emancipation was consistent, although it did not prevent him from taking action that he recognized might not withstand judicial scrutiny. In defending his revocation in September 1861 of General John C. Frémont's order to free insurgents' slaves in Missouri, Lincoln had implied that congressional authority in the matter was probably more extensive than his own; later he arrived at the conclusion that the war powers of Congress were less ample than those of the commander in chief. In framing a veto of the Confiscation Act of July 1862, one made public but never exercised, Lincoln struggled with the problem of how to emancipate legally. He criticized the bill's provisions for freeing the slaves of rebels only to suggest a restatement that would strengthen their legal force: "It is startling to say that congress can free a slave within a state; and yet if it were said the ownership of the slave had first been transferred to the nation, and that congress had then liberated, him, the difficulty would at once vanish."[15]

Until the final Emancipation Proclamation, Lincoln left open an avenue of retreat from executive action, which aroused misgivings among antislavery men. Yet the possibility embodied in the September proclamation that rebel states renew their allegiance before January and thereby escape emancipation, was highly unlikely. Moreover, Lincoln's plea in December for his constitutional amendment was a clear indication that any southern state returning would be subject to continuing pressure to end slavery. The "hundred days" between proclamations simply strengthened the case Lincoln had been building for his action.

It was characteristic of Lincoln that between his July decision for emancipation and the September proclamation he could keep his intent secret from the public, even appear to deny it. There is the well-known reply to Greeley of August 22 where he vowed that his paramount object was to save the Union, whether that meant freeing no slave, freeing all slaves, or "freeing some and leaving others alone." In reply to a petition presented on behalf of Chicago Christians of all denominations, Lincoln likened an emancipation proclamation to "the Pope's bull against the comet" and engaged in an hour of discussion raising objections and drawing out counterarguments. Significantly, he raised "no objections against it on legal or constitutional grounds; for, as commander-in-chief of the army and navy, in time of war, I suppose I have a right to take any measure which may best subdue the enemy."[16]

The rub was whether a presidential proclamation of emancipation would "best subdue the enemy." While few except Lincoln's political opponents have questioned the military and foreign policy advantages of the Emancipation Proclamation, another commander in chief no less committed to victory, but not equally moved by the principles of the Declaration of Independence and the evil of slavery, would not necessarily have agreed with Lincoln that the proclamation was his only alternative to "surrendering the Union." Its consequences could not be projected with certainty; its effect upon enlistments, upon the loyalty of border states, upon the morale of fighting men South as well as North held potential dangers for the Union cause. It was a policy, to use Lincoln's own words, "about which hope, and fear, and doubt contended in uncertain conflict." In choosing it "I hoped for greater gain than loss; but of this, I was not entirely confident."[17] Lincoln's concern that the proclamation might hinder rather than advance Union fortunes was quieted only after the event.

It must have taken great restraint for a man with so eloquent a way with words and so firm a conviction of the wrong of slavery to have fashioned the Emancipation Proclamation in a style that has been likened to that of a bill of lading. An obscure news item appearing the day before its issuance is worth quoting at length for its explicit and apparently authoritative explanation:[18]

The President has been strongly pressed to place the Proclamation of Freedom *upon high moral grounds, and to introduce into the instrument unequivocal language testifying to the negroes' right to freedom upon the precise principles expounded by* the Emancipationists of both Old and New England. This claim is resisted, for the reasons that policy requires that the Proclamation be issued as a war measure, and not a measure of morality; and that Law and Justice require that the slaves should be enabled to plead the Proclamation hereafter if necessary to establish judicially their title to freedom. They can do this, the President says, on a proclamation *proceeding as a war measure from the Commander-in-Chief of the Army, but not on one issuing from the bosom of philanthropy.*

[13]

Lincoln clearly recognized that as president he had no legal power to act against slavery because it was a moral wrong. That he struggled to subordinate his antislavery convictions to his conception of the powers and duty of the presidency cannot be doubted. To those who opposed his antislavery initiatives, or found them difficult to support, Lincoln was quick to defend his motives as those of commander in chief rather than of moralist by earnestly affirming his "good faith" and arguing the "necessity" of emancipation. At times he seemed to deny any connection between his moral conviction and his official action, but on occasion he presented his case with more subtlety. Most revealing of his justifications was the "little speech" which he made to two influential Kentuckians who in the spring of 1864 came to confer with him about border-state dissatisfaction with his policy. At their request he subsequently put its substance into writing. Lincoln opened with the unqualified statement that he was "naturally antislavery. If slavery is not wrong, nothing is wrong." Yet he understood that the presidency did not confer "upon me an *unrestricted* right to act officially upon this judgment and feeling. . . . And I aver that, to this day, I have done no official act in *mere* deference to my abstract judgment and feeling on slavery." Lincoln continued with the argument of "indispensable necessity" for emancipation and arming blacks, but at the same time acknowledged as quoted above that he had not been entirely confident of results. In closing he added to what he had said earlier the eloquent passage disclaiming any "compliment to my own sagacity" and attributing to God's will "the removal of a great wrong," to which events were "tending."[19]

In issuing the Emancipation Proclamation, Lincoln is sometimes seen as lagging behind Congress, which had passed the Second Confiscation Act on July 17, 1862. Yet the first draft of his proclamation was presented to the cabinet just five days later and his decision had been made earlier, at least by July 13—that is, before Congress acted. When his advisers convinced him to delay until a Union victory, Lincoln promptly issued the first paragraph of his draft as a separate proclamation giving warning that all persons who did not return to their allegiance would be subject, as provided by the Confiscation Act, to forfeitures and seizures.[20] The preliminary Emancipation Proclamation of September specifically enjoined all military personnel to observe and enforce the act's provisions concerning fugitive slaves and emancipation, and this was done despite Lincoln's misgivings as to the legality of congressional emancipation.

In substance, as well as in timing, Lincoln's decision for emancipation compares favorably with that of Congress. The Confiscation Act was directed primarily at slaves *within Union lines* belonging to *persons in rebellion.* The Emancipation Proclamation applied to Confederate-held areas, even those which might never be occupied by Union forces; and it applied to *all* slaves within Confederate lines whatever the allegiance of their masters. The congressional act would free slaves "as captives of war," the presidential proclamation as "a fit and necessary war measure."[21] The omission of enemy areas under Union control from the force of Lincoln's proclamation represented not a concession to slavery, as often assumed, but a concern that freedom by presidential fiat be legally defensible. When Secretary Chase urged an end to the exemptions, Lincoln answered that military necessity had not applied and still did not apply to such areas, and continued: "If I take the step must I not do so, without the argument of military necessity, and so, without any argument, except the one that I think the measure politically expedient, and morally right? Would I not thus give up all footing upon constitution or law?"[22] Lincoln and the congressional majority had made up their minds about the same time; Lincoln's proclamations had recognized and supplemented congressional legislation; his action as compared to that of Congress was more dramatic and far-reaching. Whether either act of Congress or proclamation of commander in chief could secure freedom against future hostile legislation or adverse judicial decision was problematic.

Lincoln's effort to extend freedom and insure its future safety was varied and persistent. Beginning quietly behind the scenes in the spring of 1863, he moved to obtain emancipation in occupied states through state action, a piecemeal but constitutionally unchallengeable solution. Most striking is the record of his influence on Reconstruction proceedings in Louisiana, which will be treated in some detail in the chapters that follow. In Tennessee and Arkansas presidential pressure was also exerted. In early September 1863 Lincoln wrote Andrew Johnson, his military governor in Tennessee, urging him to waste "not a moment" in reestablishing a loyal state government. Noting that Johnson had declared for emancipation "for which, may God bless you," Lincoln enjoined him to "get emancipation into your new State government—Constitution—and there will be no such word as fail for your case." The following January, when Reconstruction efforts began in Arkansas with confusion as to timing and procedure, Lincoln made it clear that the one essential was abolition. Other questions could be left for resolution to local leaders and military governor, but "be sure to retain the [proposed] free State constitutional provision in some unquestionable form."[23]

By January 1864 Lincoln had turned to still another legal support for the structure of freedom—the presidential power to pardon. His Reconstruction Proclamation of December 8, 1863, in exchange for amnesty exacted an oath to support all wartime acts and proclamations in reference to slaves. Lincoln's deference to law dictated the qualification "so long and so far as not repealed, modified or declared void by Congress, or by decision of the Supreme Court." The plan of Reconstruction outlined in his proclamation specified that the reestablished state government "should be republican, and in no wise contravening said oath." A "republican government," as the term was being used by Republicans, implied one without slavery, and the additional reference to the oath made Lincoln's meaning unmistakable.

The end in view, destruction of slavery, might still prove elusive. During the dark days following the Wilderness campaign, with victory uncertain, war weariness in the North, and mounting pressure to forswear freedom as war aim and condition of peace, Lincoln called upon Frederick Douglass to help him devise some way of getting more slaves within Union lines so that they would be free should he be forced into peace terms that left those beyond the lines in bondage. On this occasion, Douglass felt that Lincoln "showed a deeper moral conviction against slavery than I had ever seen before in any thing spoken or written by him. . . . evidence conclusive that the [Emancipation] proclamation, so far at least as he was concerned, was not effected merely as a [military] 'necessity.' " The plan, Douglass observed, was "very soon rendered unnecessary" by an improved military situation.[24]

A month earlier Lincoln had made "abandonment of slavery" a condition for peace negotiations, which brought him under bitter political attack as standing in the way of peace. A friendly War Democrat asked his help in finding "tenable grounds" on which to persuade his fellows to continue support for the administration. The response Lincoln drafted is the document most often cited to indicate that Lincoln wavered on the slavery issue. It opened with the semantic quibble that "saying re-union and abandonment of slavery would be considered, if offered, is not saying that nothing *else* or *less* would be considered," and ended with the challenge that if Jefferson Davis wanted "to know what I would do, if he were to offer peace and re-union, saying nothing about slavery, let him try me." On the very day Douglass arrived for their conference, August 19, 1864, Lincoln discussed the draft of the letter with Alexander Randall; indeed he may have been doing so while his guest waited in the reception room. The draft letter, considered so damaging to Lincoln's antislavery reputation, was never sent.[25] Like the exchange with Douglass, it may have reflected a passing despair of ultimate success, or it may survive as evidence only of Lincoln's skill at dissembling for the purpose of persuasion. Significantly, the body of the letter did not retreat from emancipation but rather eloquently justified keeping the promise of the Emancipation Proclamation both as a "matter of morals" and a "matter of policy."

For the attainment of emancipation there was both political and military hazard. A Democratic presidential victory in 1864 as certainly as military reverses would jeopardize the extinction of slavery as a condition of peace and reunion. There was urgency in Lincoln's concern that occupied Louisiana, Tennessee, and Arkansas organize loyal governments repudiating slavery. "It is something on the question of *time,*" he had written Andrew Johnson in September 1863, "to remember that it can not be known who is next to occupy the position I now hold, nor what he will do." A few days earlier, in rejecting Chase's pressure to extend the limits of emancipation beyond those Lincoln thought

[17]

defensible "upon constitution or law," he raised the problem of political effect: "Would it not lose us the elections, and with them, the very cause we seek to advance?" Chase himself was "full of anxiety," dreading "the unutterably loathsome infamy of consent to the reenslavement of men made free by a great historical act—or rather by two great national acts; by the Proclamation & by the act of Congress." Frederick Douglass, even in retrospect, saw slavery by mid-1864 as "only wounded and crippled, not disabled and killed." A victory for the Democratic party in the presidential elections "would have been a fatal calamity. All that had been done toward suppressing the rebellion and abolishing slavery would have proved of no avail" and the final settlement "would have been left to tear and rend the country again at no distant future."[26]

Lincoln made certain that the Republican national convention held in June 1864 would include a plank calling for the "utter and complete extirpation" of slavery through constitutional amendment. He called in the Republican national chairman to ask that it be made the core of the chairman's keynote address. During the bitter and sometimes seemingly hopeless campaign that followed, it was not without risk that in the face of war weariness the antislavery plank held firm. In the campaign the issue was clearly joined. With victory, Lincoln moved at once to make good on the commitment, calling upon the very same House that had failed to pass the amendment in June to reconsider and act in deference to "the voice of the people. . . . simply because it is the will of the majority." The measure would surely pass the next Congress, but "may we not agree that the sooner the better."[27] Passage through the House, however, did not come readily; indeed, its fate was in doubt even as the vote was being taken January 31, 1865. Lincoln used his powers of persuasion and patronage in the cause. These were supplemented by the work of an incredible lobby, mostly of Democrats, organized and directed by Secretary of State Seward, undoubtedly with Lincoln's knowledge and approval. Its members worked at the capital and in New York City to neutralize Democratic opposition where they could not convert it into support. Their efforts were of critical importance for passage of the amendment. Even so, it might have failed without a further assist from Lincoln, one which in effect though not in wording constituted a false denial of fact. When rumors circulated that southern peace commissioners were on their way to Washington, James Ashley, floor manager for the amendment, feared it would be lost unless Lincoln authorized denial of the report. Pressed, Lincoln sent a one-sentence, carefully phrased response: "So far as I know, there are no peace commissioners in the city, or likely to be in it." Peace commissioners, as Lincoln well knew, were on their way—but to Fortress Monroe rather than to "the city."[28]

The day after passage of the amendment, in response to a serenade, Lincoln relaxed his usual self-restraint to the extent of including "himself" in the congratulations due "the country and the whole world upon this great moral victory." He began his remarks on a characteristically restrained, pragmatic note: ". . . there is a task yet before us—to go forward and consummate by the votes of the States that which Congress so nobly began yesterday." Enthusiasm shone through his words. The amendment was the "King's cure for all the evils." It put to rest the questions of legality and scope that could be raised against the Emancipation Proclamation; it removed all cause of disturbance in the future by rooting out "the original disturbing cause." And in this moment of near-victory Lincoln expressed modest but unmistakable pride in his own antislavery role. According to the newspaper account, "he thought all would bear him witness that he had never shrunk from doing all that he could to eradicate Slavery by issuing an emancipation proclamation. [Applause.]"[29]

Was Lincoln "doing all that he could" not only to destroy slavery but to make freedom substantive, to transform slave into citizen? The Louisiana story affords the best answer, and that will be examined in the chapters that follow. Some observations of a more general nature are first pertinent. The controversy over Lincoln's racial attitudes suggests the question of whether they were of a nature and intensity to stand in the way of presidential support for equal citizenship. Since Richard N. Current's influential essays on *The Lincoln Nobody*

Knows, published in 1958, historians generally have accepted his conclusion that Lincoln entered the White House sharing the race prejudices of his neighbors and there outgrew them. Spokesmen of the turbulent 1960s emphasized Lincoln's "racism" and minimized his "growth," but they were too impatient with moderation as well as with race prejudice to demonstrate the presumed link between prejudice and presidential policy. In the mid-1970s Don Fehrenbacher challenged the assumption that Lincoln's racial attitudes were deeply rooted and that they "determined or even strongly influenced" his actions in relations to the Negro.[30]

My reexamination of the evidence has suggested a perspective that owes much to the insights of Current and Fehrenbacher but sees a larger consistency between the presidential and pre-presidential Lincoln. The progressive development during the 1860s in Lincoln's perception of the role of the black man in American society becomes as much an expansion as a rejection of the attitudes with which he took office. The tone and nuance of Lincoln's much quoted statements of the 1850s, made under pressure of a political opposition seeking to exploit his basic equalitarianism as an affront to white supremacy, foreshadowed the position at which he was to arrive before the end of his presidency. In them can be seen a tentativeness in his acceptance of the prevailing concept of racial inferiority and subordination, an undercurrent of distaste for appeals to prejudice, and a precision in phrasing that more often than not delimited his concessions on the race issue. Though familiar, they warrant another scrutiny.

In 1854 Lincoln stated that had he the power, he would free the slaves but would be at a loss to know what next step to take. He would not make them "politically and socially, our equals." His feelings would "not admit of this; and if mine would, we well know that those of the great mass of white people will not. Whether this feeling accords with justice and sound judgment" was not the question. "A universal feeling, whether well or ill-founded, can not be safely disregarded." But he could not embrace the idea of freeing the blacks and then "keep[ing] them among us as underlings," for there was no certainty "that this betters their condition." Three years later, in supporting black colonization abroad, he argued that "the negro is a man" and with bitterness and irony charged that "Democrats deny his manhood; deny, or dwarf to insignificance, the wrong of his bondage; . . . excite hatred and disgust against him; compliment themselves as Union-savers for doing so." The following year he was asking an end to "all this *quibbling* about this man and the other man—this race and that race and the other race being inferior, and therefore they must be placed in an inferior position." "Who shall say, 'I am the superior, and you are the inferior?' "[31]

[When pressed by Douglas in the famous debates, Lincoln made the statements that have been accepted as straightforward denial of any wish for black equality beyond freedom from bondage. "I have no purpose to introduce political and social equality between the white and the black races." "I am not nor ever have been in favor of making voters or jurors of negroes, nor of qualifying them to hold office, nor to intermarry with white people." What he was denying was that he had in the past championed these issues, or was doing so in the present. He never conceded that such exclusions accorded with justice, never agreed with Douglas that "a negro is not a citizen, cannot be, and ought not to be." His concessions to the basic ideological underpinning for slavery and discrimination, black inferiority, were equivocal. The Negro "is not my equal in many respects—*certainly not in color, perhaps not* in moral or intellectual endowment." He pointed to the "*physical* difference" between the white and black races "which in my judgment will *probably* forbid their living together upon the footing of *perfect* equality." He admitted that he was in favor of "having the superior position *assigned* to the white race, . . . *inasmuch* as . . . there must be the position of superior and inferior."[32] In short, his phraseology was a formulation that accepted rather than championed white dominance. Clearly Lincoln lacked the conviction that marked a committed white supremacist. Among his fragmentary notes on the Douglas debates there is one that can be read as scorn for his opponent's appeal to prejudice, and scorn for those who applauded that appeal: "Negro equality! Fudge!! How long, in the government of a God, great enough to make and maintain this Universe, shall there continue knaves to vend, and fools to gulp, so low a piece of demagougeism as this."[33]

During his presidency Lincoln did not reaffirm the disavowals of support for equality beyond freedom which he had made during the campaigning of the 1850s. He did not explicitly disown them, but their repudiation was implicit in his actions and his words. More prescient for his presidential record than his concessions to racism was Lincoln's prewar resistance to embracing white supremacy wholeheartedly. Of equal import for the future was Lincoln's prewar intransigence in holding to the principle that a slave was a man entitled to rights as a man. Fehrenbacher sees this principle as the keystone of Lincoln's antislavery philosophy but not as the core of his attitude toward race. Yet no less can be said of Lincoln's view of the free black or the freedman than that he perceived him as a man. The logic of Lincoln's position argued that limits on the equality of rights for the black man were a matter of "necessity," not a matter of principle. War tended to dissolve the perceived necessities that upheld slavery, but was a less effective solvent on that "universal feeling . . . well or ill-founded," which recoiled from political and social equality between the races.

Lincoln's changing approach to the race problem as president was consistent with his basic assumptions and the tenuous character of his allegiance to white supremacy. In their prewar rivalry, Douglas had sought to exploit the inconsistency between Lincoln's principles and his disavowal of interest in making blacks political equals. He charged that black citizenship and equality under the law followed from Lincoln's insistence that all men are created equal, without exception. Although deflecting its political impact with wit and verbal dexterity, Lincoln could scarcely have been oblivious to the validity of Douglas' logic, and he may have found it troublesome.

The experiences of wartime, as well as his political principles and his attitude toward slavery and race, moved Lincoln toward an active commitment to equality beyond freedom from bondage. He felt a special responsibility for men and women made free through his executive action and a special obligation, infused with respect, toward blacks whose performance in the fighting forces exceeded his expectations.

Lincoln was quick to turn the military service of black men into an argument for sustaining his emancipation policy; later he used it as one basis for asking suffrage for black males. To doubting whites, he explained that black men in the armed forces were indispensable to victory. To Frederick Douglass, Lincoln suggested another purpose. When Douglass sought Lincoln's aid to end racial discrimination in military pay, the president responded that "ultimately they [black soldiers] would receive the same," but the inequality had "seemed a necessary concession to smooth the way to their employment at all as soldiers." Blacks in uniform gave "serious offense to popular prejudice" while representing "a great gain to the colored people," who "had larger motives for being soldiers than white men." Douglass left "in the full belief that the true course to the black man's freedom and citizenship was over the battlefield, and that my business was to get every black man I could into the Union armies." As this incident suggests, Lincoln perceived military service as affording blacks an opportunity to attain a larger measure of equality. In mid-century, both friend and foe of racial equality recognized a close historic linkage between bearing arms and citizenship.[34]

There is no mistaking the fact that by 1865 Lincoln's concern for the future of the freed people was directed to their condition and rights at home, rather than abroad. Whether he retained a lingering interest in colonization, whether his vigorous advocacy of voluntary emigration in 1861 and 1862 was meant to undermine opposition to emancipation rather than to provide a solution for the race problem[35]— these are questions that need not be settled in order to recognize Lincoln's realistic acceptance of the obvious, that the freed slave would be a continuing presence in the nation's future. His Louisiana policy, his signature of the Freedmen's Bureau bill, his last public address with its support for qualified black male suffrage—to cite only the more obvious evidence, are incompatible with any other conclusion.

Lincoln's policy toward free blacks and freedmen as it was emerging at war's end was based upon tacit assumptions that differed markedly from those he held in the 1850s and during the first years of warfare. At least as late as August 1862 Lincoln saw white America as unmovably hostile to the acceptance of black America on a basis of equality. In that month he appealed to black leaders for support of colonization. The argument upon which he relied to move them was that as free men in America they could not realize the aspiration of all men to enjoy equality: ". . . not a single man of your race is made the equal of a single man of ours. Go where you are treated the best, and the ban is still upon you." Lincoln would not discuss the right or wrong of the situation, though the implication was clear that he considered it an injustice. "It [the ban] is a fact, about which we all think and feel alike, I and you."[36] What changed between 1862 and 1865 was the possibility of obtaining justice from American whites for blacks as free men, if not in full measure, at least to a degree that appeared unobtainable a few years earlier.

By 1865 Lincoln had shown, in many ways, a predilection to subvert "the ban" rather than sustain it. Rejection of a second-class legal status for freedmen in reconstructing the South was foreshadowed by the quiet action of Lincoln's administration in recognizing the citizenship of freeborn blacks. This was a deliberate repudiation of the Dred Scott dictum that blacks were not citizens of the United States and had no rights as such under the Constitution. The official opinion came in November 1862 from the most conservative member of Lincoln's cabinet, Attorney General Edward Bates, at the request of the most radical one, Secretary of Treasury Salmon P. Chase. Although the opinion did not deal with the freed slave, its logic was inconsistent with the legal recognition of any class of residents "intermediate between citizens and aliens"—whether free born or freedmen. According to the attorney general, citizenship was based upon place of birth, and neither color nor race could disqualify under the Constitution or the practice of nations.[37]

Lincoln's personal relations with blacks, as well as the legal stance taken by his administration, indicated his readiness to alter "the ban" of racial discrimination where it lay within his power to do so. Well attested is his respectful regard for Frederick Douglass, and this despite the latter's ambivalent and often sharply critical attitude toward the president. Almost in the same breath with which he criticized Lincoln

[24]

for the limits of his emancipation policy, Douglass gave testimony of Lincoln's personal lack of deference to the color line: "Perhaps you would like to know how I, a negro, was received at the White House by the President of the United States. Why, precisely as one gentleman would be received by another." Lincoln characterized Douglass as "one of the most meritorious men in America." Lincoln's ease in dealing with blacks, and his complete lack of disdain, would seem to belie the passing reference in 1854 to his own feelings as not admitting the acceptance of freed slaves as social equals. George Fredrickson has speculated that Lincoln felt a strong distaste for the Negro's color and an emotional commitment to whiteness and white supremacy but could control his prejudices because he recognized their irrational character. With so little evidence, and that weighted against racial antipathy, Fredrickson's argument is extremely tenuous. If emotion did indeed contend with logic in Lincoln the president, logic was clearly the victor. One circumspect outburst, however, suggests that the prejudice of whites rather than the presence of blacks taxed Lincoln's capacity for restraint. In the summer of 1864 a telegram from a Pennsylvanian urged his attention to "Equal Rights and Justice to all white men in the United States forever. White men is in class number one and black men is in class number two & must be governed by white men forever." Lincoln drafted a caustic reply, but had it sent over the signature of his secretary:[38]

I will thank you to inform me, for his [the President's] use, whether you are either a white man or black one, because in either case, you can not be regarded as an entirely impartial judge. It may be that you belong to a third or fourth class of *yellow* or *red* men, in which case the impartiality of your judgment would be more apparent.

For the freedmen, Lincoln's concern was paternal but not paternalistic in the sense of assuming for them an inherent or permanent status as dependents. He wished the doors of educational opportunity to be opened; he recognized that in fighting for the Union, black men had demonstrated a right to suffrage; his indignation with the correspondent quoted above was triggered by the claim that blacks must be kept forever subordinate. Having indicated a willingness to accept a

[25]

transitional apprenticeship status for freed people (Lincoln used the phrase "reasonable temporary State arrangement"), he noted with evident satisfaction in his last public address that none had been adopted in reconstructing Louisiana. It was Secretary Chase who had warned of the danger of apprenticeship, and Lincoln took the warning to heart. He publicly affirmed the power of the national executive to protect freedmen from abuse and then quietly abandoned the suggestion of apprenticeship. He had offered it as a means of softening both white resistance to emancipation and the potential suffering of blacks cut adrift. Even as he had searched for "some practical system by which the two races could gradually live themselves out of their old relation to each other, and both come out better prepared for the new," he had doubts of any "temporary arrangement." His personal inclination, Lincoln wrote in August 1863, was to favor "the power or element, of 'contract' " as "sufficient for this probationary period."[39]

With the destruction of slavery, Lincoln expected a new relation to follow, one compatible with his economic concept of a free society. As G. S. Boritt has made unmistakably evident, for Lincoln, American freedom meant the opportunity to rise in life. "When one starts poor, as most do in the race of life, free society is such that he knows he can better his condition."

The prudent, penniless beginner in the world, labors for wages awhile, saves a surplus with which to buy tools or land for himself; then labors on his own account another while, and at length hires another new beginner to help him. This is the just, and generous, and prosperous system, which opens the way to all—gives hope to all, and consequent energy, and progress, and improvement of condition to all.

Nothing in Lincoln's record suggests that he would exempt the black man from the dictum that "there is not, of necessity, any such thing as the free hired laborer being fixed to that condition for life." On one occasion at least he stated explicitly his belief that, like every man, "a black man is entitled" to look forward to rising from hired man to self-employed, to employer of others.[40] Such upward mobility Lincoln saw as dependent upon a man's own effort, but he was not so doctrinaire as to preclude giving the black man an assist.

[26]

How far Lincoln was prepared to go in giving governmental support to the freedmen's aspiration for landownership could be known only had he lived out his postwar term of office. In announcing his plan of Reconstruction, he referred with compassion but without protest to former slaves as "a laboring, landless, and homeless class." Just three weeks later, however, he was issuing instructions giving freedmen on the Union-held Sea Islands a priority claim through preemption to the lands that had come into United States possession under the direct tax law. The previous February, in accordance with amendments to the law, Lincoln had directed the tax commissioners for South Carolina to select from the lands that would otherwise have been sold to private individuals an unlimited number of tracts for military needs and for educational and charitable purposes, the latter understood to be for the benefit of local blacks. In September, detailed instructions signed by Lincoln had directed that a substantial proportion of such lands be set aside specifically as homes for black families, to be purchased at a minimum price. Preference was to be given those who would be "examples of moral propriety and industry to those of the same race." Two of the three tax commissioners held that lands thus reserved (about 20,000 acres, one-third to one-half of the total acreage then in their possession) were sufficient for all blacks who might wish to buy. The third commissioner, Abraham D. Smith, together with other influential friends of the freedmen on the Sea Islands, contended vigorously that the bulk of all lands held by the commissioners should be made available for preemption purchase as homesteads. New instructions issued by Lincoln on December 31, 1863, represented a victory for the general homestead policy.[41]

Unfortunately, the victory was short-lived. The two dissident commissioners refused to carry out Lincoln's order, arguing that to do so would be illegal, contrary to the freedmen's best interests, and expensive for the government. They succeeded in convincing Secretary Chase, under whose jurisdiction they functioned, that they should proceed in accordance with the September plan. Chase's decision may have owed as much to their attacks upon commissioner Smith, whom they accused of being an irresponsible drunkard, as to the merits of their

[27]

position. Curiously, no new presidential order superseded the December instructions. Whether the omission was significant is impossible to determine. It can reasonably be assumed that the instructions of September and December had been issued by Lincoln at the instance of the secretary and that Chase would not have reversed administration policy without the president's consent.[42] What is established beyond question is Lincoln's readiness to place presidential authority behind the most radical land policy in the interest of freedmen presented to him during the course of the war.

Lincoln's attitude as it had developed by the end of 1863 can also be glimpsed in Secretary Chase's directives to the Treasury agent in charge of abandoned lands in the Mississippi Valley. Prompted by an interview held at Lincoln's suggestion with James E. Yeatman of the Western Sanitary Commission, whose investigation had revealed a shocking abuse of freedmen on plantations leased by northerners in the Valley, Chase urged greater concern for the freedmen's welfare and wishes. Land should be leased to them, jointly or individually, wherever possible, and the owners of plantations "should be encouraged" to sell them parcels of from forty to a hundred and twenty acres. The basis for "encouragement" was to be the suggestion that proprietors who sold to the freedmen would be relieved "from the effects of the confiscation acts." Chase was "very confident" that Lincoln would do so even though he was "not at present authorized to speak for the President."[43] It is unlikely that the secretary would have expressed such confidence without a basis for his expectation. Moreover, his intimation of presidential action was consistent with other instances in which Lincoln used Chase as a conduit for policies on which he looked with favor but was not ready to support openly. Indeed, the views of Chase and Lincoln in respect to the freedmen were not far apart. It is more than coincidence that in December 1863 Chase wished Yeatman to accept a Treasury appointment to take charge of land policy in the Valley and that two years later it was Yeatman to whom Lincoln first turned in seeking a suitable man to head the Freedmen's Bureau.

The Freedmen's Bureau bill, which Lincoln signed in March 1865 apparently without hesitation, directed the assignment of forty acres of land to each male freedman. The land was not to be presented as a gift, but was to be leased, then purchased with such title as could be conveyed. What lands might be available and the nature of the title to abandoned or confiscated lands were both uncertain. The men responsible for framing and passing the legislation undoubtedly did so with varying expectations.[44] Despite these limitations, the legislation and Lincoln's signature were a significant indication of Republican attitude. Wartime policies, which had been widely criticized as exploitative and little better than slavery, were thereby repudiated. The bill's provisions were meant to end freedmen's labor under the regulation of either provost marshals or Treasury agents. They also were a rejection of governmental support for the perpetuation of a plantation economy based upon a permanently subordinate labor force. The implied expectation was a reconstructed South with an agrarian pattern akin to that of the North.

It would be misleading to leave the impression that landownership for freed slaves was a first concern of Congress, Lincoln, or Chase during the war years. In the struggle over the postwar status of the southern Negro, emancipation had priority. To convince doubters that freedom for the slave was practicable as well as just, antislavery men were eager to establish the black man's capacity and willingness to labor without the constraints of slavery. Proslavery ideology denied that capacity; antislavery men sought evidence that former slaves could survive and function as free men. Proof of this basic fact was high on Lincoln's priorities. From his talks with Lincoln, Chaplain John Eaton, to whom General Grant had given responsibility for contrabands in the Mississippi Valley, understood that the president's objective "was to illustrate the capacity of these people for the privileges, duties and rights of freedom."[45]

There was widespread expectation among the Negro's friends that with freedom the upward mobility assumed open to free white men of the North would likewise be opened to black men in the South. The point was stated explicitly by Secretary Chase. In urging Lincoln to delete from his plan for Reconstruction any suggestion of special state legislation for freedmen, Chase argued not only that such laws might be perverted into virtual reenslavement but also that they were unnecessary: "The demand for labor will secure them [freedmen] employment, and freedom will enable them to buy and build with the proceeds of their labor."[46] Chase was more than willing to have the government help the process along, and Lincoln apparently was of like mind; but neither man assumed that without a government land program the ex-slave would be unable to attain substantive freedom, including the opportunity to better his economic condition.

It is understandable that in retrospect Lincoln has been faulted for paying too little attention as president to the problem of the Negro's future as freedman.[47] Yet the criticism reflects late twentieth-century conscience more accurately than mid-nineteenth-century realities. Lincoln quite properly gave priority to the destruction of slavery, and the fate of the Thirteenth Amendment was uncertain until the final vote of January 31, 1865. As the end of slavery came in sight, there is little reason to assume that Lincoln was unmindful of the difficulties that lay ahead. He had struggled with the problem of the ex-slave's status in freedom at least as early as his 1854 Peoria address; he clearly recognized the difficulty of resolving it equitably in view of the prejudices of whites. If he did not foresee the full dimension of the economic problem, he was fully aware of the racial barriers that would stand between the freedman and his enjoyment of equal rights. For Lincoln, destruction of slavery was not an abstraction. He was immensely interested in the blacks who came within Union lines, concerned for their well-being, eager to learn of their achievements. Amidst the demands of the wartime presidency Lincoln found time to inquire about the freedmen's condition, to listen, to seek further information.

There was a notable official inquiry to consider the present and future of the freedmen. Secretary of War Stanton established the Freedmen's Inquiry Commission shortly after Lincoln issued the Emancipation Proclamation; it is highly unlikely that he did so without the president's sanction. Its members were staunchly antislavery men, and they were invited to write their own directives. James McKaye, the most radical member, and Robert Dale Owen, chairman of the commission, had access to Secretary Stanton and to Lincoln through Senator Sumner and Secretary Chase. Chase gave advice and implied that he spoke for the president as well as for himself. In mid-1863 he urged the commissioners to emphasize in their report that the freedom proclaimed by the Emancipation Proclamation must be accepted as permanent. "The national honor," he wrote, "and especially the honor of the President is engaged to make this condition permanent." The commission's reports spoke for freedom, and at length; they also went beyond emancipation to outline what has been characterized as a "Blueprint for Radical Reconstruction." The blueprint included citizenship, suffrage, and landownership for the freedmen. Their reports, even the most radical signed by McKaye alone, were transmitted to Congress by the secretary of war and made widely available to the public with his consent.[48]

There is reason to believe that Lincoln may have taken a direct hand in the commission's proceedings. James McKaye told a mass meeting of New Orleans' black population early in 1864 that the president felt a great interest in them and had sent him "to inquire into their condition and to ascertain their wishes." They accepted McKaye as Lincoln's spokesman and responded with resolutions thanking the president and his cabinet "for the palpable interest they take in behalf of the once so unrighteously oppressed people of Africa's blood."[49] No evidence other than McKaye's statement has come to light to indicate Lincoln's intervention, but it would have been in character for him to act quietly behind the scenes in such a matter.

Other instances of Lincoln's interest in the freedmen and his concern for their welfare are well documented. In November 1862, after Secretary Chase had read to him a letter from Benjamin Butler, then commanding in Louisiana, which indicated that "planters were making arrangements with their negroes to pay them wages," Lincoln wrote asking that Butler "please write to me to what extent, so far as you know, this is being done." Butler responded with a lengthy letter later made available to the Freedmen's Inquiry Commission. Concerned over reports of destitution and disease among freedmen's families in the Mississippi Valley, Lincoln drafted directions for their employment and protection. If there were nearby abandoned plantations, as many freed people should be placed on them as could "draw subsistence" therefrom. For those remaining, efforts should be made to "get loyal men, of character in the vicinity, to take them temporarily on wages, to be paid to the contrabands themselves—such men obliging themselves to not let the contrabands be kidnapped, or forcibly carried away. Of course, if any voluntarily make arrangements to work for their living, you will not hinder them."[50]

Lincoln took time to pen a reply to an inquiry concerning the government's attitude toward Arkansas planters were they to hire former slaves by fair contracts—and he set guidelines. The freed people should be treated "precisely as . . . the same number of white people in the same relation and condition"; they should be given government protection; such hiring must not be used to break up plantation arrangements already made to sustain the destitute. With these qualifications, Lincoln would regard the employment of freed people by former slaveowners "with rather especial favor" "in view of its tendency to advance freedom, and restore peace and prosperity."[51]

For black soldiers and their families, Lincoln showed a special concern and attention. It was on his direct authority that army commanders in the west were pressured to stop burdening black troops with an unfair share of fatigue duty and to assume greater responsibility for the care of black dependents. He sat down and endorsed in writing a plea that "widows and children *in fact*, of colored soldiers . . . be placed in law, the same as if their marriages were legal, so that they can have the benefit of the provisions made the widows & orphans of white soldiers." His letter addressed to Senator Sumner asking that he "see & hear" the bearer has been credited with initiating legislation to provide equal treatment for the dependents of black soldiers.[52]

When Lincoln looked for information and counsel on freedmen's affairs he turned more often than not to men with a reputation of being the freedmen's friend. He talked directly with Judge Abram D. Smith, the one member of the Direct Tax Commission for South Carolina who fought for preemption landholdings for freedmen. He consulted with James S. Wadsworth, the Radical general whose vigorous action as military governor of Washington, D.C., in protecting fugitive slaves embarrassed Lincoln's efforts to woo border-state support but apparently won the president's confidence. According to the general's biographer, Wadsworth was persuaded by Lincoln and Stanton to stay in Washington rather than rejoin his brigade because the president valued his work with the freedmen. Further, Lincoln would have appointed Wadsworth military governor of Florida had military reverses not aborted his plans. In October 1863 Wadsworth was selected by Lincoln and Stanton to investigate conditions in the Mississippi Valley. The general's official instructions included the directive that he report what "in his judgment" were the best means for the "protection, maintenance, employment and comfort of the colored population." On his return from the Valley, Wadsworth reported directly to the White House as well as to the secretary of war. About the same time, Lincoln received and listened sympathetically to James E. Yeatman of the Western Sanitary Commission and sent him to Secretary Chase. Not content to rely upon the reports of Wadsworth and Yeatman, in February 1864 Lincoln asked General Daniel E. Sickles to tour the Valley and report on the reaction to his Amnesty and Reconstruction Proclamation and on the condition of "the colored people—how they get along as soldiers, as laborers in our service, on leased plantations, and as hired laborers with their old masters, if there be such cases. Also learn what you can about the colored people within the rebel lines."[53]

In his retrospective account, *Grant, Lincoln and the Freedman*, John Eaton has left a lively report of his second visit with Lincoln in Washington. Troubled by "the danger and injustice to which the freedmen were exposed," which he attributed in large part to Treasury orders and to speculators who leased lands in the Valley, Eaton took his case to the president. On his arrival he went directly to the White House, and at Lincoln's request extended his stay in Washington to over a week so that he could come in after the routine of the presidential day and answer questions about blacks, especially "concerning the more remarkable colored men and women who had escaped from slavery and come within our jurisdiction." On their first meeting he found Lincoln "alert to know the facts" and "fully prepared to consider the question from every point of view." When told of the dangers and suffering of the blacks, and the conduct of the lessees, "Mr. Lincoln's keen face sharpened with indignation. 'I have signed no regulations authorizing that!' he exclaimed more than once in the course of my narrative. This indeed was literally true." Eaton thought Lincoln's "grasp of the situation was astonishing," especially in view of the many problems on his mind.[54] The visit occurred in August 1864 during the dismal summer of military and political uncertainty.

Even during the last crowded weeks of his presidency when the collapse of the Confederacy was imminent, the immediate demands of war and peace did not divert Lincoln from his continuing interest in the freedmen. A report by Thomas Conway, Superintendent of Freedmen in Louisiana, had come to Lincoln's attention and "given me much pleasure." On March 1, 1865, he sent a note to Conway expressing his firm belief that "we shall be entirely successful in our efforts [for the freedmen]. . . . The blessing of God and the efforts of good and faithful men will bring us an earlier and happier consummation than the most sanguine friends of the freedmen could reasonably expect."[55] This was the same Thomas Conway who was later forced out of the Freedmen's Bureau by pressure from President Johnson because Conway's commitment to the freedmen was offensive to local Louisiana authorities.

The most important evidence of Lincoln's concern for the freedmen's future may well be his last public address, a document well known but still freshly illuminating. It can be fully understood only in the context of developments in Louisiana, and Lincoln's role in them— matters considered in the chapters that follow. Some observations, however, are pertinent here. It was a carefully considered statement, for Lincoln had put off replying to an earlier serenade lest he "make a mistake."[56] His subject was Reconstruction and much of his comment was in effect directed to the matter of consolidating and extending freedom for "the colored man." Lincoln's defense of the reconstructed Louisiana government was based upon its action against slavery, its provision of "public schools equally to black and white," and its empowering the state legislature to enfranchise blacks. Recognizing that the black man desired the elective franchise, Lincoln argued that it would be attained sooner through sustaining rather than destroying Louisiana's fledgling

[34]

free state government. Meantime, Louisiana in the Union would guarantee an additional vote for ratification of the Thirteenth Amendment.

What becomes apparent in examining Lincoln's leadership role is his way of placing first things first, of taking one step at a time. Only after victory against southern arms on the battlefield and against slavery in the halls of Congress could Lincoln be expected to turn full attention to the problems remaining. Moreover, with his astute perception of the politically possible and his awareness of the strength of white racist feelings, it would have been surprising had Lincoln made premature pronouncements concerning the former slaves' future as free people. The heightened prejudice such statements might have evoked could endanger the *first* essential—escape from legal servitude. Beyond the acceptance of the right and capacity of blacks for freedom, the limits of the possible could not be known to Lincoln in advance. As with slavery, it was characteristic that he should keep his options open and his process of decision-making shielded from scrutiny. In short, Lincoln's style of leadership suggests that his public reserve in respect to the freedman's future can as logically be attributed to a desire for its best possible resolution as to a want of consideration for the problem.

Frederick Douglass' phrase that blacks were "only his stepchildren" is misleading as a characterization of Lincoln's attitude toward the freedman's future. The phrase fails to suggest Douglass' own understandably ambivalent attitude toward the "Great Emancipator" both during Lincoln's lifetime and in retrospect. As evidence that Lincoln was "preeminently the white man's President," Douglass cited the facts that show Lincoln placing the survival of the nation, and respect for its law, above the slave's right to freedom. Yet in the same memorial oration Douglass explicitly recognized that Lincoln could not have freed the nation from the "great crime of slavery" had he failed to take account of white America's loyalties and prejudices. After the "stepchildren" indictment, Douglass went on to say:[57]

Had he put the abolition of slavery before the salvation of the Union, he would have inevitably driven from him a powerful class of the American people and rendered resistance to rebellion impossible. Viewed from the genuine abolition ground, Mr. Lincoln seemed tardy, cold, dull, and indifferent; but

[35]

measuring him by the sentiment of his country, a sentiment he was bound as a statesman to consult, he was swift, zealous, radical, and determined.

The "stepchildren" simile obscures the essential basis of Lincoln's approach to slavery and to freedom—his commitment to the rights of man embodied in the national tradition, to reaching them "as nearly . . . as we can." Lincoln did not treat blacks as children or stepchildren but as adults. There is ample evidence to conclude that Lincoln's conception of freedom was expansive and that his personal racial feelings constituted no barrier to pushing the boundaries between slavery and freedom to whatever limit could be sustained by public consent and law. Lincoln as president, in contrast to his successor, did not stand as an obstacle to the quest for equal citizenship irrespective of race.

Lincoln exercised with vigor the powers of his office, but he did not lose sight of Congress. His reverberant query, it will be recalled, was "can *we* do better?" Older historical accounts presented executive and legislature as adversaries in an epic contest over Reconstruction involving both power and goals. The publication in 1956 of David Donald's seminal essay, "The Radicals and Lincoln," inaugurated a virtual historiographic revolution that toppled the prevailing adversary view by reducing differences to a matter of temperament and rhetoric, of faction instead of principle, of means rather than ends. No longer is it a tenable assumption that the break between president and Congress over Reconstruction, which marked Andrew Johnson's tenure in high office, would have occurred had Lincoln lived. Yet there remains from the earlier historiography an emphasis upon the differences between Lincoln and Congress over Reconstruction, differences dramatized by Lincoln's pocket veto of the Wade-Davis bill, which had been passed with near unanimity among Republicans, and by the bitter attack its sponsors then made on the president in their public manifesto. This emphasis persists despite the work of Herman Belz, which established large areas of agreement between president and party on Reconstruction, including the critical fact that Lincoln in December 1864 had reached an understanding with James Ashley, Radical member of the

House, to approve a new Reconstruction bill no less stringent than the Wade-Davis bill, except for recognition of Lincoln's Louisiana.[58]

The chapters that follow explore the way in which developments in Louisiana riled the never easy fellowship between Lincoln and Radical leaders. The more general aspects of interaction between Congress and chief executive warrant a brief review. They reflect upon the quality of Lincoln's presidential leadership and constitute an essential basis for any projection of probable national policy had he lived to help shape a new order in the postemancipation South.

It is true that the stress of an internal war and its unprecedented consitutional issues heightened a Whiggist hostility in Congress to a strong executive and sharpened congressional desire to maintain a rule of law, that fundamental constitutionalism which traditionally looked to legislature rather than to executive as the source of legitimacy. Yet more typical than the clash over the Wade-Davis bill in the summer of 1864 was the cooperation between president and party that preceded and followed: Lincoln's signature on bills abolishing slavery in the District of Columbia and in the territories and requiring emancipation as a condition for admitting West Virginia; the swift accommodation over the Confiscation Act of 1862 (Congress passing the joint resolution limiting confiscation in accordance with Lincoln's constitutional view and Lincoln receding from his other objections on the bill); the early favor with which congressional leaders received Lincoln's Reconstruction Proclamation; the administration's critical help in securing passage through the House of the Thirteenth Amendment; presidential approval of the historic Freedmen's Bureau bill. Lincoln was prepared to make concessions to congressional views, and the majority of his party (even in the Wade-Davis affair) had no wish to repudiate his leadership.

Lincoln was careful not to deny to Congress a legitimate role in decision-making respecting Reconstruction of the South. Too much weight has been given his offhand comment expressing relief that Congress would not be in session when the war ended. In the Amnesty Proclamation of 1863 and again in the annual message of December 1864, Lincoln pointed out that Congress had the final decision as to readmission of secession states: "whether members sent to Congress from any State shall be admitted to seats, constitutionally rests exclusively with the respective Houses, and not to any extent with the Executive." In the message, Lincoln added that "the Executive power itself would be greatly diminished by the cessation of actual war," thereby implying an increased role for Congress. His last and most generous proposal for a southern settlement, discarded when disapproved by his cabinet, called for a joint resolution of Congress and also explicitly recognized that "upon all points not lying within executive control" he could only recommend liberality.[59] Although deeply committed to Louisiana and pressing for its admission, Lincoln did not argue that Congress had no right to keep the state waiting. Unlike his successor, he never implied that congressional power was limited to a perfunctory examination of election returns.

Similarly, in contrast to Andrew Johnson, Lincoln did not represent a potential presidential challenge to congressional authority in the interest of preserving the rights of states. In the consultations over proposed Reconstruction legislation, he raised no objection to the imposition of some degree of black suffrage upon the southern states as a condition for readmission. His doubts about a requirement of immediate universal male suffrage were based upon practical considerations, not upon constitutional theory. In other words, Lincoln's attitude toward states rights would not deny Congress the authority to set conditions before seating representatives from the secession South. Johnson, on the other hand, did take such a stand and thereby shattered cooperation between president and Congress.

Perhaps most significant in retrospect is the fact that despite his compassion and generosity, Lincoln's differences with Congress over treatment of the white South were surprisingly limited. He did not make an issue with the Republican majority over his distaste for harsh measures, nor did he allow consideration for whites to compromise freedom for blacks. Thus, in his message on the confiscation bill he stated that he perceived no objection to a section that "forever" disqualified men convicted of engaging in or aiding rebellion from holding office under the United States. The seizure of rebel property he held in principle "obviously just," simply warning that the "severest justice may not be the best policy" and that a "justly discriminating application" of confiscation would be nearly impossible. Two years later, in the special proclamation indicating his willingness to accept the procedures of the Wade-Davis bill as one blueprint for Reconstruction, Lincoln made no mention of the disfranchisement it mandated, at least temporarily, for all who had voluntarily supported the Confederacy nor of the specially onerous provision for loss of citizenship for men holding office under the Confederacy after July 1864.[60]

Older views of the harshness of the Wade-Davis bill in contrast with the leniency of Lincoln's own efforts at Reconstruction have been modified, and need even further qualification. The clear-cut distinction that appears in traditional accounts will not stand scrutiny. Revisionist scholars have pointed out that Lincoln's plan to reestablish state government was to be carried out during the conflict whereas the congressional procedures were to be implemented only after rebellion ended, which would mean that the practical consequences of the "easy" executive requirements would approximate those of the "harsh" congressional provisions. The wartime oath Lincoln required served to screen out the Confederate faithful and those who clung to slavery. Congress would achieve the same result at war's end by making past rather than present loyalty the qualification for voting and requiring state prohibition of involuntary servitude. Both president and Congress would place power in the hands of a minority of loyal southerners who could be expected to act with the national government, particularly in liquidating slavery. Congress, however, was more deferential to southern whites by not permitting a Union minority the right to proceed (as had Lincoln) without the prior consent of a majority of all white male citizens.

During wartime occupation, the congressional plan was actually softer on the white South than Lincoln's. It recognized no governmental role for the military, placing authority in the hands of a provisional governor appointed by the president with the approval of the Senate. He was charged with observing the antebellum laws of the state except as to slavery and racial discrimination in the trial and punishment of offenses.

Some members of Congress in voting for the Wade-Davis bill may have believed that they were thereby repudiating military and minority control in the occupied South. The bill is a confusing, internally inconsistent document, easily misread. The restrictive qualification for voters who would initiate Reconstruction by electing a state constitutional convention, and pass upon its work, was not stated in so many words. The bill simply provided that they take the oath of allegiance "contained in the act of Congress of July 2, 1862." This was the "iron-clad oath" which could not honestly be taken by anyone who had willingly supported the Confederacy. Yet the wording of the bill as passed implied that those entitled to vote would be "in number not less than a majority" of all white males—an obvious impossibility.[61] The inconsistency arose during the process of amending the bill, but it reflected a deep dichotomy. In fashioning their own Reconstruction program, Radical Republicans assailed Lincoln's efforts on two conflicting grounds: as undemocratic, expressing not majority will but military decision, and as too lenient, opening the possibility of control by men who could not be counted upon to act against slavery.

The necessity for the Wade-Davis bill, one proponent explained, was that if civil government were not provided there must be military government, "a thing inimical to the spirit of our institutions." Even while supporting the bill in a version that included the one-tenth provision (the requirement that a *majority* take an oath to support the Constitution before the initiation of reorganization was made in committee shortly before the final House vote), James Ashley stated openly that one-tenth was not to his liking. "I believe the democratic idea the better one, that the *majority* and not the *minority* ought to be invested with the organization and government of a State." Yet Ashley argued that safety and justice demanded that the entire authority of reconstructing states be placed in "the hands of loyal men and none others." He condemned General Banks' action in reorganizing the Louisiana government as "unwarrantable and indefensible," "a wanton and defenseless assumption of military power." At the same time Ashley conceded that Banks' presumption would have been tolerable had it coincided with the procedures initiated by the more radical wing of the local free state men. He believed Banks had endangered the adoption of a free state constitution, that he had left open the possibility of slavery's survival.[62] In short, Ashley desired civilian control with majority rule in order to secure truly "republican" government and at the same time sought power for a minority of local Radicals within a minority of southern Unionists in order to insure the destruction of slavery by state action. The contradiction in purpose was no individual idiosyncrasy.

Henry Winter Davis introduced the final "majority" version of the Wade-Davis bill with an explanation of the new provision that was succinct and misleading: "It excludes what my friend from Ohio [J. D. Cox, Democrat] objects to—the rule of one tenth, and requires a majority to concur in forming a government." Similarly, in the Senate, Ben Wade avoided discussion, blandly stating that the provisions of the bill were not "at all intricate or difficult to be understood." He took time to castigate the presidential one-tenth as antirepublican, subversive of the great principle that "Majorities must rule," and left the impression that the congressional measure met the democratic standard.[63] In neither house did anyone call attention to the incongruity of substituting a majority for a tenth in one section of the bill while retaining in another section a proscriptive oath for voters that would insure minority control over the framing of a new state constitution, and over its ratification as well.

Despite attacks upon presidential Reconstruction, the major aims of Lincoln and the congressional majority, including its Radical leaders, coincided: each sought the hegemony of Union antislavery men. Each intended to destroy slavery and to deny political power to men who had led the Confederacy. Lincoln had counseled his military governor of Tennessee in September 1863 that there would be no point in reinaugurating state government if it returned power to those who had formerly held it. "Let the reconstruction be the work of such men only as can be trusted for the Union." His message to Congress in December 1863 characterized as "simply absurd" a guarantee for a revived state government made up in predominant part of "the very element against whose hostility and violence it is to be protected." In private, he stated the political problem with cogency and directness:[64]

> When the vital question arises as to the right and privilege of the people of these States to govern themselves, I apprehend there will be little difference among loyal men. The question at once is presented in whom this power is vested: and the practical matter for decision is how to keep the rebellious populations from overwhelming and outvoting the loyal minority.

Toward the white South, Lincoln, like Congress, was unyielding on the central issues of Union and slavery and determined to promote a new structure of political power.

Nonetheless, the bitterness of the Wade-Davis response to Lincoln's pocket veto was very real, indicating more than a clash between ideologue and pragmatist or between the authority of Congress and that of the presidency. At stake, as the two Radical leaders saw it, was the survival or extinction of slavery. After the House failed to pass the antislavery amendment in June, Henry Winter Davis from his sickbed wrote Ben Wade urging him to get the Reconstruction bill through the Senate as "something practical towards emancipation. . . . The Constitutional amendment is dead—as I always knew and said it was: and never could do any practical good. . . . Pardon me this intrusion but I am sick and can't see you and I am anxious on the subject." The House bill not only mandated directly what Lincoln sought indirectly, prohibition of slavery by amendment of state constitutions, but it also decreed emancipation for the secession states on its own authority. Davis had given up on the constitutional amendment and was eager to strengthen the legal status of freedmen by the best means at hand. Lincoln was still "sincerely hoping and expecting" the amendment to be adopted, and he was unwilling "to declare a constitutional competency in Congress to abolish slavery in States."[65] He was also determined not to repudiate the steps already taken in Louisiana to realize the emancipationist goal.

What deeply embittered Davis and Wade was not only their despair of obtaining a constitutional amendment and their fear of the practical consequences of executive policy. They distrusted Lincoln's resolve as an antislavery man. Theirs was a mistaken judgment, but an understandable one. Lincoln's style of presidential leadership was as often devious as forthright; his verbal dexterity and his skill at conciliation and persuasion tended to obscure his toughness and resolution. There was a basis for suspicion and misinterpretation, for the oscillation between hope and fear with which Radicals reacted to presidential policy. What was distinctive in the Civil War friction between zealous advocacy and political implementation was Lincoln's tolerance of the excesses of the former even while they embarrassed the possibilities of the latter. In mid-1864, at the time of the passage of the Wade-Davis bill, Radical misunderstanding and distrust were inflamed by the uncertainties of the military and political battlefields, and even more by events in Louisiana—or rather, by the version of events in Louisiana that reached Washington from local Radical dissidents. Fully to understand the rift between president and Radical leaders, the objectives and priorities of Lincoln's concern with Reconstruction, and the nature of his presidential leadership, it is essential to examine the course of Reconstruction in Louisiana.

Lincoln and Louisiana

Creation of a Free State

New Orleans and a number of nearby parishes became Union-occupied territory in the spring of 1862, thanks to Admiral David Farragut and his fleet. The army took over control with Benjamin Butler as commanding general and soon with another army officer, George F. Shepley, made military governor. In late December, Butler was replaced by Nathaniel P. Banks, like Butler, a political general from Massachusetts but with a reputation for greater moderation. Eager for early reunion to undermine Confederate morale, Lincoln pressed for Unionist elections. As a result, in early December with Butler still in command, elections were held in two congressional districts. The congressmen-elect, Benjamin Flanders and Michael Hahn, proceeded to Washington where, after considerable debate, the House of Representatives accepted their credentials on February 17, 1863. However, the Thirty-Seventh Congress came to an end on March 3 without having passed an elections bill to regularize the process of restoration. Louisiana's status was left in limbo. During 1863 a second effort was made for reunion, one more comprehensive than that of 1862 and more reliant upon local Unionist leaders. However, months passed and little was achieved.

The president took a continuing special interest in the Louisiana situation. The record of wartime Reconstruction there, particularly during 1863 and 1864, reveals much about Lincoln's use of presidential power and influence—his combination of caution and daring, of conciliation and coercion, of flexible ambiguity and tenacious resolve.

It shows him putting first things first, securing one position before advancing to the next objective. Dealing with matters of political delicacy and hazard, he preferred to have his way through a word spoken in confidence or a mere "wish" or "suggestion" committed to writing. Yet when indirection failed, Lincoln acted boldly. In the face of what he perceived as imminent danger to emancipation, he wielded the power of the presidency vigorously. His direction of affairs in Louisiana discloses a style of leadership that was resolute while giving the appearance of being vacillating. In retrospect his goals, and his consistency in pursuing them, emerge clear and unmistakable.

In a letter of frustration and barely restrained anger, on November 5, 1863, Lincoln demanded the establishment without further delay of an elected state government in Louisiana. Not *any* state government, not even any *Unionist* government; Lincoln now demanded a loyal government committed to the destruction of slavery by state action. If he could not have a state free of slavery, he would have none. The prospect of a government controlled by proslavery Unionists deeply alarmed him. "Time is important," he wrote. "There is danger, even now, that the adverse element seeks insidiously to pre-occupy the ground." Should "professedly loyal men" succeed in their design to set up a state government "repudiating the emancipation proclamation, and reestablishing slavery," he could not "recognize or sustain their work." His word was "out," he declared, "to be *for* and not *against*" the former slaves "on the question of their permanent freedom."[1] Lincoln sent the letter as a directive to General Banks; he also used it as unofficial instructions for the civilian antislavery leaders of the state.

This action was taken a month before the issuance of the Proclamation of Amnesty and Reconstruction in which Lincoln for the first time openly, though indirectly, linked Reconstruction to emancipation. In the public proclamation he avoided a straightforward statement that abolition of slavery would be a precondition for state recognition and restoration, although such was its import. Lincoln's policy thus appeared to remain open or at least ambiguous as to the future of slavery, while his role behind the scenes in Louisiana, upon which he had earlier embarked with characteristic circumspection and understatement, became increasingly explicit and unequivocal as to its destruction. Though thrust upon him by circumstances, Lincoln's direct intervention in Louisiana from the letter of November 5, 1863, through the ratification of a new Free State constitution the following September 1864 represented the culmination of a policy begun early in 1863.

During the previous year, Lincoln had seemed to hold out the bait of preserving slavery as an inducement to establish a loyal state government. To a spokesman for conservative Louisiana Unionists, in a letter of July 28, 1862, marked "private," he wrote that once the people had set up a loyal government they could "upon the old Constitutional terms, govern themselves to their own liking." Three months later, after issuing the preliminary Emancipation Proclamation, he urged elections in Louisiana with the argument that they would bring "peace again upon the old terms under the constitution of the United States. . . . All see how such action will connect with, and affect the proclamation of September 22nd."[2]

It was not so plain to see as Lincoln implied that the action he urged upon conservative loyalists would protect the institution of slavery. In March 1862 Lincoln's special message to Congress had linked emancipation in the loyal border states to the war effort; by July he had decided to use a proclamation of emancipation for the secession states as an instrument of war. When in that month Louisiana Unionists complained that the actions of the military were undermining slavery, his irritation was barely disguised. It was all their own fault, he countered; they had only "to take their place in the Union upon the old terms," but if they did not act promptly "should they not receive harder blows rather than lighter ones?" And they should consider "whether they have not already had *time* enough to do this." The sooner Louisiana took her place in the Union, "the smaller will be the amount of that which will be past mending" but there were "already broken eggs" which could not be mended. When a conflict developed between Benjamin Butler, the general then commanding at New Orleans, and his abolitionist subordinate, John W. Phelps, over the latter's policy of welcoming black refugees from slavery into Union lines, and using them as soldiers (policies abhorrent to loyal planters), Lincoln discreetly but effectively supported Phelps' position. Butler received first a cautiously phrased directive from Secretary of War Stanton on behalf of the president, then more explicit but less official prodding through Secretary Chase.[3] In short, before Lincoln issued the final Emancipation Proclamation of January 1, 1863, he may have been prepared to welcome back a secession state without emancipation as a precondition, but clearly he was not extending himself to preserve the institution of slavery in the interest of reunion. What should not be "past mending" in 1862 may have appeared to Lincoln not slavery but only its immediate, uncompensated destruction.

Not long after the final Emancipation Proclamation and months before issuing his plan of Reconstruction, at least as early as April 1863, Lincoln began discreetly to link restoration and emancipation. Quietly, he took steps to ensure that a reorganized Louisiana would be a "free state," a seemingly innocuous term heavily freighted with meaning. Signals went out from the White House sometime before May and coincided with a movement initiated in New Orleans on February 28 by Thomas J. Durant, an eloquent orator and able local attorney with a penchant for constitutional argumentation. The aim was to establish procedures for electing delegates to a state constitutional convention that would abolish slavery. As his intermediaries with the local antislavery men, Lincoln turned to two loyal Unionists who like Durant were long-time citizens of Louisiana, though not native sons. Lincoln's efforts in 1862 to reestablish civil government had resulted in elections in two congressional districts that sent to Washington Michael Hahn and Benjamin F. Flanders. Both men quickly came to enjoy Lincoln's personal acquaintance and confidence. Together with Durant, they were treated by the president as trusted leaders of the Free State movement and patronage consultants. Flanders was given an appointment as supervising special agent of the Treasury in New Orleans. He later reminded Lincoln that on his arrival in Washington as congressman "you took me by the hand and said there was a strong effort to break down your administration and asked me to support you. . . . I did it then to the extent of my influence and have ever since."[4]

From New Orleans in early May 1863, Flanders sent Secretary

Chase two letters marked private, one meant especially for the president's eye. They concerned pending patronage appointments recommended by himself, Hahn, and Durant after extensive consultation. The task of loyal men to "reestablish Louisiana as a *free* state" was a "stupendous" undertaking, he wrote. It was of highest importance that no mistake or blunder be made. "We rely upon the administration's so disposing its offices, favors and influence as to aid our efforts to the utmost." The appointments recommended "would be good and satisfactory, and would promote the free Union cause in this State." Michael Hahn wrote directly to Lincoln assuring him that the candidates for office jointly recommended were "intensely devoted to the Union and to your policy on the slavery question. Indeed in this last particular they are far ahead of me." "If you deem proper," Hahn continued, "write me a letter on the same subject (organization of a civilian government) which I can show to the people. Some office holders here are attempting to make the impression that you are opposed to the formation of a State government here and are thus retarding the movement."[5] Apparently Lincoln was not yet ready to put his intentions in writing, for no such letter to Hahn is extant. However, the president did send a clear message. The three men recommended by Hahn, Flanders, and Durant were promptly appointed to the offices of judge of the United States District Court, district attorney, and United States marshal. The latter appointee became secretary of the key General Committee of the Union Associations, a group that included all leaders of the Free State movement with Durant as president.

Before leaving Washington, Hahn had sent home word that Lincoln, with whom he had talked, would strongly support the convention plan. Durant's proposal was under intense debate among New Orleans Unionists. Hahn's letter, plus the reassurances as to Lincoln's wishes which he and Flanders must have given on their return home, proved decisive. Details were worked out for the registration of voters and the holding of an election for convention delegates. On May 21 a comprehensive proposal, largely the work of Durant, was adopted by a convention of the Union clubs of the city for presentation to Military Governor George F. Shepley. The proposal did not state directly that the constitutional convention would abolish slavery, but this was clearly understood. The stated intent to frame a new constitution "adapted to the change of circumstances and conditions produced by the rebellion," General Shepley explained, meant making the Louisiana constitution conform to "the policy of the Government in relation to the institution of slavery." Shepley agreed to carry out the suggestion for a registration of voters and to refer other aspects of the plan to Washington for definite instructions. On May 28 he sent the General Committee's proposals and his reply to Secretary of War Stanton to lay before the president, with the explanation of intent quoted above and with the request for instructions. Apparently the plan was discussed and at least tacit approval given by the Administration, although there is no record of a reply at this time from Secretary Stanton to General Shepley. On June 12, 1863, Shepley appointed Durant commissioner of registration and attorney general of the state. On July 24, the General Committee of the Union Associations by a vote of 38 to 4 required their own members to take an oath of loyalty that included support for a "free State Government." The loyalty oath devised for the registration of voters required commitment only to the organizing of a loyal state government.[6] It is worthy of note that the Durant-Union plan included no obligation to support emancipation as a precondition for voting.

In Washington those who were knowledgeable caught the direction of administration policy and the importance of developments in Louisiana. Before the end of May, George Boutwell, a Radical congressman from Massachusetts and a lifelong friend of Banks, had inferred "from what is printed in the newspapers that steps will be taken for the formation of a new constitution in La., with slavery excluded." He warmly welcomed such a development and in a letter to General Banks dangled before him the prospect "for you to add to your numerous public services the great service of tendering a free State to the restored Union." Public sentiment was "moving rapidly toward the conclusion that the eleven states shall not be admitted to the Union with slavery. *The contest on this point will be bitter.* If a precedent should be established such as would be made by the reconstruction of La. the issue would be avoided."[7] In short, victory over slavery was still precarious, and Banks might gain glory by tipping the balance in favor of freedom.

Banks would prove more than willing to try, and Boutwell would act as unofficial intermediary between president and general. Without Boutwell's prompting, and despite concentration on military operations, Banks had already reported to Lincoln a developing sentiment for restoration. Indeed, his appointment to replace Butler had been understood as a gesture of conciliation toward Louisianians whom Butler had antagonized, an effort to nurture the loyalty needed to justify readmission to the Union. Until Lincoln's November 5 letter, however, the promotion of efforts to reestablish a civil government was considered the responsibility of General Shepley as military governor rather than of General Banks as commanding general.

In pushing for the election of congressmen in November 1862, Lincoln had informed General Shepley that "I wish it to be a movement of the people . . . and not a movement of our military and quasi-military, authorities there. I merely wish our authorities to give the people a chance—to protect them against secession interference." In a second letter of the same day which Shepley made public as a poster, Lincoln had given assurances that northern officeholders would not be "set up as candidates." To send such men to Congress, "elected as would be understood, (and perhaps really so,) at the point of the bayonet, would be disgusting and outrageous."[8] Throughout 1863 General Shepley and leaders of the Free State committee acted on the assumption that Lincoln wished a local movement with substantial public acceptance and the least possible appearance of military direction or interference. There seems little doubt that their assumption was correct. By the end of the year, however, Lincoln drastically relaxed the preconditions for reorganization as a free state.

Lincoln's first open, but indirect, indication of support for the Free State movement was forced by pressure from the proslavery opposition. Loyal planters, meeting in New Orleans on May 1, sent a delegation to ask Lincoln for "full recognition of all the rights of the State, as they existed previous to the passage of an act of secession, upon the principle of the existence of the State Constitution unimpaired," and for a directive to General Shepley to order a November election. They assured Lincoln that with recognition of the old constitution "the State wishes to return to its full allegiance"—an enticement they undoubtedly considered irresistible to the president. The leader of the delegation, Thomas Cottman, had worked closely with Lincoln in his 1862 effort to reorganize Louisiana. All three delegates were recognized as influential men. Secretary Chase's "Chief Cook & bottle washer" in New Orleans, young George Denison, who held various Treasury posts and reported regularly to the secretary, had sent them off with a letter of introduction. Privately he wrote Chase that they should be made friends, "*your* friends"; they could do harm as enemies. Denison was equally direct in informing the secretary that they were opponents of emancipation; Cottman was "pro-slavery" and "always will be." Lincoln as well as Chase was forearmed. Michael Hahn had reported that Union men in Louisiana were divided on the issue of recognizing the old constitution or framing a new one. Those who desired to preserve slavery were satisfied with the old, which gave them disproportionate representation in the legislature. In favor of a convention and new constitution were "the more radical or free-soil Union men, and [they] expect to succeed in making a free-soil Constitution."[9]

Lincoln handled the situation gingerly. He kept the planter delegation waiting until two had departed and only Thomas Cottman remained. Then on June 19, 1863, he wrote a reply intended for the press as well as for the petitioners, incorporating their letter in full in his answer. He had learned that "a respectable portion of the Louisiana people, desire to amend their State constitution, and contemplate holding a convention for that object. This fact alone, as it seems to me, is a sufficient reason why the general government should not give the committal you seek, to the existing State constitution." There was abundant time for an election in November, and he assured the delegation that the people of Louisiana "shall not lack an opportunity of a fair election for both Federal and State officers, by want of anything within my power to give them."[10]

When reports reached New Orleans of the delegation's reception, the proslavery *True Delta*, in an editorial headed "Refusing Admittance," at first expressed disbelief. It had received correspondence warranting the inference that the planters' "reasonable and just proposition" had been submitted to the cabinet and "contemptuously rejected," a report the editor could not believe, nor could he accept accounts that Louisiana would not be admitted unless slavery was abolished. This was "so monstrous, so revolutionary . . . that we cannot bring ourselves to admit its possibility." When Lincoln's letter appeared in the press, the *True Delta* published it with a comment that placed the onus not upon Lincoln but upon Secretary Chase, "his abolitionist associates," and the political Radicals. They "simply mean, if they can accomplish it, that none of the States committed to the rebellion shall be restored to the Union without being shorn of the institution of slavery."[11] Lincoln had rebuffed the proslavery Unionists without alienating them or fully disclosing the extent of his support for the Free State men. His careful response did not crush their hope for control in Louisiana and concessions to slavery. That hope would prove a future hazard, but no less danger lay in a course that would forfeit their loyalty and support. In Louisiana, Confederate sympathies were strong and Union men were a minority. In his effort to restore the state, Lincoln tried to keep the minority united, but not at the cost of perpetuating slavery. It was a task that challenged the political skill even of an Abraham Lincoln. Ironically, those who first broke with his policy were not the Conservatives but rather a group of Free State leaders upon whom Lincoln counted for support against slavery.

Secretary Chase, the most outspoken antislavery member of Lincoln's cabinet, was playing the same game of propitiating proslavery leaders and simultaneously using them in the antislavery cause, but without Lincoln's finesse. After consultation with the president, in November 1862 Chase had appointed Cuthbert Bullitt, as "an old resident of New Orleans," collector of the Custom House, making the place available by shifting his own kinsman Denison to another Treasury post. Bullitt was the brother-in-law of Hugh Kennedy, owner and editor of the proslavery *True Delta*. Both Kennedy and Bullitt were close to Cottman and other Conservative leaders. About three weeks after Lincoln's response to the planter delegation, Secretary Chase wrote

Bullitt a sharp scolding letter. He reminded the collector that "before your appointment I explained to you most candidly my views of the necessity and wisdom of the President's proclamation of emancipation, and understood you, if not altogether concurring with them, yet as ready to accept the policy of the proclamation as fixed and to give it your hearty support." He had also understood that Kennedy would do the same. It was now clear that he had been mistaken as to both of them. Chase had read the columns of the *True Delta*, and he had learned that "neither your official or personal influence is given to that cause [emancipation]." Chase warned that their official relations could not be maintained unless Bullitt avoided dissensions with other officers of the government and gave cordial support to the policy of the president, "whether in respect to Emancipation or the War. . . . I trust you will appreciate the harshness with which I write," he concluded, "and receive what is written in the same spirit of kindness with which I subscribe myself. Very sincerely your friend."[12]

Cuthbert Bullitt was not one to rest his case lightly. He presumed upon the president's "friendship for me" with letters protesting interference from Denison and Flanders, parading his political loyalty to Lincoln, and attributing his troubles to an unwillingness to give support to Chase's presidential ambition. Nothing was said about emancipation. Lincoln did not intervene; the warning from Chase stood. When Cottman returned to Washington in the fall, Lincoln apparently went out of his way to speak kindly of Bullitt, for the latter wrote Lincoln with extravagant thanks for "this mark of your confidence." He reported that "the various departments of the customs are now in harmony, the hatchet is buried."[13] The combination of sugar and spice appeared for the moment to have been effective.

Despite Chase's presidential ambitions and his self-conscious role as cabinet spokesman for the antislavery vanguard, he and Lincoln worked closely together during 1863 in formulating and implementing administration policy in Louisiana. Most of the patronage appointments for the state were in the Treasury, and they were used to support Lincoln's policy, if not his prospects for renomination. Chase did not hesitate to urge measures more far-reaching than Lincoln's, but his letters left their readers in no confusion as to when he spoke for the administration and when he spoke only from his own antislavery convictions. In seeking the destruction of slavery, Chase spoke in Lincoln's name. He did so in July when he advised members of the Freedmen's Inquiry Commission that their forthcoming report should distinctly declare that "no state which has carried rebellion into a formal act of secession and included in the proclamation can be readmitted into the full enjoyment of the rights of a member of the Union until it has by a fundamental provision or act incorporated in its Constitution recognized and sanctioned the condition established by the Proclamation."

A month later, in language more obscure than was characteristic, Chase spoke for Lincoln in informing General A. J. Hamilton of his appointment as assistant special agent of the Treasury with the expectation that he would be given responsibility for reconstructing a loyal government in Texas when "the time comes for doing so with advantage." He informed Hamilton that in a conversation with the president on Texas matters, Lincoln had expressed a deep interest in the "reestablishment of a State Government under a Constitution recognizing the condition of persons established by the Proclamation." The president had also expressed his concern for the "just claims" of southerners such as Hamilton who had suffered for their devotion to the Union. "It is of great importance that the President should not be misunderstood by the earnest and loyal men of the insurrectionary states and that he should not misunderstand them." To this letter Lincoln added his personal endorsement: "Having heard the above read, I most cheerfully endorse every word of it. A. Lincoln." In early October, Chase sent Horace Greeley reassurance that "Mr. Lincoln . . . advances slowly but yet advances. On the whole, when one thinks of the short time, and immense distance, in the matter of personal Freedom, between the 1st of March 1861 and the 1st of October 1863 the progressives cannot be dissatisfied with results."[14]

In Louisiana, meanwhile, the efforts of Free State men to begin the process of reorganization had bogged down. Developments there, or rather the lack of them, led to two written directives from Lincoln in August 1863. One was an official order through Secretary of War Stanton, formulated after consultation with General Shepley, who had come to Washington for that purpose, and with Secretary Chase as well. In effect, it ordered Shepley to carry out the plan of the Free State men. He was directed to aid the "loyal citizens of Louisiana [who] desire to form a new State constitution and to reestablish civil government in conformity with the Constitution and laws of the United States." As military governor he was to proceed with a registration of loyal citizens, order an election for delegates to a constitutional convention, apportion delegates according to a designated formula that undercut the political power of planters, preside at the elections, open the returns, and notify the persons elected of the time and place of holding the convention. The order followed generally the proposal formulated by the Free State leaders and transmitted to Washington in May. General Shepley had not acted decisively during the summer. This may have been in part the result of his concern that "no shadow of suspicion of military dictation should darken the future page of the brilliant record of returning loyalty and renewed devotion to the Union and the Constitution." His apprehension, quite justified in the light of Lincoln's 1862 public commitment and private directive, was resolved by the official order issued August 24. If there was to be a "suspicion of military dictation" the onus would not rest upon General Shepley but upon his superiors.[15] Even with this assurance, Shepley did not act with vigor.

The second August directive on Reconstruction in Louisiana went as an informal letter to General Banks from Lincoln with copies sent by the president to Flanders, Hahn, and Durant. It was precipitated indirectly by Banks and directly by his friend Congressman Boutwell, who on August 4 received a letter from the general which the following day he read in part to Lincoln. The letter to Boutwell has not survived, but we know that it was written immediately after Durant, on behalf of the Free State general committee, had appealed to Banks upon the general's return to New Orleans after the fall of Port Hudson in July 1863. The Free State men sought his aid in cutting through delays and difficulties in implementing voter registration and effecting their plans for a constitutional convention.

[57]

Judging from Lincoln's response and Banks' later letters, what Boutwell read to the president probably expressed in embryo views the general later formulated in detail. From later documents we know that Banks wished the administration to act more openly to insure victory over slavery. He would have elections ordered under the old state constitution but with all provisions upholding slavery set aside by military authority. Apparently Banks believed this would bring quick united action. It would cut the Gordian knot of dissension among Union men over the status of the antebellum constitution. Whether that document was still valid, whether its repudiation would concede the legality of secession (Banks thought it would) were legal issues that had taken on a life of their own in the political arena, promoting as well as reflecting division among Unionists. Banks' approach was meant to give technical advantage to the proslavery men by recognizing the old constitution and substantive victory to the Free State forces by repudiating its slavery provisions and changing its basis of representation. Voting under his stipulations could in effect, as he saw it, establish a free state before slavery was extinguished through convention and ratification procedures. However, Banks' plan had the disadvantages of an undisguised role for the military in the reorganization of civilian government and questionable legality in voiding *de jure* slavery in areas exempted by Lincoln's Proclamation. If Banks' letter to Boutwell had indeed suggested some such procedure, Lincoln was not prepared in August 1863 to act in so vulnerable and open a manner.

Boutwell reported back to Banks immediately. "He [Lincoln] said that he desired the return of the states upon the old basis, substantially, making provision for emancipation of the slaves, and if possible, securing them homes; that, as far as he understood your views from the letter and from Gen. Shepley, he agreed with you; but that in the course of a few days he would write you, and give you his views at length."[16] Better than his word, Lincoln wrote that very day, August 5, 1863. His discreet but critically important communication in turn led to the letter of November 5 quoted earlier and to Lincoln's subsequent direct intervention in Louisiana's organization as a free state. His August letter to Banks merits careful examination.

Lincoln wrote that he knew what he "would be glad for Louisiana to do" but that it was "quite a different thing for me to assume direction." He wanted Louisiana to make a new constitution adopting emancipation, and phrased the matter carefully so that the action would both recognize the Emancipation Proclamation and extend freedom to those parts of the state which the proclamation had exempted. He wanted education "for young blacks." He had no objection to some practical temporary system by which the two races "could gradually live themselves out of their old relation to each other, and both come out better prepared for the new," but his preference was for using the simple element of contract during the transition period. Lincoln was hoping that conservative men who clung to slavery could be persuaded to agree to its destruction. He recognized that they did not have the same "motive to desire emancipation" that he had as "an anti-slavery man," but argued that there were strong reasons for them to come back "under the shield of the Union" and "to thus perpetually hedge" against the recurrence of sectional conflict. He approved of the voter registration for the election of a constitutional convention which "Gov. Shepley has informed me that Mr. Durant is now taking," and indirectly suggested that his own views on emancipation be made known to the convention when it convened. Without indirection, he stated that "the thing should be pushed forward" so that the convention's work would reach Washington before Congress met in December. Banks was to confer with "intelligent and trusty citizens of the State," specifically with Flanders, Hahn, and Durant (the names of Cottman and Bullitt are conspicuously absent), but Lincoln's letter was not to be made "generally public."[17]

The carefully phrased letter of August 5 can be misread as merely suggestion and comment. Lincoln's succinct endorsement on the copies sent to Flanders, Hahn, and Durant, however, carry a quite different implication, one confirmed by subsequent events. "The within is a copy of a letter to Gen. Banks," he wrote. "Please observe my *directions* to him." In acknowledging the letter, Banks expressed not only his concurrence in Lincoln's views but also his readiness to "execute your *orders*" in respect to the "reorganization of Government."[18] By the time the letter reached him, however, the general was deeply involved in planning a military expedition to Texas, and Shepley had been ordered to proceed with voter registration and elections. Until December, Banks assumed that the implementation of Lincoln's wishes rested in the hands of Shepley and the Free State leaders.

In view of the split that later developed among Free State men, it is important to note that there existed no such division in 1863. Lincoln assumed, correctly, that Durant and Flanders, with Hahn and Banks, were working for a common objective. The research of Peyton McCrary has established the error of earlier historians in projecting backward the two Free State factions of 1864 and in defining Treasury patronage or General Butler's legacy as a dividing line between Radicals and moderates. Despite the absence of two adversary factions in 1863, various differences of opinion existed among even antislavery Unionists. For example, the vote in the general committee instructing Durant, its president, to call upon General Banks for assistance in mid-July had been close, 17 to 16, for reasons not disclosed in the minute book.[19] The vote may have reflected a hesitancy to appeal so openly for military support. Or it may have arisen from lack of confidence or animosity toward General Banks. His early conciliatory gestures toward Confederate sympathizers, his continuing good relations with proslavery Unionists, the clashes that arose between military and civilian officers over the cotton trade, plantation management, and the policing of New Orleans, all gave rise to tensions, suspicions, and personal hostilities. Moreover, the generally inept military record of Banks as commanding general, only temporarily obscured by the fall of Port Hudson, aroused intermittent criticism and demand for his replacement. One suspected source clearly was not responsible for precipitating the friction that developed between Flanders and Durant, on the one hand, and General Banks; the repudiation of Banks by local Radical leaders did not reflect the policy of Secretary Chase. His personal and official correspondence with Banks was cordial, even when admonishing the general. Chase was interested in tending a relationship through which he could influence affairs in Louisiana.[20] In addition, the general's chief civilian aide, B. Rush Plumly, enjoyed a close tie to the secretary, from whom he had received a mark of confidence at a time of personal trouble and to whose presidential ambitions he was devoted.

In mid-September, about six weeks after the Boutwell interview with Lincoln, Plumly arrived in Washington filled with plans for recruiting black soldiers, at which he proved very successful. A northerner transplanted south by the war, Plumly was the most stalwart and seasoned abolitionist among the men of influence in New Orleans who were working for a free state. Under Banks he had some responsibility for improving the lot of freedmen on plantations and later, as Banks' appointed chairman of the Board of Education, deserved considerable credit for the success in establishing schools for freedmen during 1864 and 1865. While in Washington, Plumly, whose zest for politics was second only to his devotion to the abolition cause, did not confine himself to strictly military matters. Chase invited him to breakfast and gained a "clear inside view of military and civil affairs at New Orleans." On two occasions, Plumly had invitations to meet with the president.[21] We do not know what passed between Lincoln and the old abolitionist, but it is improbable that their exchange was perfunctory. Part of Lincoln's presidential style was to make use of informal couriers to keep informed and to transmit his wishes unofficially. This becomes apparent from fleeting references, such as those in Plumly's letters, together with notes introducing visitors and communications sent outside regular channels that appear in the presidential papers. Before Plumly left Washington, Flanders had been ordered to the capital for consultations. Lincoln would use him to spur Free State leaders to action.

To understand Lincoln's concern and increasing involvement during 1863 and 1864 with Reconstruction in Louisiana, it is necessary to keep in mind the uncertainty surrounding the final extinction of slavery. Leaders of the antislavery vanguard, including Secretary Chase, Henry Winter Davis, and Frederick Douglass as indicated earlier, were fearful that victory over slavery might yet be lost or compromised. The political pressures upon Lincoln to retreat from emancipation were great, the political dilemma formidable. A resolute antislavery stance might mean Republican defeat in 1864, with renewed life for slavery nourished by the solicitude of northern Democrats for the "Union as it was, and the Constitution as it is." Concessions by the Republican standard-bearer might bring political victory, but at the price of perpetuating or at least prolonging the existence of the "peculiar institution."

✗ ⌊In urging upon General Banks the task of making Louisiana a free state, his friend Representative Boutwell had succinctly outlined a strategy to safeguard the antislavery goal in the event of political defeat. ⌈The return of a state with a new [antislavery] constitution, and by readmission into the Union, puts the question of slavery beyond the hazards of politics, and the vagaries or corruption of judges." The problem and the solution were readily grasped by Banks. A free state in Louisiana could and should be organized before the presidential contest began. "It certainly ought not to be dependent upon that issue," he wrote Boutwell in December 1863, "and settled, not only independent of it, but before it opens." With Lincoln, Banks made the same point. Delay might be fatal "in view of events possible in another year and leaves the result as to freedom or slavery to accident or chance." The issue of slavery should be settled in Louisiana before "the country is convulsed with the struggles of a Presidential contest, and no man is wise enough to predict with certainty the result."[22]

Lincoln did not need counsel to recognize the hazard to emancipation. Nor was he sanguine of military and political success. His sense of urgency accounts for the deadline clearly stated in the August 5 letter he sent to Banks, Flanders, Hahn, and Durant, in which he asked that a free state constitution be completed before Congress assembled in December 1863. It also explains his injunction in November that reorganization proceed "without waiting for more territory"—i.e., for military successes that would bring more of Louisiana under Union control. The Free State men had expected to hold elections only after a majority of the state's population was securely within Union lines, a military goal that proved elusive despite Banks' optimism.

Two alarming developments precipitated Lincoln's decisions of November and December 1863, decisions that marked a break not in his policy but in his manner of implementing it. Proslavery leaders in Louisiana attempted a coup; the work of their Free State rivals, despite Stanton's supportive order of the previous August, had come to a standstill.

Without sanction from authorities either in Louisiana or Washington, but spreading false rumors of Lincoln's support, proslavery Unionists in September and October set about organizing an election of sorts and actually sent to the Capitol for the opening of Congress Thomas Cottman and A. P. Field as claimants of House seats. Their expectation of being seated, as indeed they temporarily were, was apparently linked with a conspiracy between Democratic leaders and Emerson Etheridge, the acting clerk of the House of Representatives and a Tennessee Unionist hostile to the administration's emancipation policy. Through a coalition of Democrats and border-state Unionists, the plan was to control the organization of the House after Etheridge had invalidated the credentials of several Republicans. Lincoln learned of the danger on October 23, at once alerted Republican leaders, and with them countered the maneuver.[23]

As a signal of displeasure to the Louisiana Conservatives, and as a reprimand to Cuthbert Bullitt for his suspected or reported cooperation in their efforts, Bullitt was summarily demoted from customs collector to naval officer. His protest to Lincoln against the "stunning" blow, one "so humiliating & unjust" that he found it difficult "to believe you have given it your sanction," went unanswered. For a second time Lincoln rebuffed Louisiana Conservatives but without rejecting the fidelity they professed for him. In a letter of December 15, 1863, to Cottman, who had expressed a desire to be guided by the president's wishes, Lincoln made clear that to sustain the Emancipation Proclamation was "indispensable" and to place the whole state on the same footing of freedom would be "fortunate." He also admonished "all sincere Union men" to "eschew cliqueism, and . . . all work together." He ended his response to Cottman by stating that he went no further "because I wish to avoid both the substance and the appearance of dictation." Though Lincoln's wishes were made unmistakable, his reply to Cottman was less than candid. When a fellow Conservative protested that the effort to call a convention being made by "a comparatively small party of over zealous men . . . greatly in the minority," was violating provisions of the state constitution and would "not be concurred in voluntarily" by "the great mass of the loyal citizens," who were nonetheless prepared to support the Reconstruction Proclamation, Lincoln kept silent. His notation on the letter read: "I do not wish to say more than I have publicly said, and said in the letter delivered to Dr. Cottman yesterday."[24] Either alienated, or shown presidential favor, conservative Unionists would be in a position to defeat Lincoln's purpose of making Louisiana a free state before the presidential election.

About the time Lincoln learned of the Etheridge plot and the bold initiative of Cottman and his associates in Louisiana, there arrived on his desk a seven page letter from the man who was commissioner of registration, state attorney general, and leader of the Free State movement, Thomas J. Durant. The lengthy, disputatious epistle could only have shocked, exasperated, and alarmed a president already deeply troubled for the future of his emancipation policy. After weeks of delay, Durant was acknowledging in October receipt of the copy of the August 5 letter to Banks, sent with Lincoln's endorsement to "please observe my directions to him." The first four pages of Durant's letter were an argument, mostly legalistic, against the perpetuation or reestablishment of slavery. Durant implied that Lincoln was contemplating the retraction of the Emancipation Proclamation or the return to slavery of those it had declared free, and more explicitly linked the hopes of slavery's advocates to the exemptions in Lincoln's Emancipation Proclamation. As if announcing a revelation, Durant concluded sententiously that "we in Louisiana, are now so situated that we must choose between the systems of slavery and freedom: I do not hesitate to choose the latter. . . . To put the matter at rest we must abolish the principle of property in man by a [state] constitutional enactment."

Then came the startling substance of Durant's reply. Before slavery could be abolished by state action "the public mind must be educated." Lincoln was mistaken in thinking that a registration of voters was under way for the election of a constitutional convention; "such is not the case." General Shepley was understood to have instructions from

Washington on the subject but they had not been made public. First, the military must have undisturbed control of more territory. All military officers and public officeholders, including local provost marshals, "should be urged and required to exert themselves to the full extent of their ability to promote the formation of a free state Government." How long all this would take "it is difficult to say." Durant was quite definite that it would not be possible "to have the work completed by the next Session of Congress." Finally, Durant denied any need for haste. "It is not likely that any serious evil may result from the absence, for a time, from the House of Representatives of members from Louisiana."[25] Despite Lincoln's support for the Free State movement, Durant understood neither Lincoln's commitment to freedom nor his sense of urgency.

After receipt of such a letter, it is not surprising that Lincoln turned to Banks and that when Banks and Durant clashed he sustained the general. In view of the split that developed, several aspects of Durant's position as presented to the president are worthy of special note: his expressed concern was with emancipation rather than with the status of freed blacks; his implicit assumption was that the destruction of slavery could not for some time command majority support in occupied Louisiana; and no scruples prevented his calling for administration pressure upon officeholders and military to act as political partisans on behalf of a free-state government.

Lincoln did not invite a conflict between Banks and Durant. Quite the contrary. His November letter enjoined General Banks to give "hearty sympathy and support" to Shepley and the Free State leaders entrusted with reorganization. But above all he wanted "both you and them, to lose no more time." Lincoln's exasperation, especially with Durant, was evident despite his effort to temper it. He had sent Durant a copy of his August letter for he had understood "that Mr. Durant was taking a registry of citizens."

I now have his letter, written two months after, acknowledging receipt, and saying he is not taking such registry; and he does not let me know that he personally is expecting to do so. Mr. Flanders, to whom I also sent a copy [of the August 5 letter], is now here, and he says nothing has yet been done. This disappoints me bitterly; yet I do not throw blame on you or on them.

Lincoln gave Flanders a copy of this November letter to Banks for the information of the Free State men. And he personally authorized Flanders to say that the president would recognize and sustain a state government organized in any part of the state in Union hands; an election should not wait upon Union control of more territory or population.[26] Whether an oversight or a deliberate signal, Lincoln did not send a copy of the letter to Governor Shepley.

The ten percent provision of Lincoln's December 1863 Reconstruction Proclamation made general and official his November decision to settle in Louisiana for a "tangible nucleus" based upon smaller numbers and territory than had previously been considered both desirable and practicable. Lincoln's intent, in the words of the proclamation, was to make possible "a rallying point—a plan of action" that would bring Unionists "to act sooner than they otherwise would." The general plan also reflected his purpose of making Louisiana, and all other returning states, free states. Significantly, the loyalty oath of the presidential proclamation went beyond the loyalty oath which the Free State movement required of Louisiana voters. The latter included no commitment to emancipation, while Lincoln specified an oath to support all acts of Congress and all presidential proclamations "with reference to slaves" and a state government "republican, and in no wise contravening said oath." Since most of occupied Louisiana had been exempted from the Emancipation Proclamation, and the Confiscation Act did not cover slaves of loyal owners or apply to the disloyal before mid-1862, enough ambiguity remained to enable Lincoln to keep the posture of persuading rather than coercing Louisiana's proslavery Unionists—to make a distinction with Cottman between action that was "indispensable" and action that would be "fortunate."

In the wording of the Reconstruction Proclamation, Lincoln left himself an ample loophole, one that could be used both to conciliate Conservatives and to sustain "over zealous men": His plan "must not be understood" as the only one that "would be acceptable." It was no "Procrustean bed," he wrote reassuringly to Cottman, then added "in

Louisiana particularly, I wish that labor already done . . . may not be thrown away." Another indication of Lincoln's flexibility as to means, as distinct from the end in view, was the sketchy nature of the procedure outlined in the proclamation. Those who took the oath were simply to "re-establish a State government." Most importantly for the Louisiana situation, the proclamation contained no mention of convening a convention to initiate reorganization, although there was nothing that could be interpreted as rejecting one. The document did suggest as "not improper" maintaining the antebellum state constitution and general code of laws subject "only" to modifications made necessary by the proclamation "and such others . . . which may be deemed expedient by those framing the new State government."[27] Lincoln's thinking was precise and his command of language enviable; he also had a genius for being ambiguous and indeterminate when those qualities served his purpose.

Returning to New Orleans after his interview with Lincoln, Flanders reported back on December 11 that he had shown the November 5 letter to Durant, Hahn, Judge Whitaker, and other prominent Union men, "and it gives to all of them great encouragement and satisfaction." Lincoln's letter, wrote Flanders, had also stimulated military leaders to action. There would now be unity "in the movement to form a State, a *free* State government for Louisiana. The measures taken for this great object will I think be stamped with prudence, and we hope their result will meet your expectations." Durant wrote Chase that Lincoln's letter to Banks when presented by Flanders to the Free State Committee caused them to visit Governor Shepley and ask that he name a day for the election of convention delegates, suggesting January 25. Lincoln's initiative had rekindled activity for a free state. The mood of Free State leaders shifted from pessimism to optimism. They began predicting both an early election and a victory that would result in a convention dominated by men who favored the abolition of slavery, a result previously thought doubtful. Governor Shepley held back from setting a date for the election, and there was some lingering fear that the call for a convention was "premature"; but the Free State men were buoyant, energetic, and united. Flanders reported to Chase that even Michael

Hahn, whose earnestness in the antislavery cause had at times been suspect, "has behaved well; he is thouroughly with us, in our free state movement, and in other matters he will be right." The Free State leaders expected to prevail.[28]

Back in Washington, however, Lincoln remained apprehensive over the success of speedy reorganization under the direction of Durant and General Shepley. In his eagerness to attain this goal, Lincoln wrote Flanders on November 9, four days after his letter to Banks, suggesting that a preliminary vote be taken on whether there should be a state convention to remodel the constitution or on "any proper question" if that would have "the effect of crystallizing" action.[29] The suggested strategy was not very dissimilar from the one General Banks would shortly present him in detail. By December 1863 the views of president and general were converging.

Banks could recognize a rebuke even when disavowed. Lincoln's November letter did not reach him until December 2 on his return from Texas. The reprimand that he perceived in it stung the general. He checked all orders he had received. They only confirmed his sense of being unfairly held accountable for a matter in which he had not been given responsibility. To Lincoln he wrote three long replies, one on December 6, the second on the sixteenth, and the third on December 27, with a duplicate dated the thirtieth. He also sent off a letter to Boutwell on December 11.

When Boutwell received Banks' letter on the twenty-first, he hurried to see the president as soon as the House adjourned. The very same day he wrote Banks a long report of the interview. The president, who had received by then Banks' first letter, showed it to Boutwell together with a file of previous correspondence with the general. Lincoln stated that neither General Shepley nor any other person "was clothed, intentionally, with separate or independent powers." Although uncertain "that your language authorized me to so do," Boutwell then read to Lincoln the letter from Banks.

It made a deep impression upon the President and in no manner unfriendly to you. After some further conversation he said he should write to you saying that he understood and expected you to exercise supreme and undivided

[68]

authority and to take the matter of State organization into your own hands. ... The President is still anxious to have La. organized as a free State, and I believe he fully agreed with my suggestion that it could be well and speedily accomplished only by putting the power in your hands.

Boutwell's report was accurate. Three days later, on December 24, Lincoln wrote Banks to "tell you that you are a master of all, and that I wish you to take the case as you find it, and give us a free-state reorganization of Louisiana, in the shortest possible time."[30]

Banks' letter to Boutwell has not survived, but those to Lincoln are intact.[31] The first constituted a strong statement of his concurrence in Lincoln's desire for speedy reorganization, his lack of authority over the matter, and his conviction that in "the initial reconstruction" a free state could be achieved "beyond the possibility of failure." It expressed surprise that Lincoln "attached responsibility to my actions in regard to the execution of your wishes." Governor Shepley and Durant believed that all decisions as to state elections and reorganization were in their hands, and he himself had so understood. Last October he had urged them to act "by the quickest methods" but they were not interested in his advice; in view of their attitude, he had refrained from sending Lincoln a lengthy letter he had drafted presenting his own views.[32] "How then can I be in any just sense responsible for the result?" A free state could be created within sixty days, but not under the direction of those understood to be responsible. Their abstract theories and private interests, according to Banks, repelled the necessary unity of action. Banks did not spell out the plan he had in mind, but this first letter clearly implied early action other than an election for convention delegates. Banks' second letter dealt not with the problem of Reconstruction but with other frustrations occasioned by obstacles he had encountered from the U.S. District Court, Treasury agents, and city officials acting under the authority of General Shepley as military governor. Banks urged that the division of authority in New Orleans either be unified or clearly defined.[33]

The third letter was written after Banks had seen the December 8 Proclamation of Amnesty and Reconstruction but before he had received Lincoln's response to his first letter. Now Banks presented his

[69]

plan to order an election for governor and other state officials under the antebellum constitution with its slavery provisions declared inoperative and void by military authority. The registration of voters would conform with the president's proclamation and at the same time would recognize steps already taken that were not inconsistent with it. A convention for the revision of the state constitution would be held after the government was organized, thus breaking with Durant's plan to call a convention before establishing an elected state government.[34] Banks argued that the procedure being followed "does not seem to promise results so speedy or certain." A convention that met before the establishment of local government would consider "every theory connected with human legislation," thus entailing "an inevitable and dangerous, if not fatal delay."

It is impossible to determine whether details of Banks' plan for action had been indicated in the earlier letters to Boutwell and thus known to Lincoln when he made his decision to give Banks full authority to proceed with Reconstruction. There is no doubt, however, that Lincoln approved the procedure Banks outlined despite its abandoning of his 1862 injunction against a reorganization movement initiated by the military. On receiving the general's third letter, the president wrote that he was "much in hope that, on the authority of my letter, of December 24th, you have already begun the work." Banks was to "proceed with all possible despatch, using your own absolute discretion" so long as he did not depart from what he had written the president or from the December 8 annual message and proclamation. The only other limitation Lincoln placed upon Banks was in his letter of December 24 in which he stated that work already done was not to be thrown away nor "war" made upon Governor Shepley or anyone else "unless it be found that they will not co-operate with you."[35]

Banks' third letter gave Lincoln full knowledge that the general intended to use military authority openly to initiate Reconstruction and obtain acquiescence in emancipation; it also explained his rationale. Banks stated that he was opposed to any settlement of the slavery issue except upon the basis of immediate emancipation. He argued that the procedure he outlined would gain consent from southerners who would not vote directly against slavery but would accept its destruction as the result of war. He thought it better to secure freedom "by consent than by force, better still by consent *and* force." From the start the new state government would be based upon the absolute prohibition of slavery. The electors by voting would in effect be accepting immediate unqualified emancipation, and the subsequent convention would confirm the decision by revising the constitution. Were a convention to be held first, while the country was in the throes of a presidential contest, and should it raise issues, regarding blacks "beyond emancipation" or in respect to the status of the secession states of a nature "unacceptable to moderate men, although successful here," it might "imperil the results of the election in other states." Banks continued: "The *history* of the world shows that Revolutions which are not controlled, and held within reasonable limits, produce counter Revolutions. We are not likely to prove an exception to this general law." Earlier in the letter Banks had argued that if the Negro "gains freedom, education, the right to bear arms . . . his best friend may rest content for another year at least." That is to say, Banks thought suffrage for blacks could wait.

With characteristic optimism, and an uncharacteristic forthrightness, Banks predicted that his plan could not fail, and explained why. Success of the new government and of emancipation would be assured by the support of the army and navy and the influence of civil officials and the administration. These influences would also secure the election of "proper men."

Banks did not rest his case upon written persuasion alone. On January 2, George Denison, Secretary Chase's most intimate and regular informant among New Orleans officialdom, left for Washington after an evening conference of several hours with Banks and Plumly.[36] He carried a letter from Banks to the president asking an interview so that Denison might "give you information in regard to the organization of a State government and other topics embraced in my reply to your letter of the 5th November." The envoy did not have to persuade the president, who had already decided that the commanding general would be "master of all." Lincoln entrusted to Denison his reply to Banks' third letter in which Lincoln urged Banks to proceed with dispatch. It ended with an expression of presidential pleasure that "Mr. Dennison, the Collector at New-Orleans" would give Banks "his full, and zealous cooperation" and with an injunction to other officeholders: "It is my wish, and purpose, that all others, holding authority from me, shall do the like; and, to spare me writing, I will thank you to make this known to them."[37] Thus Lincoln promptly invoked his influence and power as the source of federal patronage in order to ensure the success of Banks' plan. Having tried by indirection and "prudence" to obtain what he wanted—a free state in Louisiana before his tenure of office was threatened by the presidential election, Lincoln abandoned caution and openly backed "consent *and* force" as means for obtaining his goal. Once committed, he was resolute in his support of Banks.

The support of Secretary Chase did not prove so steadfast as Lincoln's, but it was readily given to Denison for Banks' proposals. The fact that Chase knew and approved the plan "heartily" is indisputable, established both by Banks' statements and by those of Denison and of Chase himself. The secretary thought the plan would work and, in his own words, "give earlier results than could be obtained in any other way."[38] Denison, who was a young man, returned to New Orleans elated and self-congratulatory. From there he wrote his uncle that during his four days in Washington "I did 4 weeks-work. Nobody comes up to the scratch in such matters, as I do." He included no particulars but did comment: "Gen. Banks is doing finely here and his success both civil and military is assured. Isn't Old A. Lincoln a trump?"[39]

Banks proceeded to carry out his plan of action. On January 11, 1864, he issued a proclamation setting February 22, Washington's birthday, for the election of a governor plus six other state officials and the first Monday in April for election of delegates to a constitutional convention. The gubernatorial campaign was lively and the election brought out over 11,000 voters, more than double the presidentially required minimum. It resulted in a decisive victory for the moderate Michael Hahn over his two opponents—Benjamin Flanders, the choice of the Durant Radicals, and J. Q. A. Fellows, candidate of the proslavery Conservatives. On the following March 4, Hahn was inaugurated governor with much fanfare. Banks had presented Lincoln, as promised, a free state government within sixty days. Lincoln accepted it as such, sending Hahn congratulations "on having fixed your name in history as the first-free-state Governor of Louisiana." So did Chase, who wrote Banks as "the honored instrument" of the "good and great" work of "making Louisiana a Free State."[40]

Despite the diminution of Banks' influence caused first by his absence and then by the disasters of his Red River campaign, completion of reorganization followed under his guidance, and was largely as planned. The convention election was held March 28, a few days earlier than originally intended. There was a sharp drop in the number voting, yet more than 6,000 participated. The convention met from April 6 through July 25, 1864, making major revisions in the antebellum constitution, including the unqualified, uncompensated abolition of slavery. The constitution was ratified on September 5 by a vote of 6,836 to 1,566. At the same time, voters chose representatives to Congress from five districts and elected members to a state legislature, which met promptly in special session followed by a regular session. On October 5, that body elected two United States senators. On February 14, 1865, upon receiving the governor's message transmitting the Thirteenth Admendment, the lower house suspended its rules and adopted unanimously a resolution to ratify; three days later the state senate took like action, with one nay vote.[41] Convention, electorate, and legislature had vindicated Banks' prediction that his plan could not fail to strike down slavery.

From the perspective of early November 1863, when the momentum for reorganization appeared indefinitely stalled and the prospect of local action to destroy slavery seemed precarious and distant, the Lincoln-Banks initiative had succeeded. Yet the free state they had brought forth was an outcast, shunned or suspect by antislavery men whose cause it was meant to serve, and a precipitant of the mid-year clash between president and Congress over Reconstruction. At the nation's capital, and throughout the Northeast, Banks' actions came under immediate and continuing fire. After the September elections, the general left New Orleans for Washington and remained six months in order to help the president develop support for Louisiana's readmission to the Union. Lincoln and Banks made every effort, yet they failed to obtain recognition from either house of Congress. By the session's end, Republicans in the Senate would have seated the two Louisianians except for the filibuster of Charles Sumner; but Sumner prevailed. His intransigence was fueled by his commitment to suffrage for blacks.

CHAPTER THREE

The Struggle for Credibility

The Lincoln-Banks government was in jeopardy from its very inception in early 1864. Like other strong presidential action during the Civil War, that in Louisiana was open to the charge of dictatorship and executive usurpation of legislative responsibility. Constitutional scruple and congressional jealousy of its own authority played a role in Louisiana's failure to gain readmission, but standing alone, those concerns would not have proved decisive. What undermined a notable achievement in creating a free state in the midst of war and political uncertainty was the split in the ranks of Louisiana's original Free State men. It led to bitter suspicions, distortion of fact, and on the part of Thomas J. Durant an implacable determination to destroy what Banks and Lincoln had wrought. In the course of the contest between Banks and the Free State dissidents, from January 1864 to March 1865, the latter shifted their fighting issue from immediate emancipation, first to civilian control of Reconstruction, then to Negro suffrage and the charge that under Banks' labor regulations freedmen were not free. As leader of the opposition, Durant proved an effective and tenacious adversary. But the extent of his success owed much to Banks' blunders and to distrust of Lincoln by antislavery men.

It was ironic that the suffrage issue brought Durant victory and Lincoln defeat in the struggle over admission of Louisiana in the winter of 1864-1865. Suffrage had not been the main thrust of Durant's attack nor was it a question on which he and Lincoln substantially disagreed. When Durant turned on Lincoln in February 1864, and did so with the charge that Banks was made "master" out of fear that "those termed radicals" were about to urge suffrage for blacks, Durant, Lincoln, and Salmon P. Chase, the recognized Radical of Lincoln's cabinet, all stood on common ground. They were agreed that freeborn blacks should be enrolled as voters. Lincoln's concurrence in this position was a fact not generally known, but a fact of which Durant had written evidence. To compound the irony, while Durant abandoned the suffrage issue in Louisiana after the election of Hahn as governor, Lincoln set in motion a major effort to open the door for black enfranchisement.

As late as the summer of 1862 Thomas Jefferson Durant seemed a most unlikely leader for Louisiana's antislavery movement. At the time he owned a slave woman and her children as domestic servants, and he penned a vigorous protest that reached the president on behalf of Union planters who were complaining that the military by receiving slaves within their lines were undermining the relationship between master and slave. Durant's letter brought a sharp response from Lincoln. Shortly thereafter, a visit to Washington, which included an interview with Secretary Chase, resulted in Durant's turning against slavery in the interest of Unionism.[1] By early 1863 there is no doubt but that he was a sincere and forceful Free State leader.

Durant's liberal views on suffrage, as distinct from those on slavery, developed gradually. The Free State plan of reorganization that he fathered provided that only loyal free *white* male citizens should vote. When and why he embraced a larger view is obscure. Durant's correspondence with Chase suggests that his first public reference to the desirability of black suffrage came in response to the secretary's prodding. This first statement was an ambiguous one in which Durant predicted that rebels would try to vote and that the danger would be "counteracted by the enlargement of the area of citizenship," presumably even beyond citizenship for the freeborn. Speaking "for himself he was willing to lay aside any prejudices he might have had, and adopt any necessary measures to counteract such influence." A few weeks later he clarified his position by arguing the necessity of "extending the elective franchise to the free colored citizens, most of whom were men of education and property"—i.e., to New Orleans Creoles. At the time Durant, as attorney general and commissioner of registration, refused to register "free colored citizens" apparently preferring that General Shepley as military governor assume the responsibility. He did take a notable stand by championing the seating of colored delegates at a Convention of the Friends of Freedom and won. This was in mid-December, at the time of his public support for colored Creole enfranchisement. The action was later interpreted as support for political equality, but there was nothing in Durant's very general tribute to "the great principle of equality and fraternity" or in the resolutions of the convention, over which he presided, that specifically mentioned suffrage. No hard evidence has come to light that establishes Durant's willingness at this time to support actively enfranchisement beyond that for freeborn blacks, and a good deal to suggest the contrary.[2]

By January 1864 Lincoln had twice given approval for the enrollment of freeborn Negroes as voters in Louisiana, first formally, then informally. The first and official permission was embodied in the order which Secretary of War Stanton gave at the president's express direction to Governor Shepley August 24, 1863. The relevant passage read: "you will cause a registration to be made in each parish in the State of Louisiana of *all the loyal citizens* of the United States." The omission of "white" from the orders to Shepley, which otherwise followed closely the Durant proposals, was no oversight. The evidence on this point is convincing. Of the relevant documents, the most available is a retrospective letter to Lincoln from Chief Justice Chase. Here Chase clearly implied, but did not directly state, that the order was meant to include free colored men. More direct testimony can be found in his private correspondence while secretary. Two weeks after the issuance of Stanton's order, Chase wrote Robert Dale Owen that despite his fears that slavery would be perpetuated, "progress" had been made. Sometime back, he explained, the secretary of war had sent him the plan for reorganizing Louisiana with delegates elected to a constitutional convention based upon the free white population. Chase had returned the document with comments on the absurdity of excluding any representation from those who had furnished twenty regiments of volunteers. His letter continued:[3]

Nothing was then done, but lately Gov. Shepley has been here and has gone back with authority to make districts having regard to the number of *loyal Citizens of the United States* resident in them and to call a convention to be elected by these loyal citizens and I believe he has taken with him one or more copies of the Attorney General's opinion on Citizenship. For the instructions we are indebted to Mr. Stanton and the President.

Some two months later, on November 19, Chase wrote Durant a letter meant to prod him into registering freeborn blacks. It further confirms Lincoln's awareness of the "white" omission in Stanton's order and provides an insight into the president's intent, and his caution in handling the suffrage issue.[4]

I see you are carrying on the registry. Do you register any names of colored citizens? My own impression is that it is safest as well as most just to do so; and I know that the instructions to Gen. Shepley were framed in view of the opinion of Attorney General Bates on the citizenship of colored freemen, natives of the United States. I do not know, however, nor have I any reason to believe that the instructions were intended to establish any imperative rule of registration.

What Chase was telling Durant was that Lincoln's instructions permitted, but did not mandate, the enrollment of freeborn colored men. On his own authority, Chase was advising Durant to do so.

In answering the letter, Durant did not reply directly to Chase's question or his implied advice. What Durant wrote was that he "had long and intimate business relations with the leading free men of African descent in this city," that he believed they "should be admitted to the registration," and had "advocated it in my public speeches here. These men have petitioned Gov. Shepley to allow them to be registered; to this he promised to reply but has not yet done so." While Durant ended by asking Chase to command him "as one desirous of devoting all his humble abilities to the cause of the country and of freedom," he also struck a plaintive note. "You must give your sympathies to those who for the sake of the country are willing to be called abolitionists in the extreme south: there is some sacrifice in it." A week later he read the Chase letter to the Free State General Committee. Flanders reported that it was applauded "not so much for what it expressed," apparently a reference to the suggestion to register blacks, but "because it was from Mr. Chase." Durant had received Chase's letter on November 30, four days before he made his first public reference to extending the suffrage. In that address he specifically mentioned the attorney general's opinion that all free persons born in the country were citizens. Whether Durant had been aware of the opinion and its implications for voter registration before receiving the Chase letter is not clear. A year later he stated in passing that "according to the proclamation of Gov. Shepley, the names of the colored men were to be put on the roll; but then the question was put off day to day." This was an inaccurate statement and a curious one from the former commissioner of registration, but it does suggest that Durant knew there was authorization for registering freeborn blacks though unable to acknowledge any responsibility for not having done so.[5]

It was characteristic of Chase that he did not let the matter rest with Durant's reply. By the time he had received it, Lincoln had issued the Reconstruction Proclamation with its provision for white suffrage only. Chase did not presume to outflank the president. What he did was raise the question directly with Lincoln. And he gained consent for Durant to proceed with the registration of freeborn blacks. That Lincoln gave approval for their enfranchisement conflicts with the picture of Lincoln as an obstacle to Radical objectives in Louisiana, but there is no doubt of the fact. In his next letter Chase informed Durant of his exchange with the president:

I am particularly gratified by your wise and courageous advocacy of the right of native freeborn colored citizens to participate in the reorganization of the State Governments. I informed the President of your views on this subject, and he said he could see no objection to the registering of such citizens, or to their exercise of the right of suffrage. You will have observed doubtless that in his Message and Proclamation he does not limit reorganization to the precise forms or modes proposed by him, but is willing to accept any form or mode whereby the great ends of restoration to the Union with permanent free State institutions can be best secured.

The following day Chase wrote to Lyman D. Stickney, a direct tax commissioner through whom he hoped to help shape reorganization in

Florida. The secretary informed his subordinate of the "excellent letter from Mr. Durant," who "boldly advocates the right of the freeborn native colored citizens" to participate in reorganizing Louisiana.[6] He continued: "I told the President of it, and he said he could see no objection to their enrollment and voting. I hope you in Florida will go further, and let all of full age vote who have borne arms for the country, or who can read and write, without any other distinctions at present."

Chase's assessment of the flexibility of the Reconstruction Proclamation is convincing. Lincoln himself called attention to the deliberate loopholes in the presidential plan. Passages in the proclamation and in the annual message stating that other modes of Reconstruction would be acceptable, Lincoln informed Banks, "were put into these documents on purpose that some conformity to circumstances should be admissable." After issuing the Reconstruction Proclamation with its restriction of suffrage to antebellum voters, and before the conference with Chase, Lincoln sidestepped the request of a Conservative Unionist for assurance against rumored participation "by free negroes, who do not possess the right of voting under the [antebellum state] constitution."[7].

When Lincoln made Banks "master of all," the option to enroll freeborn blacks was open. This may not have been apparent to Banks for there is no evidence that he was informed of it by Lincoln, Chase, or Durant. He may have thought there was no choice under the terms of the president's Reconstruction Proclamation. Yet it is evident that had Banks known of the option, he would not have exercised it. Banks feared the suffrage issue, that it would split the Union men, endanger the reorganization of the state on the basis of emancipation, or provoke a backlash that would undercut a victory for freedom and Union by counterrevolution. If all these hazards were avoided in Louisiana, there was still the danger that the recognition of blacks as political equals would be so distasteful in the North that it would jeopardize Republican control of the national government. Lincoln was not unmindful of the hazards, but he would minimize them by appearing merely to accede to local Unionists. The president was not ready to initiate a move for black enfranchisement, but Banks—not Lincoln—stood in the way of Creole voting in the initial elections that inaugurated the free state.

Durant did not press the issue. On January 9 when he received Chase's letter with Lincoln's approval for registering freeborn blacks as voters, Durant was more concerned with Banks having been made "master" than with the question of black suffrage. In his reply to Chase, Durant did not even acknowledge Lincoln's authorization. In his letter Chase had included suggestions for a broader black enfranchisement which he hoped the upcoming Louisiana convention would embody in a revised constitution. Durant responded perfunctorily to the secretary's "views as to the elective franchise" as "full of wisdom" and promised that were he a member of the convention "the lesson you have conveyed will not be lost upon me."[8] A fissure had opened within the ranks of those seeking a free state, and it was already swallowing up Durant.

The primary responsibility for the split lay with Banks. It was latent in Lincoln's grant of authority as "master of all." Yet unity could have been maintained had Banks handled the situation with more sensitivity and skill. There is a special irony in the political general failing to be politic. The breach widened in a tangle of affronted pride, mutual suspicion, and conflicting ambition. Had Durant been less persuasive as an advocate or less relentless as a foe the damage might have been contained or repaired. The fate of Lincoln's free state suggests the vulnerability of presidential purpose and power to ineptitude of execution, the obstinacy of human nature, and misperceptions fired by the passion of great ends linked to personal conceits.

A critical sequence of events followed upon Banks' receipt of authority to take charge and "give us a free-state re-organization of Louisiana, in the shortest possible time." When Lincoln's letter arrived, Banks at once informed Durant and asked him to come by for a conference. According to Durant's account, Banks read Lincoln's letter and then "informed me that he intended to order an election of state officers, and members of Congress, and that the Governor to be elected could appoint two Senators." Durant rejoined that Banks or Shepley could order an election in three weeks for a convention, which could form a new constitution under which officers could be elected. When Banks objected that this would take too long, Durant, "being very familiar with the whole subject," assured him that it could be done long before August. Banks "replied in a preemptory tone that it could not. I said no more of course on that point." Durant then argued that members of Congress could not be elected legally until there was a new districting according to the census of 1860. Apparently there was no discussion of the possibility of colored Creoles voting. "The interview terminated without either of us making an impression on the other calculated to effect a change of opinion." In other accounts of his exchange with Banks, Durant wrote that "the word *MASTER* . . . grated harshly upon my ears," that the letter to Banks had been "inspired by incorrect information," and that with Lincoln's taking reorganization "out of our hands. . . . I will not deny that I was deeply mortified."[9]

According to Banks' version of the incident, his first move "after receiving the instructions of the President" was to seek Durant's cooperation. Durant's response was "a distinct declaration, that while he should not oppose the measures that might be adopted he should not under any circumstances assist in their execution." To Banks, this position seemed "indefensible" because Durant based his opposition "entirely upon the *methods* adopted to obtain results and not to the results we hope to produce which are identical in spirit as in form with those advocated by himself"—namely, restoration, "abolition of Slavery at once, and the education, & the recognition of all the rights of the oppressed races." Banks characterized Durant as honest and able in his profession (law) but a blind follower of precedent and wholly "impracticable." It was impossible to obtain his cooperation: "He does not act with other men."[10]

Under Durant's direction, and in response to the message from Lincoln carried by Flanders, the Free State men had been working hard to invigorate the registration process and hold an election for convention delegates on January 25, 1864. They had called a mass meeting for the very evening of the eighth in order to bring pressure upon General Shepley to set the date. The military governor had at first agreed to order the early election requested and then hesitated to act.[11] As

Flanders, who was to preside, entered the meeting, Durant took him aside to tell him of Lincoln's letter and Banks' intentions. The meeting went forward with Durant, an effective orator, receiving an enthusiastic reception for a speech of over an hour which led to resolutions declaring that the "people want a constitutional convention *first* and the election of state officers *second*; and they called upon the Governor to order the election." Durant had defied Banks and had proceeded as if there had been no Lincoln letter or interview. For his part, Banks made no concession to Durant's views in issuing the election proclamation three days later. Yet he sent a copy to Lincoln with the optimistic assurance that the plan would have very general support. Those "who had organized the previous movement, and were confident of being able to control the power of the State," and others who held "lucrative offices" would resist, but their opposition "cannot avail or last long." Banks pledged that no parties would be excluded from "the results of the election" and "every possible effort will be made to harmonize all interests and to have all classes justly represented."[12] Ominously, on the publication of the proclamation Durant promptly resigned as attorney general and as commissioner of registration.

The Free State men were confused, surprised, hurt, angry, and fearful. Yet among them were voices calling for restraint and cooperation. On January 13, the General Committee, with Durant presiding, restated its position but agreed to take part in the election. At the same time the committee issued a call for a nominating convention of Free State Union men. Two days later, the committee offered Banks an olive branch, a memorial requesting that he order the election for convention delegates for the same date as that for state officers. Flanders considered this concession so important that the very next day he wrote Lincoln a troubled, emotional letter stating that he feared Banks would not agree and urging the president "to direct him to comply. This would satisfy the Free State men and cure the dissatisfaction which is universal" among those "who had worked day and night to bring the people up to the support of *all* your measures." He saw a danger that copperheads and proslavery men would unite in an effort to elect state officers who "will bring back slavery and fasten it upon us for years." Requir-

[83]

ing an oath to uphold the Emancipation Proclamation was no safe-guard for "you have not abolished slavery but only emancipated slaves in a portion of the State. There is nothing to prevent the continuance of this as a Slave State if the pro-slavery party gets control." Flanders identified those "against us" as "Cottman, Dr. Kennedy of the *True Delta*, Roselius, and others of the kind." In writing Chase, Flanders was more open in his attack on Banks. He had "no faith whatever in him" and referred to "the Copperhead Conservative faction" as "led by the Maj. General." There is evidence that Flanders had been outspo-kenly hostile to Banks even before the general assumed direction of reorganization, and his animus was fueled by bad relations with Plumly, who supported Banks and wanted Flanders' Treasury post. Flanders' resentment extended to Lincoln. He wrote Chase that "Mr. Lincoln has lost by his letter to Gen. Banks much of the friendship which he previously enjoyed of the loyal men here."[13]

Only hours after writing the president, on January 16, Flanders together with two other designated members of the General Commit-tee met with General Banks. Contrary to Flanders' expectation, the interview went well, with Banks agreeing to order the convention elec-tion for February 22 as requested. He also assured the Free State men that elections would be based upon white population, as they had planned, not upon total population as set by the antebellum constitu-tion (a provision that placed power in the hands of planters) and that all voters would have to take the oath prescribed by the president. The three men departed satisfied and prepared a report expressing their pleasure that Banks had granted "all that we asked." The next day the local press carried the news. In the same issue, the New Orleans *Times*, which was then under the control of Denison and Plumly, urged Free State men to agree on one ticket that would unite all loyal people within and without the party organization. The "great and sincere di-vergence of opinion among free State men" on "the question of negro suffrage and kindred topics" should not be made test questions in the coming canvass; it would be time enough after the election to organize around such questions with a view to amending the state constitution.[14]

The possibility for reconciliation and unity was short-lived.

Within five days word was out that Banks had changed his mind on the date for election of convention delegates, a report that was made official in a letter from Banks to the General Committee dated January 29. For a time Banks even wavered on the requirement of the presidential oath for those who had qualified to vote in 1862 as loyal men. On the latter issue, he was under heavy pressure from Conservatives and faced the possibility that so many might refuse to vote as to jeopardize the needed ten percent participation. Banks referred the question to Lincoln, but held to the original requirement.

Why Banks did not honor his commitment to the Free State men on the date for the convention is not at all clear. A draft of the letter he sent them suggests by its deletions, interlineations, and variant pagination that he labored over an explanation. Careful consideration, he wrote, had convinced him that a February 22 election would not provide enough time to settle the many difficult questions involved in determining the basis of representation. He wished these problems to be fairly considered and all interested parties heard. More vaguely stated was his fear that precipitant action might "peril the great objects in view." The new consitution should provide a model for all the secession states. The "magnitude of the propositions connected with the selection of delegates" required time "for their full and mature consideration." Peyton McCrary has found a note which strongly suggests that Michael Hahn persuaded Banks to change his mind. No record remains, however, of the arguments Hahn may have used. Banks later tried to explain his decision to the Judiciary Committee of the Senate. He had thought it desirable to "ascertain the condition of the public mind" by the general election before committing himself to the election of a convention that would have power to change the fundamental law. If the first balloting had shown the voters "disloyal in the election of candidates" or so few as to discredit the election, the persons elected "would have been without power," and "further proceedings in the restoration of the government could have been suspended without difficulty." In Banks' convoluted prose, this was a discreet admission that he had not been certain of the election outcome and had been prepared to set aside a conservative victory. Evidence which emerged several years later suggests that Lincoln had given prior approval for such action.[15]

For whatever reason made, repudiation of the concession to the Free State Committee was a major blunder. Banks' action could only confirm Durant and Flanders in their suspicions of the general and his plan for reorganization. It was probably the point of no return, leaving a residue of unbridgeable distrust that precluded unity on a Free State gubernatorial candidate or in the subsequent convention election.

In Washington, however, the attack of Durant dissidents on Banks was not at first taken very seriously. In a dispatch from the capital January 23, Whitelaw Reid, the young but widely respected correspondent of the Cincinnati *Gazette*, characterized the anti-Banks protest that had reached the city as "neither temperate nor quite just." He suggested that complaints grew out of a clash of ambition; both Free State leaders and General Banks sought credit for bringing back into the Union the first rebel state with slavery abolished. Reid thought the issues technical rather than substantial and anticipated conciliation. His views probably reflected those of the administration. Although without ready access to the White House, he was close to Secretary Chase, whose presidential ambitions he supported.[16]

Following close upon Banks' about-face on the convention election, reports circulated that Michael Hahn was the general's candidate for governor. Flanders was convinced that Banks intended to manipulate the election in Hahn's favor by the registration of soldiers whose votes Banks would control through his officers and by a last minute disqualification of Free State voters on technicalities. Once elected, Hahn was expect to appoint as senators two of the most extreme proslavery Unionists. The feeling of the old Union men against Banks, Flanders wrote Chase, "is getting to be intense." When the Free State nominating convention met February 1, it was a scene of uproar with the Durant forces trying to maintain control through strict requirements for seating delegates and the Hahn forces disrupting proceedings. The former adjourned to smaller quarters and nominated Flanders. The latter took over the convention hall and nominated Hahn. Each faction claimed to represent the majority. Before adjourning, the Hahn men unanimously approved Banks' plan, the universal immediate extinction of the institution of slavery, and its embodiment in the state constitution. In his acceptance address Hahn pledged that if elected there would not be a slave in the state after February 22.[17]

Up to this point, except for the theoretical implications that could be drawn from the timing of the convention election, what of principle was at stake in the developing battle as perceived by the Durant-Flanders forces was emancipation—immediate emancipation. They feared that a victory for Banks and Hahn, at the very best, would result in a delay such as that voted in Missouri, where after a protracted factional fight an ordinance of emancipation had been passed to take effect in 1870. In a stormy meeting of the Free State General Committee a few days after the convention, a resolution was presented sustaining the Flanders nomination and asking for Flanders the support of all Union men "who in the establishment of civil government in Louisiana, demand, without hesitation or reservation, that slavery shall at once and forever be abolished within our limits." The resolution implied that Hahn was not resolutely committed to the same goal. Opposition to its passage was led by Dr. A. P. Dostie, an outstanding and thoroughly Radical member, who supported Hahn because he thought Banks' plan would work. He was refused the right to address the chair, and the resolution was passed, 49 to 12, with Dostie in a "loud tone" and "violent manner" accusing his associates of foul play. About the same time Durant was charged by the opposition faction with acting from personal motives; he replied that his objection to Mr. Hahn "is purely because I think he heads a reaction." In writing to Secretary Chase, Durant referred to Hahn as "a trickster and a trimming politician." Even as late as the election, just before and again just after, John Hutchins, a partisan of the Durant-Flanders men and an Ohio Radical whom Chase had recently sent to New Orleans as a Treasury agent, wrote the secretary that Banks' plan and Hahn's election, if accepted by Congress, would put the immediate abolition of slavery in jeopardy, even postpone it "to an indefinite future."[18]

Despite such apprehensions, immediate emancipation was never in hazard in the hands of Banks and Hahn. Had the Conservative ticket triumphed, there might have been a danger, but in that event Banks was prepared to disallow the election results. The possibility of such a proslavery victory was in fact remote. Lincoln's tactful firmness, reinforced by a concern for the loaves and fishes, had resulted in the capitulation of an influential group of Conservatives to the president's wish to destroy slavery. In mid-November Hahn had written Lincoln that Cottman who "has differed with us considerably of late on the 'negro question' . . . is coming over all right." By year's end, Cuthbert Bullitt had persuaded his brother-in-law Hugh Kennedy to sell the *True Delta* to Hahn, and the paper announced editorially that its previous views on slavery would no longer be maintained. Hahn's longstanding friendship with these men made it easy for them to embrace his candidacy. Indeed, after the election, Bullitt as president of the "Lincoln Club" tried to take credit with Lincoln both for Hahn's nomination and for his victory![19] Lincoln rewarded Bullitt with the office of United States marshal but, unlike his successor, Andrew Johnson, who received similar blandishments, took care to keep the cooperating Conservatives in a subordinate role. Lincoln used them whereas Johnson was used by Bullitt, Cottman, and Kennedy.

Bullitt had sought to turn the gubernatorial campaign into a Lincoln versus Chase contest, getting some New York reporters newly arrived on the scene to send out news stories identifying the " 'Hahn and Bullitt' party" as the "Lincoln party," and Flanders' supporters as "the Chase party." Denison set the reporters straight. The only distinction Denison saw between the Hahn and Flanders candidacy, as he wrote Chase shortly after the nominations, was that "one is a Banks and the other an Anti-Banks party. In conformity with what I understood to be the wishes of the President and yourself, I have followed Gen. Banks' lead and support Hahn." About the same time, the special correspondent of the New York *Tribune* sent a dispatch from New Orleans reporting that he could find no "essential matter of principle" dividing the two tickets. The "rancor and bitterness between the parties" he attributed solely to "conflicting personal preferences," which he hoped would abate in time "and leave the earnest Free State men of Louisiana to act in harmony." Even after the election, Denison pronounced the "whole contest . . . a personal one, and I have failed to detect any differences in the principles of the two parties, of which one is as radical as the other."[20] No differences in principle clearly emerged, but an ominous difference in tone distinguished the two camps as the campaigning for Hahn took on a decidedly racist coloration.

With the able, educated, free black community of New Orleans demanding a voice in the reorganization of the state, it was perhaps inevitable that the prejudice of race should become an element in the campaign. Had the Free State men remained united behind one candidate, however, it is highly unlikely that racist appeals to voters would have originated in their camp. Twelve days after the nominations, Hutchins reported to Chase that the *Era*, a local newspaper considered Banks' organ, was injecting the rhetoric of "negro-suffrage, negro equality, colored excitement &c" into the campaign to discredit Flanders. A few days later Flanders sent Chase clippings that aroused the secretary's indignation and firmly allied his sympathies with Durant and Flanders.[21] The apparent willingness of Banks to tolerate the sorry tactic of appeal to race prejudice not only was unconscionable for a Massachusetts man but constituted a second major tactical blunder in Banks' effort to establish a free state. In the eyes of antislavery men, the nature of the attack on Flanders' candidacy validated the credentials of Flanders and Durant as the only "earnest and thorough" friends of the colored man.

Curiously, it was Durant who precipitated the black suffrage question into the campaign. At a well-publicized meeting of the General Committee held shortly after the gubernatorial nominations, he practically invited an attack upon the Flanders' candidacy from opponents of black enfranchisement. He did so even though neither he nor Flanders was prepared to make suffrage an issue in the election. This political ineptitude would seem to have arisen from Durant's inability to perceive that his own October letter to Lincoln had some relation to the president's decision to give Banks authority over reorganization. Although Durant had read Lincoln's November 5 letter with its explicit statement of bitter disappointment, he could write the president, apparently in all honesty, that he "was ignorant of having caused any dissatisfaction, until the 8th Janaury 1864, when the Major General Commanding this Department read to me your letter to him of 24th December." Durant had to look for another explanation, and the one he found was that "the men of the Post Master General Blair school have induced the President" to alter the plan to call a constitutional convention. At the General Committee meeting Durant voiced his suspicions openly and extended them further. "He thought the change [in plans for reorganization] was ordered in consequence of a fear at Washington that the people here were getting too radical." He noted that the change was not proposed until after the meeting of the Friends of Freedom at Lyceum Hall on December 15 in which the free black delegation was seated. He believed it was "induced by a fear that negro suffrage would be urged by what was termed radicals. How far this might have been the case, or what might have been the effect if these fears were realized he was not prepared to say."[22] As we have seen, Durant had reason to know from the information Chase had sent him that the accusation against Lincoln was false.

Durant also charged that the election of state officers was "a reactionary movement detrimental to public welfare and therefore hostile to public liberty." This accusation was too much for the *Era*. Picking up the charge of reaction, its editor replied with equal stridency, even while stating that "it has been our desire to avoid this issue of negro suffrage." The *Era* accepted Durant's version of the administration's position on suffrage, though acknowledging that it had no "official information on this point." The *Era* also was ready to plead guilty to Durant's charge of being reactionary "if to free every slave, to educate every black child, and at the same time, to withhold the right of suffrage until the blacks are fit to exercise it, be 'reactionary.'" What the *Era* desired was that Flanders drop out of the race. While some subsequent editorials asserted that he had radical views on black suffrage, others ignored the question or accepted his assurance that black suffrage was not an issue in the campaign. This equivocal position was displaced the day before elections with a blatant racist editorial equating a vote for Flanders with a vote "in favor of negro equality, negro suffrage," and a belief "that the black race is superior to the white race." Hahn's paper, the *True Delta*, avoided the suffrage issue in its editorial columns until the day after the gubernatorial election when it labeled Flanders' party "The Negrohead Ticket." Editorial restraint did not affect news columns nor speakers at pro-Hahn meetings. So far as one can judge from reports in the local papers, Hahn himself, like the *True Delta*, generally avoided the suffrage issue.[23]

Despite the considerable campaign rhetoric, black suffrage was not a clear-cut issue in the contest between Flanders and Hahn. According to the early *Era* editorial, Flanders believed the right should be extended to blacks while Hahn believed "that the time has not yet arrived for negroes to be admitted to political privileges on an equality with the whites." Flanders publicly denied that black suffrage was an issue, that he had ever advocated it, or that he "deemed it practicable." Durant charged that accusations against Flanders on the issue were unfair, that he (Durant) did not know Flanders' opinion, nor did he care, and that for himself "he did not believe in negro equality in the sense in which it was generally used, but he did believe in giving equal justice to them." Hutchins wrote Chase that Flanders was opposed to unrestricted black suffrage while approving black suffrage with "an educational qualification properly guarded," but did not consider the question at issue in the election for governor. After his defeat, Flanders explained to Chase his position on the "question of negro suffrage & equality which was invoked to defeat me."[24]

> I never advocated negro suffrage; have always said as I did to you that I was not ready for that question; but when the charge was made against me by the "Era" I refused to commit myself against negro suffrage. I knew it must at sometime hereafter be conceded to the colored man as a right.

In his reply to that letter, Chase noted that the terms hurled at Flanders and his friends were ones with which antislavery men had always been assailed. He added: "I am only sorry that the epithets were not better deserved." To his old abolitionist friend Plumly, whom Flanders had succeeded in discrediting as placing the election of Hahn above "his life-long principles," Chase sent a reprimand that also reflected upon Durant and Flanders. It "looked a little strange," he wrote, to read Plumly's name among "the stigmatizers" instead of among those stigmatized as " 'Negro-heads' and 'Negro-Equality men'. . . . I supposed that you were in advance of of Mr. Flanders on this question. I am. He goes, I believe, no further than Mr. Durant, if so far; and Mr. Durant limits his advocacy of colored suffrage to Creoles." Plumly indignantly responded that Chase had "readily accepted protests against me from accidental & eleventh hour men, who were, at best, but defeated aspirants for office, not one of whom was 'radical' in our sense."[25]

In short, black suffrage was at stake in the election only in the sense that the race prejudice aroused by its rhetoric, and apparently justified by Hahn's victory, would constitute a formidable obstacle to the grant of any rights to blacks beyond freedom—a point effectively made by Peyton McCrary. It cannot be assumed, however, that had the rhetoric not been invoked by Hahn's partisans, racist opposition would have laid dormant in the face of an effort to extend voting rights to blacks, freeborn or freed. The Era's warning that nineteen out of every twenty voters were against extending the suffrage to blacks, was probably not far afield. Denison believed that such action was "too much in advance of the times."[26] Interestingly, statements on suffrage from both the Hahn and the Flanders camps were made in general terms, thereby avoiding discussion of granting the vote to freeborn blacks or to all who could meet such requirements as Chase had suggested.

Durant, the epitome of Louisiana Radicalism, was not prepared to fight for black suffrage. Chase had urged him to do so assuming that he would be a member of the forthcoming constitutional convention. After Hahn's victory, however, Durant refused to have anything to do with the election of delegates and carried the day in the General Committee for such a policy. For a time, Flanders flirted with the possibility of cooperating with the Conservatives in order to gain control of the convention and oust Hahn, a joint effort obviously not in the interest of a broader suffrage. Chase was so shocked he refused to believe that the reports could be true.[27]

Through written admonitions and through Frank E. Howe as intermediary, Chase tried to remain even-handed and reestablish unity, even after Hahn won the governorship. He wrote the defeated Flanders urging that "all friends of State Organization on the basis of the prohibition of Slavery . . . now act together and secure that main object." To Denison he made clear that his personal preference would have been for Flanders as the more "earnest" man, but assured his protégé that it had been "natural and almost inevitable" for him to have supported Hahn. Chase continued: "If Mr. Hahn redeems his pledges, and goes in earnest for a prompt establishment of a free State, unsullied by compromises in the form of negro apprenticeships or like devices for the continuance of servitude, there can be no ground for permanent division."[28]

For Durant such considerations were not persuasive. With loss of the first round of elections, he called for a repudiation of the whole election procedure as a mere exercise of military power and intimidation. To permit Banks' creation to stand would "inaugurate a system favorable to nothing but military despotism and corruption." Such a departure from constitution and law was not to be tolerated: "It is true we were Abolitionists," Durant explained some months later, "but we were also friends of constitutional government and of individual liberty." At the time, he wrote Chase that the upcoming election for convention delegates would simply mean that General Banks would declare who the members shall be and what the convention shall do "and all these to make seven votes for somebody in the Presidential election." The only hope was "in Congress." A few Durant Radicals did run for election in order to help write the best constitution possible, but they were defeated. The Hahn forces had considered, then summarily dropped, a gesture of conciliation. The bitterness and suspicion that were rife may have been as persuasive as the temptation for the victors to take all. Thus the continuing split in Free State ranks had serious consequences for the composition of the convention. It diminished the number of delegates who could be counted upon as friends of freedom and the black man.[29]

In this vacuum of local white leadership, a movement to open suffrage to blacks was mounted by Lincoln himself, mounted behind the scenes with caution but with unmistakable presidential pressure. The

[93]

congratulatory message Lincoln sent off to Hahn just nine days after his inaugural as governor dealt with the suffrage question in words usually read as casual and indecisive:

> Now you are about to have a Convention which, among other things, will probably define the elective franchise. I barely suggest for your private consideration, whether some of the colored people may not be let in—as, for instance, the very intelligent, and especially those who have fought gallantly in our ranks. They would probably help, in some trying time to come, to keep the jewel of liberty within the family of freedom. But this is only a suggestion, not to the public, but to you alone.

On the surface, this appears a weak, tentative expression of preference. In fact, it represented a presidential directive, tactfully stated but not meant to be taken lightly. The parallel is striking between this admonition on suffrage and the August letter on emancipation that Lincoln had sent to Banks, Hahn, Flanders, and Durant. Lincoln's seeming lack of firmness was both a hedge against the hazard of a presidential stand on black suffrage with an election impending and a means of stimulating action while appearing to defer to local initiative. Hahn and Banks recognized the presidential intent, and acted accordingly. Hahn respected Lincoln's wish to avoid making the letter public but understood that he might use it within discreet limits. Two days after the suffrage letter, Lincoln strengthened Hahn's position generally by investing him "with the powers exercised hitherto by the Military Governor of Louisiana."[30]

Lincoln's "suggestion" to Governor Hahn of March 13 is believed to have been precipitated by an interview the previous day with a delegation of free blacks from New Orleans. They brought a petition with a thousand signatures asking to be registered as voters and pointing out that their application to Governor Shepley and General Banks had brought no response. At the meeting, Lincoln expressed regret that circumstances did not permit the government to confer the right upon them. He gave no indication of the letter he was about to write Hahn, nor any intimation of previous decisions in their favor. The treatment of the delegation again suggests a parallel, this time to Lincoln's fending off requests for an emancipation proclamation during the period

[94]

when he had decided to issue one but awaited a propitious moment to do so. The following news account of his exchange with the New Orleans Creoles, originating in Washington and published in the New Orleans *Era*, has a familiar ring:[31]

In their interview with President Lincoln, he declined to act upon their petition, taking the ground that having the restoration of the Union paramount to all other questions, he would do nothing that would hinder that consummation, or omit anything that would accomplish it. He told them that, therefore, he did nothing in matters of this kind upon moral grounds, but solely upon political necessities. Their petition asking to become citizens and voters being placed solely on moral grounds, did not furnish him with any inducements to accede to their wishes, but that he would do so whenever they could show that such accession would be necessary to the readmission of Louisiana as a State in the Union.

In writing Hahn the next day, Lincoln used an argument that qualified as one of "political necessity," vaguely stated and beautifully embellished, but "political necessity" nonetheless: "To keep the jewel of liberty within the family of freedom."

The most surprising aspect of what Lincoln asked of Hahn was that the president's formulation for suffrage extension went beyond that publicly supported by Durant before the elections and compares favorably with the broader proposals being made at the time by Chase. Durant, it will be recalled, was supporting the vote for freeborn blacks; Lincoln made no distinction between the freeborn and the freed. Chase wished a suffrage requirement which made no distinction as to race, one he termed "universal suffrage." The specifics of his suggestion, however, would neither bring universal suffrage as the term is now generally understood nor equate the requirements for white voters with those for black voters. In effect, he and Lincoln were both pushing for qualified suffrage for blacks, and, of the two proposals, that of Chase was the more susceptible to discriminatory manipulation. Since this conclusion runs contrary to the generally accepted view of the differences between the "Radical" Chase and the "moderate" Lincoln, Chase's advice to Durant sent December 28, 1863, is quoted at length.

I hope your Convention will be wise enough to adopt the principle of universal suffrage of all men, unconvicted of crime, who can read and write, and have a fair knowledge of the Constitution of the State and of the United States. What a glory for Louisiana to be the first State to adopt a Constitution basing the right of suffrage on virtue and intelligence alone. The object might be easily attained by establishing commissions to make examinations, and give certificates for which a small fee, fifty cents or a dollar, might be required. These certificates would naturalize the recipients into the great electoral community.

Chase outlined like procedures for Florida and proposed to Horace Greeley that the editor advocate the plan.[32]

The basic convergence of the views of Chase and Lincoln on black suffrage during this crucial period is also evident in the secretary's reaction to the president's December Proclamation of Amnesty and Reconstruction. Provided with a draft and asked for comment, Chase wrote a critique advising modification in three respects, most importantly by omitting the reference to apprenticeship. Chase made no mention of the desirability of change in the suffrage provisions, which would give only whites the vote in initiating reorganization. More than a year later, in his last public address, Lincoln alluded to Chase's approval of the Reconstruction Proclamation except in the three limited aspects. Chase, then Chief Justice, wrote Lincoln that, according to his memory, he had also objected to the restriction of the initial electorate to those qualified as antebellum voters; he had believed from the beginning that black loyalists should be allowed to participate in Reconstruction. Undoubtedly, such had been his preference, and it is possible that he had expressed it orally with specific reference to the proclamation. Yet, as Chase himself admitted, "I did not, however, say much about the restriction."[33] He most certainly did not allude to it in his written advice on the proclamation. On that occasion Chase apparently recognized the need to defer to political reality. Even behind the scenes, he was urging for the first round of voting in Louisiana no more than that freeborn blacks be allowed to register and participate. To that recommendation Lincoln had agreed.

The "Radical" and the "moderate" were also agreed on the desirability of broader enfranchisement. Until victory for emancipation in Louisiana was assured, Lincoln made no overt move but he stood ready to approve local initiative. Chase recognized this in his December letter to Durant urging a provision for "universal suffrage" in the revised state constitution. "The lever and the fulcrum are give [by the President]," he wrote. "Let voluntary work do the rest." When the volunteers proved wanting, Lincoln turned to professionals who respected presidential purpose and power.

When the Louisiana constitutional convention met in April 1864, there was consensus in favor of the destruction of slavery but it did not extend to measures that would place black men on a level of civil and political equality with whites. What was achieved toward that goal was the result of pressure from Governor Hahn and General Banks with the steadfast support of 21 out of a convention membership of 96. On civil rights short of the ballot, the influence of the general and the governor was consistent with their convictions; on qualified black suffrage, however, they went beyond their personal views of what should be attempted in mid-1864. There can be no doubt that the effort to obtain an extension of the suffrage was made in response to Lincoln. His "suggestion" of March 13 to Hahn was of key import. It may not have been the only signal sent. In view of Banks' conviction three months earlier that the matter could wait at least a year, a passage in a letter to Lincoln of February 25 strongly suggests that the president, before he wrote Hahn, had conveyed to Banks through some intermediary a wish for convention action on qualified black suffrage. Banks wrote reassuringly of the results of the gubernatorial election and the future work of the convention:

> The convention for revision of the constitution will confirm the absolute extinction of slavery upon which the election has proceded and to which every voter has assented, and *provide for such extension of suffrage as will meet the demands of the age*. I have been and still am unable to write as fully as I could wish. . . .

Meeting the "demands of the age" was the euphemism that Banks had used in early references to destroying slavery. By the end of March, he was somewhat more direct, going on record with the Freedmen's In-

[97]

quiry Commission as favoring for freedmen "participation in all the privileges of citizenship according to the development of intelligence and capacity."[34]

On the very day the convention opened, April 6, 1864, Banks from field headquarters on the Red River sent a letter marked "Confidential" to Edward H. Durell, an able New Orleans lawyer who was to play a prominent role in the convention. He had been appointed judge of the district court by Lincoln, with Banks commending Durell as a man of ability and integrity whose "opinions are in concurrence with the policy of your administration." Although there was a general expectation that an eminent Conservative would be elected president of the convention, the Banks-Hahn men apparently had arranged for the office to go to Durell. "Something tells me you will be President of the Convention which meets today," Banks began. Without his usual circumlocutions, he then informed Durell that there was much interest "at Washington" in the question of suffrage. If some system could be established that would secure suffrage on the basis of intelligence and taxation without distinction of color, it would be "advantageous to the state and general government." The constitution of New York, Banks suggested, might offer a good model. "Please give the subject your best consideration."

At the same time, Banks wrote to another member of the convention, Thomas B. Thorpe, apparently making a like suggestion. Thorpe replied at length. He pointed out that the free colored Creole population, which had enjoyed French citizenship and "came into the Union entitled to all the immunities of free white men," could form "a link between the white and the slave emancipated populations and make workable the 'New York clause' of a property qualification." He thought the Negro question difficult, and that the convention would ignore it "unless the property qualification comes in as a middle ground." Banks was impressed with Thorpe's reply and in the midst of military disaster had a copy sent to Boutwell and also to Chase. The latter had written Banks urging that suffrage be extended to all qualified by service in the field or by ability to read, write, and comprehend the state and national constitutions, a letter Banks received some three

[98]

weeks after sending his urgent request to Durell and Thorpe.[35]

The "Negro question" did indeed prove difficult. The convention provided suffrage for whites only. At one point in its proceedings an amendment was passed by an overwhelming majority that would have prohibited the legislature from ever passing an act authorizing free blacks to vote! By pressure and stratagem the liberal forces backed by Banks and Hahn succeeded in reversing that decision and obtaining a constitutional provision authorizing the legislature to enfranchise non-whites on the basis of military service, taxation, or intellectual fitness. The suffrage clause was permissive, not mandatory, and thus fell short of Lincoln's goal. Nonetheless it was a notable achievement in view of the racial bias dominant in the convention, an attitude that mirrored public opinion. Denison thought the constitutional provision "a great deal"—in his view "more than reasonably could have been expected." He explained to Chase that the authorization had been very difficult to get through the convention. Its passage was made possible "only by unremitting efforts by Gov. Hahn, Gen. Banks and others," who succeeded in changing nearly forty votes. "In this matter," Denison reported, "Gov. Hahn worked faithfully and well." Anything more in the present state of public opinion could not be sustained and would render whites "permanently and bitterly hostile, so that they cannot be made friends to the Gov't." Denison had seen great progress in the racial attitude of whites during the past two years and thought it would continue and grow as blacks became educated and whites became accustomed to the new relationship. And political realities would help. By November, Denison was predicting that when the rest of the state returned to the Union and "the opposite party strives to get the power, the present dominant party, through the Legislature, will immediately confer suffrage on all colored men, so that by their assistance they may retain control of public affairs."[36]

Opposition in the convention to publicly supported education for black children, while less virulent than opposition to black suffrage, was formidable. Again, the liberal forces finally carried the day, writing into the revised constitution a mandate to the legislature to "provide for the education of all children of the State, between the ages of six and eighteen years, by maintenance of free public schools by taxation or otherwise." Although the general expectation was that separate schools for the two races would be maintained, nothing in the constitution required separation or prevented integration.

There were additional changes from the antebellum constitution with benign implications for the Negro in freedom. The restriction of militia service to "free white men" was amended to read: "All able-bodied men in the State shall be armed and disciplined for its defense." The implications were far-reaching in view of the traditional relation between militia service and citizenship and white disapproval of blacks bearing arms. Representation in the state legislature was to be based upon the number of eligible voters, thus undercutting the old planter predominance without specifying that apportionment be according to white population, as had both Durant and Banks in initiating Reconstruction. Traditional civil rights provisions not in the antebellum constitution were added to safeguard against excessive bail, excessive fines, cruel and unusual punishment, or unreasonable searches and seizures. Most important was a new article reading: "All courts shall be open; and every person, for any injury done him, in lands, goods, person, or reputation, shall have remedy by due course of law, and right and justice administered without denial or unreasonable delay." All such protections were understood as applying equally to both races.[37]

Lincoln's March 13 letter to Hahn, though sent in confidence and phrased as mere suggestion, had been effectively used by the governor. Shortly after Lincoln's death when asked to make the text public, Hahn did so explaining that the letter "although marked 'private,' was no doubt intended to be seen by other Union men in Louisiana beside myself, and was consequently shown to many members of our Constitutional Convention and leading free-State men." Hahn's characterization of Lincoln's style and his evaluation of Lincoln's influence are revealing: "The letter, written in the mild and graceful tone which imparted so much weight to Mr. Lincoln's simple suggestions, no doubt had great effect on the action of the Louisiana Convention in all matters appertaining to the colored man"—of which Hahn listed "instantaneous, uncompensated emancipation," provision for "the education of all children, without distinction of color," "enrollment of all men, white and black, in the militia," and investing the legislature "with power to extend to the colored man the highest privilege of citizenship."[38]

As soon as the convention finished its work, Hahn left for Washington to inform the president of its achievements and of the perils ahead. At the same time, Banks wrote Lincoln summarizing the constitutional provisions affecting blacks. He recommended that those who had "labored so faithfully in this work" receive recognition from the government, and reported that with very few exceptions, one of them Denison, the civil officers of the Treasury and judiciary had been in "open and unreasoning hostility."[39]

With the new constitution facing another round of elections for ratification, Lincoln mobilized the power of his office. On August 9 he sent Banks a succinct directive and authorization. He had just seen the new constitution, he wrote, and was "anxious that it shall be ratified. . . . I will thank you to let the civil officers in Louisiana, holding under me, know that this, is my wish, and to let me know at once who of them openly declare for the constitution, and who of them, if any, decline to so declare." Banks used the patronage threat with effect although not with complete success in mobilizing officeholders. Denison had been absolved by Banks of any culpability. Yet he was so concerned that damaging reports would be sent to Washington by the Bullitt Conservatives, who were supporting the constitution, that after the election he sent directly to Lincoln an accounting of the vote of every local Treasury appointee! Eight had been absent on leave, twenty-five were under the age of 21, forty-one had not resided in the state for the requisite one year, thirty-four were out of the city on official duty, eighty-five had voted for the constitution. "Those who ought to have voted but did not" numbered forty. Denison commented: "I regard the obligation on a Gov't official to vote, as imperative. These [40] persons were reminded by me of their duty, and they shall soon learn that it was not for their interest to disregard it."[40]

Without the push from Lincoln, the new constitution might have been in danger, not so much from "no" ballots as from nonvoting. The convention and its record were under strong attack. Its members were deprecated as nonentities, ignorant, vulgar, irresponsible, extravagant, and corrupt. Indeed, the disrepute of the 1864 convention parallels that which long obscured the achievements of the Radical Reconstruction conventions of 1868. Historical scholarship has been more tardy in reassessing the reputation of the Lincoln-Banks body. Peyton McCrary has now established that its delegates were overwhelmingly middle class, from the professions and the business community or local office-holders. His account is generally sympathetic to Durant and critical of Banks, yet he has characterized the convention's record as "impressive." The achievements were the more remarkable in view of the handicaps under which the forward-looking leaders of the convention functioned, limitations far more severe than those faced in the Radical conventions two years later. A sudden change in General Banks' fortune and popularity had followed upon the debacle of the Red River campaign and threatened to undermine his influence. The military situation so demoralized the convention that Judge Durell as presiding officer was subsequently credited by "his firmness and sound judgment" with preventing it from dissolving in a panic. Though still nominal commander of the department, Banks was stripped of military responsibilities, which were assigned to General E.R.S. Canby. Moreover, from first to last, the convention was a target for attack not only from the Conservative old-elite right but from the Durant Radical left. In an open letter to Henry Winter Davis which made the front page of the New York *Evening Post*, Durant called for the rejection of the work of "the so-called consitutional convention" by Congress "no matter what might be its provisions." And he did so in the name of "all the friends of freedom in Louisiana."[41]

To insure ratification, and a sizable vote, Banks did not rely upon the power of patronage alone. There were paid canvassers, mass meetings, rallies, a torchlight parade, pressures subtle and not so subtle. To Dostie, still faithful, still Radical, Banks entrusted the selection and supervision of canvassers who would "induce men to register." "There should not be too strong a demand for affirmative votes upon the Constitution," he counseled Dostie. Ratification could not be defeated but the constitution might face "serious opposition elsewhere, and the thrusts of our enemies" would be "as successfully parried . . . by a negative vote . . . as by a vote in its favor."[42]

With the constitution ratified by a respectable turnout, the reconstructed state would soon come knocking at the doors of Congress. Its credentials should have cheered Radical men in 1864—unqualified freedom, equality before the law, an open door to gradual enfranchisement of blacks. Except as to voting and officeholding, all distinction between white and black had been struck from the constitution. Had there been no split in the Free State forces, no racist rhetoric in the initial campaign, it is quite possible that the remaining discriminations would have been eliminated for such blacks as could meet relatively broad suffrage qualifications. Even as framed, what Hahn, Banks, and Lincoln had wrought went further than the provisions of the Wade-Davis bill toward establishing equal citizenship. The latter provided only a limited civil equality by directing that laws for the trial and punishment of white persons should extend to all persons during the interim provisional government. No civil rights requirement other than freedom was mandated for inclusion in the state constitutions that would thereafter be controlling. Nor did the Wade-Davis bill breach the suffrage barrier. Indeed, in initiating Reconstruction, Congress would have limited jury duty as well as voting to whites.[43] In comparison, the stillborn free state of Lincoln and Banks represented an advance in the status of free blacks of potentially great significance.

The Lincoln-Banks government would have received a ready welcome at the nation's capital had it arrived with the solid support of all Louisiana's Free State leaders.[44] Instead, the new order was discredited before receiving a hearing. Durant had preceded it to Washington, both in person and in a shower of letters. He had worked upon the sensitivities of the Radical leadership—their jealously of congressional authority, their suspicion of Lincoln, their fear of losing the battle against slavery, and above all their desire to realize antislavery goals without fracturing the constitutional framework of government by the consent of the governed. Reconstruction by military authority was suspect on every account. Durant made the most of traditional aversion to arbitrary government. He argued that the Louisiana elections, state government, convention, and consititution were mere projections of the will of the military commander, of no legitimacy whatsoever, an executive usurpation of power belonging rightfully and exclusively to Congress. And he made certain that his views reached a wide public by being printed in northern newspapers or as pamphlets. When Congress reassembled in December, Durant had waiting a petition signed by Louisiana citizens urging that the state's representatives not be seated. A month later he was arranging that a copy of a new protest he had written be sent to every member of Congress.[45]

Durant's influence has been succinctly assessed by Joseph Tregle: "Probably no man did so much to convince Congress and a broad segment of the American public that Presidential Reconstruction, at least in Louisiana, was a betrayal of the cause of freedom and American republicanism."[46] It can be added that Durant's impact shifted the course of Reconstruction history, despite the fact that he did not succeed in convincing a majority of congressional Republicans that the Lincoln-Banks creation was unworthy of admission, and the probability that Henry Winter Davis and Charles Sumner, leaders of the opposition, did not need convincing. Nonetheless, Durant provided Lincoln's critics with moral reassurance and ammunition for debate which hardened opposition to the president's Reconstruction efforts, making compromise difficult, volatile, and—as fate would have it—unrealized before Lincoln's death. The angry Wade-Davis Manifesto rested its case against Lincoln heavily upon Durant's version of events. The government in Louisiana it declared a mere creature of the president's will, an oligarchy "imposed on the people by military orders under the form of election, at which generals, provost marshals, soldiers and camp-followers were the chief actors, assisted by a handful of resident citizens, and urged on to premature action by private letters from the President." Sumner transformed Durant's staid prose into flowing rhetoric in his famous condemnation of Louisiana as "a mere seven-month abortion, begotten by the bayonet in criminal conjunction with the spirit of caste." Louisiana was left waiting and so was a general plan of Reconstruction upon which Lincoln and Congress might otherwise have agreed.[47]

Possibly there was one man who could have restrained Durant or offset the damage of his attack. That man was Salmon P. Chase. For reasons not difficult to understand, his role was ambiguous. Although Chase deplored the division among Free State men in Louisiana and counseled unity, he exerted no pressure upon Durant or Flanders to forbear criticism. Indeed, his reply to Durant's first relatively restrained report of Banks' action could easily have been read, or misread, by Durant as an invitation to defy the general and appeal to Congress. Chase expressed hope that every effort would be made to organize a free state "under the same lead as would have controlled it" had the original plan been followed. He regretted that Durant would not permit his name "to be used for Governor," assuring him that he had the confidence of the country "to an extent of which you have probably a very imperfect conception" and could render a most important service in the reestablishment of the Union on the basis of freedom. Then he ended the letter with the following paragraph:

There is considerable feeling in Congress about the proclamation of General Banks. A majority, and probably a large majority, of the Union Senators and Representatives look with distrust upon the reorganization under military proclamation. They think that such organization should take place in pursuance of some settled principles established by law,—and calculated to secure the national peace against future attempts at secessions and rebellion.

In answer, Durant said nothing of Chase's hope that all Free State men would unite in bringing back Louisiana into the Union on the basis of freedom. He attacked Hahn as a trickster, Banks as a political partisan, their supporters as hostile to liberty, and the administration as having erred in trying to hurry civil reorganization. The present danger was that the new constitution to be framed would "fasten upon us a form of state government founded on no higher sentiment than the 'epidermic prejudice' "; the remedy: "Congress should assume control of the whole matter and fix on an immutable basis the civil and political status of the population of African descent, before any state shall be readmitted into the Union."[48] As Flanders' defeat loomed in sight, Durant had decided that he would appeal to Congress to upset the Lincoln-Banks government. His play upon Chase's passionate antiracist convictions effectively defused any protest that Chase might otherwise have made to Durant's challenge of administration policy.

Chase never repudiated the Banks government or broke with Banks personally. However, he took no effective supportive action, though it was well within his power to do so. For example, it had been understood that Flanders would resign his office as Treasury special agent on assuming the presidency of the newly established national bank, yet when Durant interceded and Flanders clung to the office, Chase acquiesced despite the political implications of this favor. "It will be entirely agreeable to me that you retain the Agency," he finally wrote Flanders, "and I fully agree with you that the Free State Party should be sustained [even?] if all its members do [cannot?] be fully approved. Let us [do?] our full duty & let others be responsible for [their own?] course." Earlier Flanders had let Chase know of the plan to publish a statement showing that the election was carried for Hahn by "military dictation throughout"; Chase had offered no objection.[49] The Cabinet's Radical had no stomach for disciplining "earnest" men, and with his predicament one can sympathize.

Of a different order was the reluctance to support Lincoln's policy growing out of Chase's bitterness at having to bow out of the presidential race and then to leave the cabinet. In the very letter by which Horace Greeley learned of Chase's decision to withdraw as candidate, the secretary stated that he had written "to call your attention to the aspects in Louisiana. Messrs Durant, Flanders & our truest men are set aside because they are willing that intelligent creoles should vote without regard to complexion, and the paper owned & edited by the Governor elect calls them 'Negroheads.' " When the president accepted his resignation, Chase's pained reaction led him to distort Lincoln's policy even more explicitly. "It is well known to the country," he wrote Frank Howe, "that Mr. Lincoln & I have not for a long time been accordant in our views." Chase continued:

He thought the best policy was to have no policy. I thought definite ideas and decisive action upon them important. He was slow and reluctant in coming to the conclusion that all loyal men in rebel states ought to be free men and should be organized for armed defense of themselves & the Union—& even yet though willing to put arms into their hands he is not willing to put ballots. Within the last few days he has pocketed the great act of Congress for the reorganization of loyal governments in rebel states on the basis of universal freedom. In all other matters my views & his are opposite.

Blinded by his sense of grievance and his conviction of moral superiority, Chase could not recognize, even in private, that he and Lincoln were in substantial accord on Reconstruction policy in Louisiana, including support for qualified black suffrage. Months later as Chief Justice, when Chase had recovered some balance in respect to Lincoln, he still could not acknowledge the concurrence. It is not surprising that when Durant called upon him in July 1864 to discuss Louisiana matters, a few days after Lincoln had accepted his resignation as secretary, Chase was in no mood to deflect a battle against Lincoln, Banks, and the fledgling regime in Louisiana. His diary entry for the day referred to the "almost proslavery course of the President."[50]

Durant had laid the foundations for his attack before he arrived in Washington. Ironically, Banks had assisted him. The verbal excesses of Banks' official pronouncements as commanding general were his third major blunder, for they immensely strengthened Durant's hand. Actually, the theoretical position Banks took was defensible. As occupied territory in time of war, New Orleans and adjacent parishes were in fact under military control. Any self-government conceded would be accountable to the military. Before Banks was made "master," Durant himself did not challenge military authority emanating from presidential directives. Indeed, he eagerly sought its active support. His earliest letters attacking Banks recognized that what had changed since January 8, when the general assumed control of reorganization, was a matter of appearance rather than a matter of legality or constitutional legitimacy. Given an unprecedented situation without any one obvious, safe, and uncontestably logical constitutional resolution of the restoration problem—and no action by Congress, Banks' concept of gradually surrendering increments of military authority to elected officials as they and the electorate met the tests of loyalty and "the demands of the age," was as reasonable and legitimate a method of Reconstruction as any.[51]

Unfortunately for Banks, he felt that he must proceed with a flourish. His proclamation ordering elections for state officers ended with a grand and quite unnecessary declamation. "The fundamental law of the State is martial law," it asserted, then went on and on, denouncing faction as treason while liberty was in peril, invoking the "wish of the President," and urging the people of Louisiana to immortal fame by announcing "to the world the coming restoration of the Union in which the ages that follow us have a deeper interest than our own. . . ." As if proclaiming martial law from the house tops were not blunder enough, Banks followed with an additional pronouncement some days later which stated that all those eligible should take the oath and vote, and added: "Indifference will be treated as a crime, and faction as treason." In all fairness it should be added that beneath Banks' inept and grandiose proclamations lay a deep conviction that the hour was momentous, with the extirpation of slavery at stake not only in Louisiana, but by virtue of Louisiana's example, in all the confederate South.

Banks' actions, though vulnerable, did not equal his rhetoric. To make them appear equally damning, Durant used every available contention. Some of his argumentation was strained and inconsistent with his own record. Thus he urged that Hahn's election be set aside because Banks had not conducted the election in strict accord with the antebellum constitution and laws of Louisiana. Louisiana residents who had enlisted as Union soldiers were permitted to vote; the state constitution did not permit it. Regular election law provided that registration in New Orleans be ended three days before the election; General Banks had kept registration open on the very eve of balloting. No matter that Durant himself held the old constitution had died with secession or that he espoused a plan to reorder its allocation of power. No matter that the Free State General Committee the previous August had resolved "that a citizen enlisting in defence of our Country does not and ought not, and ought not [sic] to lose his right to vote." Banks had accepted the constitution of 1852 as in force and Lincoln's Proclamation of Reconstruction had stated that voters must be qualified as such by the election law of the state preceding secession. Durant even argued that by inviting the reestablishment of a "state government," Lincoln in his proclamation had necessarily meant a government of all three branches, executive, legislative, and judicial, and therefore Banks' state government, being only the first, could not qualify as a government at all![52]

Leaving aside Banks' rhetoric and Durant's exaltation of logic over reality, there was still a clear case of military influence upon the Louisiana elections. Yet Durant's contention that the whole process which Banks initiated was meaningless as an expression of civilian preference and decision is exceedingly tenuous. A large majority of those going to the polls did by that act in effect accept the unequivocal destruction of slavery. The contest for governor had been lively, the number voting had exceeded expectations, and Banks's preference for Hahn had not, despite claims to the contrary, lost Durant's candidate the office of governor. Denison saw Flanders as an unpopular man incapable of coalescing with others, one of "great zeal but no wisdom," whose "very integrity is offensive, because offensively displayed." His holding a high Treasury office while being a candidate, Denison also considered a liability. On the other hand, Hahn was a popular man with a special appeal to Germans, Irish, and his old Conservative associates. Without special favor, he was a natural to win. Durant's case was vulnerable, yet he could and did marshal an impressive lawyer's brief. And when Henry Winter Davis asked for additional facts and figures, Durant obliged. However, he answered lamely when Davis pointedly asked: "Why did your people go to the polls *at all* to lend countenance to an election where you could not succeed, and which gained power by the fact of your recognizing it."[53] In short, Durant's actions during the gubernatorial campaign had been inconsistent with his basic argument after the event that the whole process of reorganization under Banks had been nothing more than a military usurpation of legitimate authority.

The least defensible aspect of Durant's special pleading was his attack upon Lincoln. We have already noted his false accusation following upon the imbroglio of the Free State gubernatorial nominating convention, a rash statement which might find an excuse in the hot temper of the hour. Durant's most savage assault, however, appeared months later in the New York *Evening Post* of August 5, 1864, orchestrated with that of Davis and Wade. It was a letter "reviewing Mr. Lincoln's policy of reconstruction," addressed to Henry Winter Davis and "handed to us by the writer, Mr. Durant, of New Orleans, for publication." In it he characterized Lincoln's Emancipation Proclamation as the means by which "he maintained slavery" in occupied Louisiana and his Louisiana policy as "the infidelity to freedom which had been the essential characteristics of Executive administration in our state." According to Durant, Lincoln's pocket veto of the Wade-Davis bill had prompted "the gravest accusations of insincerity on the part of the Executive in regard to the question of slavery" without affording defenders of the nation "a plausible reply." Durant ridiculed Lincoln as a jokester and added that those who laughed with him, "in secret . . . deplore the calamity of a choice they dare not repudiate, from the unfounded fear that opposition would secure the success of an anti-national candidate. No nation will vote its own destruction, though the catastrophe may be accomplished by voting for incompetent men."[54] Unlike Wade and Davis, Durant had knowledge of the support Lincoln had given throughout 1863 to the Free State movement then under Durant's leadership. He knew that under Stanton's order, directed by the president, freeborn blacks might have been enrolled as voters, and he had evidence that Lincoln confirmed through Secretary Chase his approval for such action. It is difficult to reconcile Durant's honorable reputation with his attack upon the president. Quite possibly he was self-deceived, blinded by his sense of outrage that Lincoln had granted to Banks authority as "master of all," for Durant, like Chase, appears to have been a self-righteous and a self-esteeming man.

As president of the Free State General Committee, Durant had established contacts with northern antislavery leaders and his open letter in the *Post* was mindful of their concerns. "*No free State constitution*" had yet "*been adopted or installed*," he asserted, in a technically correct but grossly misleading statement. The constitutional change making Louisiana a free state had been adopted by the convention but the constitution had not yet been ratified. With like distortion Durant wrote

that "the so-called constitutional convention now sitting in New Orleans ... evinces the same aversion as the Governor to that principle
which in Louisiana can alone 'establish justice and ensure domestic
tranquillity'—equality of all men before the law—the failure to recognize which is, indeed, a defect in your bill, not pointed out by the Executive." Durant was chiding not Congress for the inadequacy of the
Wade-Davis bill in its limited provision of civil equality for blacks but
Lincoln for not criticizing the flaw! Yet Lincoln, Banks, and Hahn had
made certain that the Louisiana constitution provided "equality of all
men before the law" as that phrase was generally understood. In addition, they had opened the door to black suffrage. Months later, after
the constitution had been ratified, Durant in another open letter to
Davis again denied that it provided equality before the law. This time,
however, he hedged the accusation: "If the assertion is intended to
mean that men are made by the Constitution politically equal, it is a
wide error."[55]

In early 1865, when the prospect for Louisiana's admission
seemed promising, Durant's view of the "New 'State' of Louisiana"
was prominent in the antislavery press and helped Wendell Phillips persuade the movement to oppose its admission despite Garrison's defense
of Banks. By then, Durant was supplementing his condemnation of the
state's reorganization as military usurpation with the argument that the
black laborer in Louisiana was not really free and that under the existing state structure there was no hope for extending the suffrage. Durant
was cited as authority for the statement that "there is no such thing in
Louisiana as negro Liberty" and that what was called a constitution
was "only N. P. Banks' private memorandum book." Phillips posed
"the great issue" as: "Shall Louisiana be admitted into the Union with
her present slavery?" The Boston *Commonwealth* told its readers that
the Banks government would be overthrown by returning confederates
as soon as the war ended unless blacks were allowed to vote, "and that
[allowing blacks to vote] the President and Gen. Banks, and their fol-
lowers, are determined not to do."[56]

Defeat before Battle

Neither Banks nor Lincoln had ever implied that the Louisiana constitution had made blacks "politically equal," but both men did intend that the constitutional opening for black suffrage be meaningfully implemented. They did not expect to leave the decision to enfranchise the black man, freeborn or freed, to the unconstrained preferences of Louisiana's white residents or to permit a return of political power to exconfederate leaders while blacks were denied any access to the ballot box. When, after months at the nation's capital championing the state's claim to readmission, Banks returned to Louisiana with the president's backing, he expected (as he sent word to Lincoln's successor) to settle "every question connected with the reconstruction of the govt . . . and satisfactorily to the country. Even to the question of negro suffrage . . ."[1] Having turned around the vote in the constitutional convention on the suffrage issue, he was confident of a like success with the state legislature. And he had no intention of permitting recapture of ascendancy by the antebellum elite. Banks was prepared to oust "Rebels" and "Copperheads" from office.

There can be no doubt but that Lincoln, unlike Andrew Johnson, would have supported Banks wholeheartedly. Banks had been understandably reluctant to return to the scene associated with the bitter disappointment of his hope for military glory and for national acclaim as the statesman of freedom and reunion. Lincoln had insisted that he do so, even while refusing to give Banks top military authority in the area. "I wish not to be argued with further . . . I have told you why I can not

order Gen. Canby from the Department of the Gulf. . . . Yet I do believe that you, of all men, can best perform the part of advancing the
new State government of Louisiana." Lincoln was sending Banks back
to New Orleans to "hatch the egg," including that desire of the black
man for the franchise which, on the eve of Banks' return, Lincoln
would publicly argue could be attained "sooner by saving the already
advanced steps toward it, than by running backward over them."[2]

Banks' departure was delayed beyond Lincoln's original decision,
made in late November 1864, apparently because the fortunes of Lincoln's free state appeared even more precarious at the Capitol than in
New Orleans. Lincoln's concern for its local vitality, however, is unmistakable. Shortly after Banks had left New Orleans for Washington
in late September, Governor Hahn had let Lincoln know that he could
"hardly hope to get along" without the general's "counsels and powerful aid." A month later Hahn was reporting to Lincoln that the military officers in power in New Orleans seemed determined to undermine
the civil government and urged the president to "lose no delay in sending to us Gen. Banks or some man to take charge of the Department of
the Gulf, who will have the *power and the desire* to aid us." A week
later Hahn warned that "to build up a Free State, at the mouth of the
Mississippi, the Federal, State and Military authorities must cooperate
and act in harmony which, *I regret to say*, is far from being the case
now." This letter was followed in a few days by one asking Lincoln's
help in an effort about to be made "to give certain rights [suffrage] to
some of our colored population which have hitherto been withheld
from them" and again urging Banks' return. "Without him, or some
man of his views and character, we must break down in our efforts to
build up a loyal State government here." Lincoln had Banks telegraph
Hahn to send all the facts in relation to Louisiana. In his own hand on
November 14, 1864, the president drafted and signed a blistering letter
marked "private" to General Stephen A. Hurlbut, an old friend who
had replaced Banks as commanding general in New Orleans.[3] It
opened with a sharp reprimand: "Few things, since I have been here,
have impressed me more painfully than what, for four or five months
past, has appeared as bitter military opposition to the new State Gov-

ernment of Louisiana." Lincoln's anger, and his determination, are clearly evident as the letter continued, and ended in a threat:

A very fair proportion of the people of Louisiana have inaugerated a new State Government, making an excellent new constitution—better for the poor black man than we have in Illinois. This was done under military protection, directed by me, in the belief, still sincerely entertained, that with such a nucleous around which to build, we could get the State into position again sooner than otherwise. In this belief a general promise of protection and support, applicable alike to Louisiana and other states, was given in the last annual message. . . . Every Unionist ought to wish the new government to succeed; and every disunionist must desire it to fail. It's failure would gladden the heart of Slidell in Europe, and of every enemy of the old flag in the world. Every advocate of slavery naturally desires to see blasted, and crushed, the liberty promised the black man by the new constitution. But why Gen. Canby and Gen. Hurlburt should join on the same side is to me incomprehensible.

To make assurance against misunderstanding, I repeat that in the existing condition of things in Louisiana, the military must not be thwarted by the civil authority; and I add that on points of difference the commanding general must be judge and master. But I also add that in the exercise of this judgment and control, a purpose, obvious, and scarcely unavowed, to transcend all military necessity, in order to crush out the civil government, will not be overlooked. Yours truly   A. LINCOLN

General Hurlbut's reply indicates his perception that Lincoln's concern for the state government was also a concern for the freedmen. The general argued that whatever was being done for the freedmen was being done by the military, not by the state government, and cited the fact that he had organized black troops in West Tennessee as evidence of his own attitude toward the Negro. "Your Excellency has known me long enough to feel assured that on principle and practice, I am disposed to do everything in my power to advance the condition of the Colored Race both as a measure of humanity and justice and as the sole condition of eventual safety and unity of the American nation." The letter could hardly have been altogether reassuring for it revealed Hurlbut's resentment of the military's role as "Tutor and Guardian of these people," together with the expense involved, as "onerous and harassing duties" not properly a military responsibility. Moreover, he flatly stated that the state government could "never successfully go into full operation" until armed resistance ceased. There was no pledge of cooperation with Governor Hahn. Later General Hurlbut would explicitly and publicly take the position held by enemies of the free state that it was "the creature of the Executive authority exercised through the then Commanding General" and would recommend that the ambiguity of the situation be resolved.[4]

Lincoln was a master of ambiguities when they served his purpose, and he was not about to resolve those of the Louisiana situation, at least not until he knew the result of Banks' return. The possibility that Banks might fail may well have been what Lincoln had in mind when on April 11, 1865, he publicly reaffirmed his promise to support the Louisiana government, but with a qualification. "I shall treat this as a bad promise, and break it, whenever I shall be convinced that keeping it is adverse to the public interest. But I have not yet been so convinced." By then, Lincoln was well aware that the situation in Louisiana had deteriorated. The Free State forces had been demoralized by their problems with the military commander and by failure to gain congressional recognition. Michael Hahn, whom Lincoln could trust to carry out his policies, had escaped from the harassment and frustration of his situation by resigning the governorship to accept election as senator, and his place had been taken by the lieutenant governor, J. Madison Wells, a wealthy Unionist planter. When Lincoln spoke out on Reconstruction and Louisiana in his last public address, he may or may not have learned that three weeks earlier the new governor, with General Hurlbut's endorsement, had removed Banks' appointee as mayor of New Orleans and placed in that key position of local power the former proslavery editor and owner of the *True Delta*, Hugh Kennedy, brother-in-law of Cuthbert Bullitt. However that may be, Lincoln had already hesitated to give Wells authority for such appointments. Wells had written Lincoln on March 6 asking for the same power the president had granted Hahn by designating him military governor. Lincoln may have noted with misgiving that the first three of the seven signatures endorsing the request were those of Kennedy, Cottman, and J. L. Riddell (Conservatives whom he had out-maneuvered in 1863), and the seventh was that of Benjamin F. Flanders, Durant's candidate for governor whom Hahn had defeated in 1864. Unlike most decisions in respect to Louisiana's civil government, Lincoln referred this one to Secretary of War Stanton, who recommended against appointing a military governor.[5]

Thus, when Nathaniel Banks left Washington for New Orleans in early April 1865 in order to sustain the free state government, he did so with undiluted "plenary power," to use Stanton's phrase. Lincoln was with Grant in Virginia, personally visiting Petersburg and Richmond as Lee's forces left them. His thoughts were too occupied to give the last minute directions Banks requested, but Lincoln wired by military telegraph that Banks should be off without awaiting his return to the capital "and you and I will correspond, when desired by either." Even without further directives, Banks had the opportunity to know more of Lincoln's purpose in respect to Louisiana, and at first hand, than any other man. For several months he had worked closely with Lincoln in their joint effort to obtain congressional approval for the free state. Lincoln had vouched for the validity of Banks' testimony before the Senate Judiciary Committee in "all the statements which lie within the range of my knowledge," and Banks spoke for the president. Before the congressional session opened, when his departure seemed imminent, Banks had asked "to know from you what shall be done by me in the execution of orders" since the "Secretary of War has said to me that in civil matters you had generally given directions yourself."[6] Lincoln had already sent John Nicolay to ask Banks to call at the White House that evening at seven.

Just a week after Lincoln's death, General Banks addressed a memorial mass meeting at Lafayette Square in New Orleans, where he had finally arrived after a circuitous lengthy journey. Lincoln's influence, he assured the audience, was still strong and would be consummated by the return of Louisiana into the Union. "You know how deeply he was interested in the destinies of Louisiana. It was among the first wishes of his heart that improvements may be perfected during his administration." Then he spoke directly to the blacks in the mass gathering:[7]

To the colored people of this State, I will say that the work is still going on; and by being patient, they will see that the day is not far distant when they will be in the enjoyment of all rights. . . . Abraham Lincoln gave his word that you will be free, and enjoy all the rights invested to all citizens. [Great cheering.]

In the name of Lincoln, Banks had promised that suffrage would be extended to blacks. Commenting on the speech, the Radical black New Orleans *Tribune*, which supported Durant and was generally hostile to Hahn, Banks, and Lincoln, did "not hesitate to acknowledge that Gen. Banks is willing—in principle—to give the franchise to the colored citizens of the United States"; but according to the *Tribune* he could not fulfill the promise. General Banks "does not make laws and constitutions. In that matter his sole power is his personal influence. . . . He has been all the time powerless to grant us what he considered our due." The *Tribune* counseled its black readers to claim their rights and look to "higher and more powerful authorities" than General Banks, apparently referring to their friends in Congress. The editorial failed to recognize that Banks had spoken in Lincoln's name.[8]

A month later the paper published on its front page an "important communication" to the editor, a letter within a letter, the first signed "W. D. K.," and the other "S. N. T." The first initials the *Tribune* identified as those of "that noble friend of republican principles, Wm. D. Kelley." The writer of the communication, however, was not identified, nor has it been possible to do so. From internal evidence the document appears to be authentic and its statements credible. It seems not to have been noted in the northern press although it probably led to the publication there of Lincoln's March 13, 1864, letter to Hahn in response to a request made by Kelley some weeks after writing to S. N. T. Kelley's letter, together with other evidence indicated below, bears witness to an important fact. During the struggle over Louisiana's admission, Lincoln had assured key members of Congress that he supported extension of suffrage to blacks and was prepared to use presidential influence and patronage in Louisiana to obtain it. He had shown them his letter to Hahn as evidence of both past and future intent. Kelley was surprised that his New Orleans correspondent should not have known "that Mr.

Lincoln had been earnestly anxious to promote the extension of the right of suffrage to American citizens of African descent in Louisiana." His letter continued:

> It was not a mere sentiment with Mr. Lincoln. He regarded it as an act of justice to the citizens, and a measure of sound policy for the States, and doubtless believed that those whom he invested with power were using their influence to promote so desirable an object. Of this he assured me more than once, and in the presence of others to whose memories I may safely appeal. Careful as he was not to commit himself to a step from which he might be compelled to recede, he avowed this object to Hon. Michael Hahn, immediately after hearing of his election to the gubernatorial office of your so-called Free State, in a letter of congratulation and counsel. . . . My recollection is that it was marked 'private', but this restriction was long since removed by the exhibition by Mr. Lincoln of a copy of the letter to several persons, and, as I understood from him to Mr. Hahn that it might be given to the public. I have therefore no doubt that Mr. Hahn will in justice to the memory of his illustrious friend and patron gladly show you the original. . . .

The *Tribune* commented that "Mr. Lincoln's instructions have not been heeded by the officers intrusted with his confidence." S. N. T. thought the letter had been deliberately suppressed with the result that Lincoln was generally believed to have shared "views publicly expressed in [ter]ms of prejudice against the extension [of?] the suffrage" by "those who, supported [by?] the strength of his name, organized among us their so-called Free State Government." Had the letter been published in April 1864 after the gubernatorial and before the convention election, S. N. T. speculated that it would have prevented results "admitted to be unfortunate" and "would have helped with powerful aid the cause of equality before the law."[9]

Governor Hahn had in fact used Lincoln's letter behind the scenes with members of the 1864 constitutional convention and later, after the November presidential election, he asked Lincoln's permission to make it public. An effort was about to be made in the Louisiana legislature to extend the suffrage, he wrote, and "some of our friends think that the use of a letter you wrote to me on the 13th of March 1864 (a copy of which I enclose) would prove of some service to the colored race and do you no harm." Hahn's interest in black suffrage, unrecognized among New Orleans' articulate blacks, can be explained by his understanding of Lincoln's wishes. It is altogether likely, though there is no direct evidence, that the two men discussed the extension of the suffrage when Hahn visited Washington in early August to report on the new constitution and confer on patronage and policy.[10]

In reply to his November letter, Governor Hahn received no authorization to publish Lincoln's position on black suffrage, but the omission does not mean that Lincoln ignored the request or meant to refuse it. Indeed, Kelley's recollection would suggest the contrary. At the time Hahn's letter arrived, Lincoln was insisting upon Banks returning at once to New Orleans. In early December plans were being made in New Orleans for a gala reception upon Banks' return. The general would have been the natural conduit for Lincoln's response. The length of Banks' subsequent stay in Washington was not predetermined but rested with developments on Capitol Hill. And the governor in the face of difficulties not only with the military but also with the legislature, which was "refusing to mind the reins," had been insisting that only Banks could save the local situation.[11] In effect, Lincoln recognized the request by his public statement on Reconstruction in his April 11 speech. His delay in responding is understandable, and the fact that he spoke of Reconstruction and black enfranchisement to serenaders, on an occasion when many thought it more appropriate simply to rejoice over Lee's surrender, suggests that Lincoln wanted to strengthen Banks' hand in getting an extension of suffrage through the recalcitrant Louisiana legislature.

Another response of Lincoln during the period when Congress was determining the fate of his free state may have been misinterpreted by historians in a way that obscures Lincoln's determination on the suffrage issue. In December 1864 Lincoln and congressional leaders had apparently agreed to a compromise by which Lincoln, in return for the recognition of Louisiana, would accept the provisions of the Wade-Davis bill for other states substantially unchanged except that the new measure would extend suffrage to all loyal male citizens, that is, to blacks. The first version of the bill was changed within a few days (December 15–December 20) to restore the "white" qualification except for men in the army and navy. The change has been seen as a concession to Lincoln's objection to the broader enfranchisement. This view is a reasonable but not a necessary inference based upon a passage from John Hay's diary for December 18 in which he reports a conversation between Banks and Lincoln, who had just read carefully the original version of Ashley's compromise bill. According to Hay, the president "said that he liked it with the exception of one or two things which he thought rather calculated to conceal a feature which *might be objectionable to some.*" Lincoln was not necessarily voicing an objection to universal suffrage so much as an apprehension that the provision would arouse an opposition that might obstruct the bill's passage. Banks' immediate response was, "Yes, that is to be stricken out and the qualification 'white male citizens of the U.S.' is to be restored."[12]

Banks was in close touch with his friends on the hill, and his prediction was correct. He himself believed that a grant of suffrage to blacks in the initial stage of Reconstruction would alienate local whites, and Hay quotes him as saying that under such an arrangement they would refuse to vote. This was not, however, the whole of Banks' concern. He feared the provision "would be a fatal objection to the Bill" in Congress, and thus prevent Louisiana's admission. Up until then, Radicals had been unable to pass any measure to enfranchise blacks, even for Washington, D.C., or the territory of Montana. The previous July they had eliminated black enfranchisement from the Wade-Davis bill because they had recognized that the measure could not otherwise be passed. As William Lloyd Garrison observed in an editorial on equal political rights published in early January 1865, "the primary difficulty lies in the state of public sentiment towards the negro." About the same time Banks wrote his wife that Louisiana matters did not look as well as they had at the end of December because there was "a strong desire to couple with admission the question of negro suffrage."[13]

Although Lincoln undoubtedly shared Banks' apprehension that neither northern public opinion nor a majority in Congress would sustain unqualified black suffrage, his own view of what was desirable, and perhaps of what was possible, went beyond that of the December 20 revision of the Ashley bill which would enfranchise only black soldiers. And there is good reason to be wary of assuming that Lincoln agreed completely with Banks. The general had lagged behind the president on the suffrage issue a year earlier and may still have approached it with more hesitation than Lincoln. Nonetheless, Banks stood ready to fight for a meaningful extension of suffrage in Louisiana, and expected to win. If in retrospect the hope of success appears unrealistic, it is worth noting that it was also Chase's assumption as late as April 1865. He wrote urging Lincoln to take "the shortest road" to the admission of Louisiana "by causing every proper representation to be made to the Louisiana Legislature." On a suggestion from "the National authorities," Chase felt certain that "the Legislature will promptly act." And by April, Chase expected that body to enact universal suffrage as the term is now understood, not as he had used it a year earlier. What he had read in New Orleans newspapers the past few months had made him no longer "contented by suffrage for the intelligent and for those who have been soldiers."[14]

In his effort during the fall and winter to win public support for Louisiana's admission, particularly from antislavery men, Banks tried to provide assurance that suffrage would be granted blacks. To Chase, he indicated that he was "decidedly in favor of the liberal extension of the right of suffrage to colored citizens." Speaking in Massachusetts, he pointed to the provision of the free state constitution that enabled the legislature to grant blacks the vote and interpreted the authority given as "under the circumstances . . . in the nature of a command." He made known his conviction that "the question of suffrage will be settled sooner in Louisiana than in any other State." The Boston *Commonwealth*, Radical and hostile to Banks and Lincoln, took note of the "statement which the general . . . makes, that the President subsequently [after the initial Louisiana elections], as well as Mr. Chase, desired that measures should be taken to extend suffrage to colored citizens," although the paper mentioned it only in ridicule and disbelief.[15]

From New Orleans those supporters of Banks who had won respect in antislavery circles sent north letters and reports, which Garrison published in the *Liberator*, to vindicate the general's record and affirm his continuing purpose to attain justice for the black man. They did not overlook the suffrage issue. The Reverend E. M. Wheelock, secretary of the Board of Education for Freedmen, Department of the Gulf, wrote that the "freedman in Louisiana has won, or is fast winning all his rights. He already shares our civilization; he will soon share our political equality, and the franchise of a citizen." A letter from Plumly attacked the Durant-Flanders Radicals as a mean and double-dealing faction against whom "the real friends of the administration, of reconstruction, of colored suffrage, and of universal education, have to struggle." Banks' former provost marshal, writing from New York to Garrison concerning the labor system and the conditions among blacks when Banks assumed command, stated his own conviction that in all measures concerning the freedmen "the great object he [Banks] had in view was their elevation to all the rights, natural and political, of white men."[16]

Such statements were not made for northern consumption alone. In November 1864 Plumly addressed a large meeting of free colored men in New Orleans in a very lengthy speech of which Garrison ran an extended extract on the front page of the *Liberator*. Plumly told his audience that he did not expect "an immediate rush of millions of freedmen upon the suffrage of the country" but saw a hundred reasons why colored Creoles and all free black men who had fought for their country or who could read and write should vote. "A bill framed upon that basis," he assured his black listeners, "will be passed by the Legislature, soon or late, by patient and persistent effort." The free black men needed only to unite, combine with their friends, and sustain the government in order to win the right to vote. Plumly was followed on the platform by Thomas W. Conway, Banks' superintendent of the Bureau of Free Labor and later assistant commissioner of the Freedmen's Bureau in Louisiana. He made a strong statement attacking the proposal to give suffrage to quadroons as whites and supporting the enfranchisement of colored soldiers and all other blacks who could meet property or educational qualifications. Linking the names of Sumner,

Phillips, Garrison, Beecher, Butler, Farragut, Grant, Sherman, Sheridan, and Banks with that of Lincoln ("who, though doubted by many of you, has never been doubted by me") as molders of the public mind and leaders in battle, Conway predicted triumph. "The rights of colored citizens," he asserted confidently, "will be a part of the triumph." In January, the Lincoln-Banks men appealed to an even larger audience of colored people at a giant celebration made an official holiday by Governor Hahn and Acting Mayor Hoyt of New Orleans, a Banks confidant and appointee, in honor of the emancipation acts of Missouri and Tennessee which were seen as following the precedent of the Louisiana Free State. About a thousand black men and women assembled at Lafayette Square and listened to speeches from Hahn and A. P. Dostie, the most prominent Radical among the original Free State men who supported Banks and Hahn in the 1864 split. The governor spoke of prejudices to be overcome, but assured his audience that he himself was confident that the qualities of black men entitled them to every right. Dostie was more specific, predicting that the state legislature then in session would pass laws giving them the elective franchise. The evening festivities included a giant transparency with a portrait of General Banks on one side and on the other the legend "New glories are before us."[17]

Two New Orleans newspapers closely allied with Banks' supporters followed policies consistent with an understanding that the administration meant to see that the franchise was opened to blacks. The cautious, otherwise conservative, *Daily True Delta* gave Lincoln and Banks loyal support during the months when Banks was in Washington lobbying for Louisiana and Hahn occupied the governor's chair. This was the newspaper that Hahn acquired in early 1864 from its proslavery owner-editor Hugh Kennedy and shortly thereafter turned over to William R. Fish, Hahn's close political associate and former law partner. The following January, Fish welcomed as coeditor and co-owner Alfred C. Hills, who had previously edited the *Era* as Banks' organ and was currently a member of the state senate. Fish took pride in the paper's acceptance and increased circulation under his editorship in spite of its expressing, as he saw it, "sentiments on political and kindred subjects calculated to jostle the prejudices of large and respectable classes." Actually its editorial statements were exceedingly circumspect in regard to suffrage—"the most exciting and delicate question that has ever been agitated in this community"—but its policy during this period was gently to lead its readers to favor, or at least countenance, black enfranchisement. Columns of fine print presented *in toto* the "forcible speech" of Plumly, the one sent Lincoln and printed in part by Garrison, with the editor's comment that it was delivered before a "large audience of intelligent free colored men." The speech included a lengthy, proud account of the history of the Garrisonian abolitionists, with praise for Frederick Douglass, Charles Remond, and Robert Purvis. The *True Delta* characterized the account as "valuable as a historic statement of the antislavery movement at the North, and of the devotion to principle of those men who have been so long the earnest advocates of justice to the colored race." Its editorial introduction to the speech also pointed to Plumly with obvious satisfaction as a "staunch friend of the colored men" who had given "unequivocal support" to the policy of President Lincoln and the measures of General Banks.[18]

During November, the *True Delta* gave prominence to the suffrage bills introduced in the Louisiana legislature and to the controversy they aroused, even to reprinting an editorial from the New Orleans *Tribune*. Like the *Tribune* and Conway, Hills in the state senate opposed the quadroon bill and made evident his belief that blacks were entitled to a more general grant. Unlike the *Tribune*, which took Durant's view of the illegitimacy of the free-state government and sought immediate action from Congress, Hills and the *True Delta* looked to the state legislature and kept reminding blacks that prejudices could not be summarily removed but must be attacked step by step. In the November debates, Hills voiced the dilemma of the Banks men by expressing doubt that the time had come for action while asserting in almost the same breath that "such time will come speedily."[19]

When the Convention of Colored Men of Louisiana met the following January, the *True Delta* reacted with indignation at the success of the *Tribune*-Durant forces in defeating a petition to the state legislature for enfranchisement and in passing requests that Congress enact universal suffrage and deny Louisiana readmission. The *True Delta*'s editors warned that while Congress might pass the pending amendment abolishing slavery, "the right of suffrage will probably always be determined by the individual States." If black men, "who had so much at stake," "rendered fruitless" all efforts to redeem Louisiana, their fate would be "for years at least, uncertain, and not unlikely to be as favorable as that already attained." The state legislature, they were admonished, was at least due the courtesy of a formal petition before concluding that it would not act, a surmise "as likely to be wrong as to be right." The editors urged black people to act with judgment and moderation, quoting a remark of one of the "venerable" speakers at their convention which "may be thought abrupt or homely" but was "worth thinking of now and then": " 'Remember,' said he, 'that we must make the white man our friend, and keep him so, or we can hope for nothing.' "[20]

A few days later the *True Delta* published a long communication from "A Friend of Universal Suffrage," a statement probably solicited or composed in its editorial office.[21] The piece took issue with the New Orleans *Tribune*'s arguments that the state legislature had no right under the present constitution to grant universal suffrage and that any enfranchisement it might pass would hold no security for the future. "A Friend" argued that the danger of a reactionary Congress was as real as that of a reactionary legislature, citing the insertion of "white" into the enabling act for Montana by a large majority and the fact that even William D. Kelley was insisting only upon a "partial" extension of suffrage to blacks. Furthermore, the argument went, Congress could only set conditions for admission; it could not govern the internal question of suffrage after the state was admitted. On the other hand, the writer reasoned ingeniously, the 1864 constitution gave the legislature the power to extend suffrage, even to make it universal, but not the authority to restrict suffrage. It could grant suffrage to "persons who 'by intellectual fitness, may be deemed entitled thereto.' This includes everybody; or, at least, the right of extending suffrage to everybody." White men who could not read or write nevertheless voted "because they are intellectual beings," an endowment given man as a natural gift long antedating his ability to read and write. The legislature could *"deem"* every black man entitled to the suffrage by virtue of his manhood and the intellect God had given him. And once universal male suffrage was granted under the 1864 constitution, the legislature would have no power to withdraw it! The communication ended by urging black men to petition the legislature. If that "meant a whining subserviency, a cringing of the knee, then indeed it might be deprecated. But if it means, as it does, a proper and friendly conference between men claiming a right, and men clothed with the power to accord that right, it is a proper and recommendable means."

Apparently the advice of the *True Delta* and its "Friend of Universal Suffrage" was heeded. A few weeks later, on February 17, 1865, editor Hills in his capacity as state senator presented a petition asking for the right of suffrage signed by some five thousand black men, many "serving the country in the camp and in the field." The *True Delta* published the long petition in full. Interestingly, the petitioners claimed the right of suffrage as loyal citizens on their own behalf "and on that of their brethren and their posterity forever." The petition was referred to a special committee of five with Hills' name listed first. On the same day another state senator in supporting a resolution to commend Banks' defense of the free state at the nation's capital, attacked Durant bitterly for his opposition and his inconsistency in insisting upon universal suffrage while fourteen months earlier he championed only "the cause of the favored few." If now Durant favored the "full principles of equal rights," and "if it is *real*," the speaker concluded dryly, there was still hope that he might perform some good.[22] The defenders of the Lincoln-Banks free state were moving cautiously but unmistakably toward an open commitment to a broad extension of the franchise to blacks. This reflected not only their understanding of administration policy but also their response to the growing militancy of New Orleans blacks and to what they perceived as a gross misrepresentation of Banks' policies and of the attitudes of most freedmen by the New Orleans *Tribune* in league with Durant.

The short-lived *Black Republican*, whose first issue appeared

April 15, 1865, carried as its editorial masthead a quotation from Lincoln's December message reasserting his determination to retract nothing as to slavery and concluding: "If the people should, by whatever mode or means, make it an Executive duty to re-enslave such persons, another, and not I, must be their instrument to perform it." The editor's "Address" proudly announced that the paper was issued by an association most of whose members had been bondsmen and that the editor "was born, and has lived most of his life, a slave." The paper would ask nothing, and yield nothing, on account of "complexion." It would be an instrument "to unite our people, to bind them to the great Government that gave us freedom ... and to strengthen the hands and gladden the spirit of our beloved chief magistrate, Abraham Lincoln, in whose heart is the cause of the poor." The editorials of the first issue reflected the approach of Banks' white supporters in taking note of the "cruel and dangerous prejudices that must be outlived" since "the sting of the serpent of slavery is in the hearts of the people," while at the same time affirming that "justice and righteousness ... shall succeed." As the paper's prospectus put it: "If this revolution has made us bleed and suffer, it has also given us great and noble benefits"—freedom, the right to bear arms, the opportunity to show the courage of our race on the field of battle, free schools for our children, and under General Banks orders, "we have organized Industry.... All our Rights will follow."

On suffrage, the *Black Republican* spoke out at once, and explicitly:

We desire to see our population put upon no restriction not imposed upon others in this respect, and we hope the time for that is near. But the Legislature adjourned without any action on the subject. This will be remembered in future as a sign of the unfaithfulness of that body. The men who sent the petition, and those who encouraged them to do so, have done their duty.... It is the duty of citizens to keep asking of their Government till justice is done.... We must ask and ask again. We must accept the right of suffrage when we can get it. We must strive for it till it comes.

On the front page of its May 20 issue, the editor called for a Southern

Colored Convention with delegates from all slave states to ask "the national right of suffrage."[23]

The advent of the *Black Republican* had been enthusiastically hailed and probably assisted by Plumly and Conway, both of whom at the time were being bitterly condemned by the *Tribune*-Durant leadership for carrying on Banks' policies. Conway wrote Banks that "the American negroes are indignant" at the attacks of "the rich colored men under the lead of Flanders (who was present)" and were starting a new organ "to more fully represent the cause of the black man." Plumly wrote Lincoln that the freedmen and "the American colored people here, disgusted with the 'N O Tribune'—the French Jesuit (color'd) paper, that under Durant and a few colored Creoles, has been always against us—are just starting another paper. . . . It will be out in a few days. I have been requested, by the Association to send the first copy to you, with the renewed expression of the undying gratitude and confidence of the People of Color." This was part of a long letter Plumly sent shortly after Banks' appointee, Stephen Hoyt, was summarily ousted and Hugh Kennedy installed as mayor. Plumly wanted Lincoln to know that General Hurlbut was pressing Free State men out of office in favor of "old semi-rebels and copperheads." He feared being forced out of his place on the Board of Education for Freedmen unless Lincoln intervened, but the letter was much more than a personal appeal. No man in the city felt safe, he reported; any Lincoln supporter was liable to humiliation or outrage; Negro school children and a black funeral procession had been attacked with impunity; the black people were in alarm and dismay. "In this Dept. at this time, the one petition of the popular liturgy is, "Good Lord oh send us, Banks."[24]

Plumly was no stranger to Lincoln. Like Banks and Hahn, he had enjoyed several interviews with the president, and apparently Lincoln had relaxed his usual restraint when discussing Louisiana's affairs. After a conversation in early August 1864, Plumly had written Banks, who was still in New Orleans, that Lincoln said he "stands by you, firmly & he means to. . . . His blood is up on the Wade & Winter Davis protest." Plumly thought Lincoln would be pleased with his November address, for he made available a copy to Colonel James T. Tucker, a close aide to Governor Hahn and a friend of John Hay, for forwarding to the president's private secretary. Plumly wrote Tucker that by the time Lincoln was "ready for his 'third term' we shall have 300,000 colored votes in the Restored States." In sending on the speech, Tucker clearly implied his own belief that Plumly's position represented presidential policy, an impression Tucker may have received from Governor Hahn. When the latter took his farewell of the legislators in late February he spoke openly of suffrage extension, a subject he had avoided in his October message. His remarks were guarded and defensive, yet seemed calculated to prepare the way. He may have been influenced in some measure by the views of "A Friend of Universal Suffrage" published a month earlier in the *True Delta*. "I have no hesitation in saying," he told the legislators in praising the Free State constitution, "that its terms will justify the adoption of universal suffrage, whenever it shall be deemed wise and timely."[25]

Thus the public and private statements of men working closely with Lincoln, made while Louisiana's credentials for readmission were under scrutiny, together with the policy of the two New Orleans newspapers strongly supportive of Banks and Lincoln, indirectly confirm William D. Kelley's letter to S. N. T. that credited Lincoln with pressing for an extension of suffrage to Louisiana blacks. There is direct corroboration as well. On December 22, 1864, B. Gratz Brown, senator from Missouri and like Kelley a champion of black suffrage, wrote a letter for his home constituency urging the Missouri constitutional convention to go beyond emancipation and enfranchise the emancipated, "under proper qualifications." In the course of a lengthy argument he pointed to the new Louisiana constitution as having recognized "a right of eventual suffrage." According to Brown, this showed "as with a handwriting on the wall the imperative necessity admitted on all sides for some action in that behalf." Without doubt, he stated, the insertion of the suffrage provision in the Louisiana constitution "was prompted by the executive head of our nation himself." Then he quoted an extract from the president's "note to Gov. Hahn upon that subject." The quotation, while diverging slightly from the wording of the March 13 letter, could only have been known to Senator

Brown by Lincoln's having read or shown the letter to him. And indeed, Hahn so stated when in response to Kelley's request he made public the private letter as "no impropriety" in view of Brown's direct reference to it in his "extensively published" communication with "an accurate quotation . . . as furnished by Mr. Lincoln." Hahn added: "The copy which Mr. Lincoln preserved was also read by him to a number of other gentlemen."[26]

Direct contemporary evidence of Lincoln's commitment is not limited to Brown's letter. Equally impressive is the record of the *Congressional Globe* for January 17, 1865. Thomas D. Eliot of Massachusetts, in defending readmission for Louisiana, stated that its constitution was not all he would like, but that it did provide for an extension of suffrage. "We have every reason to suppose that the Legislature will speedily take this action." In the course of his remarks, he reiterated that assurance, and made it more authoritative. "From information derived from the highest sources I am satisfied that no time will be lost in taking such legislative action as shall be right." Kelley then inquired what reason there was to believe that the legislature of Louisiana would act. For the third time Eliot asserted that it would, again basing his expectation upon "statements made here, from responsible authority, that the Legislature of Louisiana is about proceeding. There are influences bearing upon them which, I believe, will not be resisted."[27]

Some Radical congressmen and senators were unconvinced. Like Wendell Phillips, they believed, largely on Durant's authority, that such action by the "so-called Free State" was impossible. The 1864-1865 session of the Louisiana legislature did, indeed, prove intractable.[28] There are hints in private correspondence and in the press that Banks' men were looking to a fresh round of elections after his return to attain the suffrage objective. Assurances, even from "the highest sources," could not guarantee action from Louisiana's legislators. Nonetheless, the evidence establishes beyond a reasonable doubt that Lincoln and Banks intended to make every effort to persuade the legislators to enfranchise a substantial number of blacks. The effort they contemplated might have strained Chase's rubric of "proper representation" to the legislature and reinforced Durant's charges of "Executive usurpation" and "military despotism," but most certainly it would have confounded the Boston *Commonwealth*'s skepticism as to the intent of president and general. And quite possibly, had Lincoln lived to support Banks in 1865 as he had in 1864, the effort might have succeeded.

The actions Banks and Lincoln intended in respect to freedmen's labor are not so evident as those they meant to pursue in respect to black suffrage and the danger of a return to power by ex-rebels. It is clear, however, that their long-range goal was not the institutionalization of a subservient, permanently dependent, plantation labor force but rather the creation of a free labor system in which freedom meant opportunity for economic independence.[29] In retrospect, the goal may appear unrealistic, but contemporary perceptions looked to the northern agrarian past in projecting the future of the agrarian South.

The labor regulations Banks had established in 1863 and revised in 1864 came under severe attack, reflecting both genuine concern and the heat of highly partisan contention in New Orleans and in the antislavery movement. Banks required owners to pay their former slaves wages, along with housing, food, and clothing for them and their families. He forbade physical punishment, set wages, and in 1864 required planters to allot an acre of land to each family for the cultivation of crops either for use or for market. Planters also had to permit black children to attend the schools organized by the army in rural areas. The laborers were required to contract for a year's employment on plantations, but with a free choice of employer. If they refused, they still had to work and could be employed without pay under the army on public works or on "home farms" established to sustain the aged and decrepit. Those under annual contract as plantation workers were not free to leave the plantation without authorization from army officers and were subject to forfeiture of wages as penalty for not working or refusing to obey instructions. In 1864 a somewhat higher wage scale was set with half the annual compensation to be paid currently and half at the year's end, together with tighter control over the sale of crops to insure that workers would be paid. More than a century later, it is still difficult to pass fair judgment—not upon the limitations of Banks' system as one appropriate to freedom, which are readily apparent, but upon the options open to Banks in a chaotic wartime situation and a geographic location exempted from the Emancipation Proclamation.[30]

What was important for the future was the nature of the defense Banks had made against the charges that his system was for the benefit of the planter and not of the Negro. This he had vehemently denied. Without property in slaves, Banks argued, the planter's possession of land was of no value; he had to have labor, pay for it, and use it only under directives approved by the government. The inevitable result, as Banks saw it, was the break-up of land monopoly giving "every individual a chance, not only to occupy and cultivate, but to possess." The true theory of the system of labor, he stated, "is to put into the hands of the laboring population the possession as well as the occupation of land." Banks countered criticism of the prescribed wage rates by contending that the critical question was not one of wages but rather "in which manner and how soon can he [the freedman] become an owner of land himself? . . . This is the immediate and ultimate object of the labor system of Louisiana." Banks vigorously defended his system, but he justified it only as a *temporary* necessity. Thomas Conway's official report on labor in early 1865, which presented Banks' system as vindicated, made explicit the widely held assumption which Banks apparently shared that the displacement of old planters and the sale of their lands was inevitable and already under way.[31]

The *True Delta*, less enchanted than Conway with the projected disintegration of the old order, hoped that some planters could survive; but even the *True Delta* did not envisage a permanently servile labor force. Earlier it had argued that one desirable consequence of the system of withholding a half year's wages was that freedmen by receiving a sizable sum would gain "an elevated idea of themselves," a characterization meant not as ridicule but as commendation of developing self-confidence and "hopes of independence." When the *Tribune*-Durant men established an association to help freedmen work plantation land for themselves, the *True Delta* published the news in a brief but friendly report. The *Black Republican*, the authentic voice of the so-called moderates in matters affecting the former slave, announced that it would speak for "the poor as well as the rich, the freedmen as well as the freeman." It enjoined faithful labor for those who paid fairly "until we ourselves shall become employers and planters." It reported that freedmen were so far in advance of the previous year that they were hiring themselves, that the government was simply furnishing forms and managing planters more than freedmen. It predicted that General Banks on his return would bring all labor systems to an end since freedmen would have reached a point where they could claim and defend their rights. Also suggestive of the direction in which Banks' men were moving was Conway's initiative in leasing abandoned lands to freedmen after he became head of the Freedmen's Bureau in Louisiana in May 1865, an appointment for which he had solicited Banks' influence with Secretary Stanton. In a major Fourth of July address in New Orleans shortly after his fall from power, Banks himself advanced the suggestion that property be taxed "to such extent as to compel the division of large estates, and sales to small cultivators."[32]

In matters respecting blacks, Hahn tended to lag behind Banks, just as Banks had lagged behind Lincoln. Yet shortly after leaving the gubernatorial chair, Hahn assailed the Treasury regulation of freedmen's labor before a mass meeting of black people. His contention that "the blacks had equal rights with the whites in making such contracts. . . . brought down the house." His remarks were a departure from earlier attitudes. In November 1863 he had suggested stringent vagrancy laws if freed slaves would not otherwise work. When he took office as governor, his initial message to the legislators asked them to formulate a special set of laws to meet the needs arising from the "change from servile to compensated labor." The provisions of the Civil Code on contracts for letting and hiring labor he then had considered "but a scant and imperfect plan," inadequate to protect either laborers or the public interest. In response, the lower house appointed a special committee with an ominous "whereas"—whereas the condition of freedmen being ignorant, illiterate, consequently immoral and incapable of the enjoyment of liberty in the fullest sense of the word! Subsequently, the committee's chairman characterized its work as "delicate" as well as "extremely difficult" for it would be necessary to avoid all conflict with United States authorities. A member of the house objected that the committee might have "a very important and delicate labor to perform" but "I don't know what this Legislature has to do with manumitted slaves, who are, as I understand it freemen. . . . for if free, they are at liberty, under the laws of the United States and Louisiana, to do as any other freeman may. . . . I hold that these men are restricted to no other code of laws than are freemen at large." After this forceful objection nothing more was heard from the committee except that it had appointed a clerk. By the end of the session, its chairman, in another capacity, was advising the new governor of the need for quite different legislation—revision of the Statutes at Large and the Civil Code "in order that society may be fully recognized on the basis of free labor, by laws in strict accordance with the new State Constitution."[33]

Lincoln's free state, so long as it was under his and Banks' influence, escaped the dishonor of enacting the first postemancipation Black Code. This omission was consistent with Lincoln's retreat from his earlier approval of a temporary way station between slavery and freedom. In all probability, it was not unrelated to Banks' insistence in the face of his critics that the Louisiana constitution and courts recognized the Negro "as a free man entitled to all the rights and all the protection of a white man." Also, the political objectives of Banks and Hahn were not ones that maximized pressure for laws to ensure faithful laborers. They sought not to perpetuate planter dominance in state government (Hahn referred to it as an "oligarchy") but to replace it with a coalition dominated by city merchants, professionals, and white laborers with Union planters playing a subordinate role and with blacks gradually added as white prejudice was undermined by the need for black votes and by recognition that black behavior belied old proslavery stereotypes. Banks early saw Andrew Johnson's course as a reversal of political direction. He maintained in private and in public, sometimes explicitly, sometimes by implication, that Lincoln would never have similarly entrusted political power to men who had sought to destroy the Union.[34] His was an informed judgment.

Banks had no chance to prove either his commitment or his effectiveness on behalf of black suffrage and the freedmen. By the time he reached New Orleans on April 21, a week after Lincoln's assassination, a situation had developed in which he could succeed only with full presidential support. Governor Wells, who had taken office March 4, 1865, and his appointed mayor, Hugh Kennedy, were busy displacing Banks-Hahn Union men in city office, the police force, and judgeships with copperheads and returning rebels. Banks' long absence, the uncertainty of his return, and the support Wells received from General Hurlbut had eroded the Banks-Hahn influence and increased that of the "rising Sun." The New Orleans *Times* had greeted Wells' installation of Kennedy with a specially commissioned poem published on the front page. It ended: "Illustrious Hugh!—Congenial Kennedy!" The *True Delta* accepted the mayorality change with a bland friendly editorial which precipitated the departure of Alfred C. Hills as co-owner and coeditor. Thereafter its earlier effort to undermine white prejudices evaporated, even to the point of an ambiguous statement suggesting opposition to the extension of suffrage to blacks.[35]

For a few short, politically volatile weeks a change in direction appeared possible. With Banks certainly en route after many erroneous reports of his coming or not coming, then his arrival and swift decision to countermand the appointments of Wells and Kennedy, loyal supporters under A. P. Dostie's leadership rallied mass support for the general and opposition to governor and mayor. A few days after his return, on April 27, workingmen staged a giant protest against Mayor Kennedy's order lowering the wages of city laborers and passed resolutions attacking the city government as "now in the hands of Copperheads and notorious sympathizers with the accursed rebellion" and greeting "with joy . . . the return to this Department of the people's friend, Major Gen. Nathaniel P. Banks." Their demonstration with torchlights and transparencies ended in front of Banks' residence with the band playing "Hail to the Chief." On May 5, Banks sent several officers to the mayor's office to oust Kennedy and establish as acting mayor Samuel M. Quincy, scion of an old Boston family and colonel of the 73rd U.S. Colored Infantry. The next day on the front page of the New Orleans *Times*, his act was hailed as putting an end to an attempted "reign of terror"! The *True Delta* after some hesitancy as to how it should react to Banks' return had renewed its old enthusiasm for his "masterly" ways. With Kennedy displaced, it ran a series of tough editorials attacking Kennedy as the "enemy . . . in the guise of loyalty," discrediting his claim to have instituted economy in city government, and accusing him and Wells of using power to build up a party that "would make freedom a mockery" and revive "the old prejudices which have been the bane of this society." The *Black Republican* used five columns to discredit Kennedy, publishing extracts from his writings, a communication, and an editorial, all pointing to the conclusion that "every loyal man thanks God we are rid of Kennedy as Mayor." There was no visible sign that the New Orleans *Tribune* joined in the thanksgiving.[36] The *Tribune* could recognize the hand neither of God nor of Lincoln working any good through General Banks.

The climactic effort of the Banks men came on the evening of May 17 at a mass meeting in Lafayette Square described by the New Orleans *Times* reporter as one of the largest assemblages ever gathered in the city. To sustain the administration of Andrew Johnson was its stated purpose, and the published list of over three hundred "vice-presidents" or cosponsors cut across all factions. There was no mistaking, however, who engineered the call and who controlled the proceedings. The meeting was brought to order by A. C. Hills, who nominated Judge Edward Durell to preside. As chairman of the planning committee, Dostie had invited a number of the Durant group to speak; for the most part they politely declined. Dostie himself, being "loudly called for," made the closing address in which he attacked Wells, Kennedy, and the returning rebels who had boasted of how they would use power. He ended by asking cheers for the Union, the president, the soldiers who had just captured Jeff Davis—and for General Banks.

The high point of the evening was the address by Henry Clay Warmoth, a rising figure in the Banks camp. He declared that the former slave "will stand upright and free in the midst of Southern chivalry and assert his right to life, liberty, property and political equality." He called for unity under the 1864 constitution with the purpose of electing a legislature that "will give to the colored man the right to vote," disfranchise for ten years rebel officers, both civil and military, and place restrictions for a few years upon "those who have been in the rebellion in any capacity." He also declared that Louisiana's "extensive plantations will be divided up into small farms, cultivated by the industry of freemen, securing to every man an interest in the soil." How this would happen he did not say, apparently assuming it would be the natural consequence of "free labor and republican institutions." The resolutions adopted at the meeting declared for permanent disfranchisement of rebel leaders with restoration of rank-and-file confederates to the privileges of citizenship "as soon and in such manner as the safety of the Government and loyal men will allow." They were not explicit as to black suffrage. One resolution stated that in reestablishing civil government in the southern states "our only safety consists in making all loyal men equal before the law" without which no government is either "just," "equitable," or "republican."[37]

When General Banks took over the mayor's office, Wells and Kennedy protested and together with Thomas Cottman had promptly left for Washington to take their case directly to the new president. Banks at once sent warning of the consequences should governor and mayor be reinstated:[38]

There can be but one object in the course pursued by these two officers: It is to re-establish in power men of the old system of slavery—This they have threatened to do, and this will be accomplished if they are continued in power. . . .

If the Police is in the hands of men who openly sympathise with them, we cannot maintain the government. If the Parishes are filled with returned Rebel soldiers and the govt offices are filled by their friends, it is idle to talk of a Union or administration party. . . . We can carry an election triumphantly at any time if we are not disturbed—We will settle here every question connected with the reconstruction of the govt. without involving the administration in any trouble, and satisfactorily to the country. Even to the question of negro suffrage, so that other Rebel States will follow the example of Louisiana as if it were a pillar of cloud by *day & of fire by night.* But we cannot live if only Rebels are in office.

George Denison also wrote a strong letter, marked "private" and addressed to Secretary of the Treasury Hugh McCulloch, in the hope that if McCulloch understood the issues at stake he would influence President Johnson against Governor Wells' mission. Denison argued that the matter was one of grave consequence "because the struggle has just commenced or is about to commence in the reorganization of the Southern States between on the one hand the union men of these States reinforced and aided by those recently settled here from the West and North who represent and always adopt and support the policy and ideas of the administration, and on the other hand that class of politicians who have heretofore controlled the local politics of these Southern States. . . . With the aid and assistance of the former the ideas and policy of the administration and the government will be attended here with success, with the latter with failure."[39]

Other warnings reached President Johnson and the men around him but all were without effect. The president acted summarily. News of his decisions reached New Orleans just a week after the May 17 meeting. President Johnson removed Banks from his command, confirmed Wells' appointive power, and ordered Kennedy reinstated. Kennedy later informed General Canby that he regarded his appointment as coming directly from President Johnson who "assured me that no military interference with the civil administration of the city would be permitted." Wells wrote his wife from Washington that "the South will never regret his [Andrew Johnson's] being President. . . . Tell the boys we shall not again be troubled with further Yankee adventurism— Banks is the last and he is for ever killed off—this is as it should be with all wretches who would thake [sic] their arms and dance with negroes at their balls as has been proven to have been the case with this miserable man . . . so I have by the exposa [sic] of the very best people in N. Orleans killed him off for good."[40] The man whom the New Orleans *Tribune* portrayed as ineffectual had in fact become so, "killed off" at least in part by a report to the president of his having breached the color line at a ball!

On his return to New Orleans, the governor received a grand reception at Lafayette Square, presided over by J. Q. A. Fellows, the 1864 nominee of the Conservatives. Wells extolled Andrew Johnson as a conservative Democrat from whom they had nothing to fear and announced "that the Radical Aboliton party is broken up, disorganized and demoralized." He made clear to his audience that there would be no concessions on the suffrage issue, and no place of power for his former Free State associates. Radical abolitionists and "the political adventurers who have come among us," he told them, would be defeated in their intent to enfranchise the black man in an effort to "prevent the return of power to the Conservatives of the South." The meeting adjourned with three cheers for President Johnson, Governor Wells, and General Hurlbut.[41]

Before returning home from Washington, Cottman went on to Philadelphia and New York from where he wrote assuring President Johnson that the conservative element of the entire country would rally to his support. Once back in New Orleans, Cottman left a gloating note for General Banks: "Doctor Cottman presents his complements to N. P. Banks late commander of the Department of the Gulf." By repudiating General Banks, Andrew Johnson had smashed the embryo free state that Lincoln had hoped to hatch.

The Postemancipation
Outcome

Reflections on the Limits
of the Possible

The identification of the southern policy of Andrew Johnson with that of Lincoln is no longer an unquestioned verity of Reconstruction historiography, but misconceptions of Lincoln's purpose and priorities tend to obscure the distance that separated the two presidential approaches to Reconstruction. The Louisiana story contradicts the assumption, commonly accepted, that Lincoln was prepared in the interest of reunion and reconciliation to return political power to the antebellum landed elite or that in the interest of either reunion or party he stood ready to sacrifice the freedmen. It confirms that president and the radicals of his party shared an identity of purpose, if not of rhetoric and tactic, in seeking basic rights, citizenship, and political participation for former slaves.

From the Louisiana perspective, Lincoln's "Ten Percent Plan" can be recognized for what it was, not a policy of leniency but one of expediency, a means to precipitate an antislavery minority government. It reflected a first priority not, as generally assumed, for restoring an errant state as quickly as possible but priority for insuring freedom. Nor did Lincoln consider himself bound by the plan so often seen as defining his intentions. He did not view the December 1863 proclamation as a blueprint for the future. On the very day of the assassination he began with his cabinet a consideration of "the great question now before us"—Reconstruction—and urged deliberate and careful review of a proposal drawn up by Secretary Stanton. Four days earlier, on April 10, he had told Francis Pierpont, wartime governor of rump loyalist Virginia, "that he had no plan for reorganization, but must be guided by events." Stanton later testified that insofar as he knew Lincoln had not yet "matured any plan." In his carefully prepared public statement of April 11 on Reconstruction, Lincoln cautioned "that no exclusive, and inflexible plan can safely be prescribed."[1] The safety that Lincoln left undefined, for his fellow Republicans meant security for white Unionists, for freedmen, for party, and for the Union. Although he had not decided upon the best course to achieve them, there is no reason to believe that Lincoln differed from his party on basic objectives.

While Andrew Johnson might be expected to show concern for Union and for Union men, his commitment to the freedmen and to the Republican party was more tenuous. His appreciation of the need for flexibility in guiding Reconstruction was unlikely in view of the rigidity characteristic of his ideas and of his behavior. Moreover, he harbored a long-standing antipathy to antislavery Radicals that persisted despite his cooperation with them in late 1861 and early 1862 as a member of the congressional Joint Committee on the Conduct of the War. Both immediately before and immediately after, he publicly equated abolitionists and secessionists as disunionists, a term carrying an opprobrium that left no space for a measure of sympathetic tolerance.[2] In contrast to Lincoln, Johnson would never perceive Radicals as devils facing Zionwards. And notwithstanding Johnson's championship of "the people" and his assaults upon the planter aristocracy, as president he did more to resuscitate than to undercut the southern elite. It has been claimed that his goal was transfer of political power from landed wealth to plebeian and mechanic; if so, his presidential policy was ineffectual. Except in Alabama, where Sarah Wiggins has found that Unionists in 1865-1866 "had their day" at the political expense of Black Belt planters, and to a lesser extent in South Carolina, where Johnson men won from the 1865 constitutional convention a partial elimination of the political privilege enjoyed by the propertied, antebellum class leadership apparently had little difficulty in reestablishing its influence during Johnsonian restoration.[3] That this result was not entirely a matter of miscalculation or ineptness in exercising presidential power is indicated by Johnson's early decision to sustain J. Madison Wells and Hugh Kennedy and to repudiate Banks. The new president had due warning of the consequences, but he was not deterred by the prospect of returning political power to the old planter establishment.

Johnson's interviews with Wells, Cottman, and Kennedy—and his decision—came within the first weeks of his administration. Draft proclamations of reconstruction and amnesty presented in cabinet by Secretary of War Stanton and Attorney General Speed were then, Gideon Welles noted in his diary, "in the hands of the President who will shape [them] right."[4] For Johnson this may have been a period of genuine indecision, which would help explain the expectation of Radicals that he would stand with them in desiring a stern settlement with the South, even Negro suffrage. If so, the Louisiana delegation may well have influenced the course of Reconstruction in general.

At Lincoln's last cabinet meeting, the president, according to Welles, characterized Stanton's proposal for initiating reorganization as "substantially, in its general scope," one previously "talked over in Cabinet meetings." Between then and Johnson's proclamations of May 29, the proposal underwent a series of significant changes. The result was an end product at variance in important respects with Stanton's original paper and inconsistent with Lincoln's objectives, his pragmatic approach, and his stance in Louisiana. The role Stanton envisaged for the military was diminished. Unlike his design, the final plan embodied in the North Carolina proclamation and all subsequent such proclamations provided for the appointment of provisional civilian rather than military governors. It omitted authorization for a special recruitment of volunteers "to preserve the peace and enforce the laws" as support for a corps of provost marshals. Both volunteers and marshals were to have been under the direction of the secretary of war. It added a new paragraph which undercut the primacy of military authority upon which Lincoln had insisted in Louisiana. The wording strongly suggests that Johnson was reacting to the protests against Banks' action in New Orleans made by the Louisiana emissaries. The military commander of the department and all officers and personnel were not only directed to "aid and assist" the provisional governor but also specifically "enjoined to abstain from in any way hindering, impeding, or discouraging the loyal people from the organization of a State government as herein authorized." To emphasize the civilian character of the president's plan, and his respect for the state as a continuing entity of self-government, the original heading "Executive Order to Reestablish the Authority of the United States, and Execute the Laws within the Geographical Limits Known as the State of North Carolina" was discarded in favor of simply "A Proclamation." Thus from its inception Johnson's version of presidential Reconstruction departed from Lincoln's insistence upon the military being "master," and despite Lincoln's warning it became one inflexible plan. Johnson's proclamations also closed the door that Lincoln had kept open for the use of national authority in extending suffrage to blacks as part of the Reconstruction process.

In his original paper Stanton had sidestepped the matter of who might be allowed to vote in initiating reorganization. Like Lincoln, he recognized that the party was divided on the suffrage issue and sought a basis for unity. At the urging of Senator Sumner, who with other members of Congress was in his office two evenings after Lincoln's assassination, he provided in the revised draft for suffrage by "loyal citizens," that is by blacks as well as whites. When the draft came before the cabinet on May 9, Stanton's wording was criticized as "equivocal, . . . vague and uncertain." President Johnson expressed a wish that there be no room for dispute or equivocation. Then the question of whether blacks should be authorized to vote was put to the cabinet, and the six members present divided evenly. Sometime after the cabinet meeting Johnson settled the issue in favor of white-only voting by substituting for Stanton's phraseology a provision that followed Lincoln's December 1863 proclamation. Later a passage was added that in effect disavowed any right on the part of president or Congress, even under the war powers, to require enfranchisement of blacks. It read that the state convention to amend the constitution, or the legislature meeting thereafter, "will prescribe the qualification of electors . . . a power the people of the several States composing the Federal Union have rightfully exercised from the origin of the Government to the present time."[5]

No wonder that J. Madison Wells on returning home felt secure in assuring the Conservatives that Andrew Johnson would make no concession on the suffrage issue!

In New Orleans, more clearly than in the nation's capital, it was apparent that the decision Johnson made to oust General Banks and support Wells and Kennedy, a decision reached by May 17, foreshadowed the political substance of presidential policy to come. In the months ahead, to the surprise of Unionists, Johnson would generally support local officials in their clashes with the Freedmen's Bureau or the military. In doing so, he would take few precautions to protect antislavery men, white or black. Even more unexpected was Johnson's failure to use his influence as president to build political strength for Unionists generally. The course on which he had embarked by mid-May broke with Lincoln's effort to implement through local political allies and the military an antislavery policy that extended beyond emancipation. And it failed to maintain Lincoln's stand that the commanding general must be "master."

The significance of Johnson's repudiation of Banks has eluded both contemporaries and historians. What motivated his Louisiana decision is an important question, the answer as varied and speculative as the many reasons scholars have offered to explain his subsequent break with the congressional majority. Speculation is not without some supporting evidence. From the letters extant it seems evident that the Louisiana delegation played upon Johnson's desire for presidential power in his own right, the culmination of a driving ambition now generally recognized as central to his character and career. Undoubtedly the three also appealed to his long-standing constitutional views as a state rights Democrat and to the concern for the primacy of civil over military authority that cut across party lines. In addition, Wells' letters suggest that Johnson as a southerner responded to the criticism of General Banks as an outsider, a Yankee attempting to impose alien values upon the South, and to charges that Banks and his associates were plunderers out to rob the state treasury. The letter of Wells to his wife, quoted earlier, makes it unmistakable that Wells also appealed to Johnson's racial prejudice.[6]

No historian can weigh with certainty the import of that prejudice upon Johnson's southern policy, or separate the conscious from the unconscious force of his bias.[7] To recognize these imponderables, however, is not to dismiss as inconsequential Johnson's attitude toward blacks. In considering the potential of presidential leadership for helping shape the future of the freed slave, whether by action or inaction, by positions publicly taken or by influence exerted behind the scenes, a comparison of the racial attitudes of Andrew Johnson and Abraham Lincoln is inescapable. From one perspective there was not much distance between the two men. Neither stood apart from his age, an age in which a pervasive racial prejudice cut across section, party, and class; an age to which was alien the concept of racial equality that a century later would give strength and ideological authority to those who fought racial injustice. Certainly Lincoln no more than Johnson championed equality of the races. Nor did Johnson's behavior, or even his rhetoric, as military governor or as president place him, any more than Lincoln, at the opposite extreme of the racial spectrum. Yet the difference between Lincoln and Johnson in racial attitude should not be minimized as a mere matter of degree. Philosophers recognize that a variation in degree (in quantity) can result in a significant difference in kind (in quality), though not necessarily discernible from every perspective or valid for every purpose.[8] Historians might well take note. Certainly in the context of an inquiry into the possibility of a different course and outcome of Reconstruction, the distinction between the racial views of Johnson and those of Lincoln is more importantly a matter of quality than a matter of degree.

Antebellum attitudes toward slavery helped shape postwar attitudes toward blacks and their future. On slavery, the distinction between Lincoln and the Tennessean who would become his successor in presidential office was unmistakable. In the prewar years Johnson had boasted of being as "sound" as any southern man on the question of slavery. He saw himself as its defender against abolitionists and black Republicans. He believed that "negro slavery was neither a moral, social or political evil, but was right"—"a blessing." As a spokesman for the common man he saw no contradiction between democracy and slavery: "our institution, instead of being antagonistical to democracy is in perfect harmony with it." He could "wish to God every head of a family in the United States had one [slave] to take the drudgery and menial service off his family." His own ownership of slaves was evidence of the opportunity that American democracy offered to climb "Jacob's ladder" from humble origin to status and achievement. Johnson was proud to be a slaveholder "not by inheritance, but by hard labour."[9]

The exigencies of war and politics, together with the gentle prodding of Lincoln, brought Johnson reluctantly and belatedly to embrace emancipation. Yet as late as March 1862, as Lincoln's military governor in Tennessee, he sought to reassure the citizens of Nashville and Davidson County that slavery was safe within the Union. According to Johnson, Lincoln was not waging war to free the slaves. "It is very easy to talk about Lincolnites. . . . I have repeatedly asked them if the war was being directed to the institution of Slavery. Their reply has always been, 'We've got more niggers at home that we want; d--n the niggers." Johnson's personal view was made clear: "I believe that slaves should be in subordination, and will live and die so believing."[10] Earlier that month Lincoln had sent to Congress his message urging support for gradual, compensated emancipation, and less than ten days after Johnson's address, Lincoln in the White House was trying to reassure Wendell Phillips, his specially invited guest and the most radical of Radicals, that unlike border-state senators and representatives who, he said, loved slavery and meant to perpetuate it, "he [Lincoln] hated it and meant *it should die*."[11]

Unlike Lincoln, Johnson had never been tentative or qualified in his view of black men as not the equal of whites. He embraced white supremacy wholeheartedly; indeed, it is doubtful that he could conceive of a biracial society organized on any other basis. For Johnson, blacks were "not created equal in the very beginning. The distinction begins with the very germ itself." The Negro was "an inferior type of man, and incapable of advancement in his native country." Slavery had grown "necessarily out of the physical and mental structure of man." Johnson "had no hesitancy . . . upon the subject, believing and knowing, as he did, that the black race of Africa were inferior to the white man in point of intellect—better calculated in physical structure to undergo drudgery and hardship—standing, as they do, many degrees lower in the scale of gradation that expresses the relative relation between God and all that he has created." When the author of the Declaration of Independence wrote that all men are created equal, "Mr. Jefferson meant the white race, and not the African race."[12] ~report~

The certainty and intensity of Johnson's racial view were part of his southern heritage. In assailing secession in the borderlands during the fall of 1861, he made clear his identification with section: "I am a Southern man, sharing the prejudices of my section, and I am no abolitionist." The depth of his prejudice may also have reflected, as David Bowen and William Riches have argued, an insecurity and defensiveness as son of a menial servant and apprentice to a tailor never totally accepted by the local elite, an insecurity reflected in his fierce attachment to democracy and the Jacob's ladder concept—for whites only. They have concluded that Johnson, in contrast to Lincoln, could not recognize blacks as human beings in the same sense as whites, even after his conversion to antislavery. A number of Johnson's public statements suggest that he tried. But his outbursts in private, characterized by his secretary as a display of morbid feelings against blacks, indicate that he could not escape his past. Frederick Douglass, "one of the most meritorious men in America" in Lincoln's view, was for Johnson "that d--d Douglass; he's just like any nigger."[13] The Tennessean who had climbed the heights of Jacob's ladder would, indeed, "live and die" believing that "slaves [and ex-slaves] should be in subordination." Lincoln could take pleasure and satisfaction in the achievement of a black man; Johnson felt uncomfortable in the presence of a black who was not "in his place."

Johnson's commitment to whiteness distorted his perception of reality and precluded the possibility that as president he would move his fellow southerners to accept and institutionalize a substantial measure of freedom and equality for blacks. This was the great historic challenge to the political leadership of the 1860s. Bound by his heritage of section and class, Andrew Johnson was incapable of perceiving it.

He was further insulated from a sense of presidential responsibility for the future of freed slaves by his view of the proper constitutional limits of federal authority. Beyond freedom, he saw the status and condition of the black man as a matter for state, not national, decision. His drive for political power reinforced his inclination and his constitutional principles. The support of southerners and of the northern Democracy was welcome, perhaps essential, if the tailor's apprentice was to realize his ambition to be an elected president. They could not lightly be alienated. The Radicals, the old abolitionist wing of the Republican party, seemed politically expendable. An aggressive loner, stubborn, insecure, clinging to "right" principles and rejecting differing views as error or evil, Johnson could neither lead the nation nor accept the leadership of the Republicans in Congress. Whatever his conscious intent, the use Johnson made of the powers of the presidency—not only his vetoes but also his pardons, his appointments, his directives as commander in chief, his authority over the Freedmen's Bureau, erected barriers beyond which advance toward equal citizenship for blacks could be made only at the price of open and prolonged warfare between president and congressional majority.[14]

Lincoln had recognized the historic challenge. He was prepared to implement, so far as he would find practicable, "the principle that all men are created equal." The nature of presidential leadership helped shape events, and the leadership of Andrew Johnson and of Lincoln diverged markedly. Johnson lacked Lincoln's political skill, finesse, and flexibility; more importantly, he did not face in the same direction. Lincoln would expand freedom for blacks; Johnson was content to have their freedom contained. Both men held, to use Lincoln's words, that "important principles may, and must, be inflexible"; the operative principles of Lincoln and Johnson simply did not coincide. During his presidency, though not during his period as war governor, Johnson clung to a narrow concept of the powers of the national government as "right" principle. Lincoln's constitutional scruples, on the other hand, did not preclude the expansion of federal authority. He had exercised broadly the war powers of commander in chief, and his readiness to continue to do so in reconstructing the states was indicated both by his sending General Banks back to Louisiana and by his initiating cabinet consultations in preparation for making "some new announcement to the people of the South," after Congress had adjourned without agreeing upon a southern policy. Lincoln took to heart the warning of William Whiting, solicitor of the War Department, to which Phillip Paludan has called attention. He saw the danger in recognizing a doctrine of state existence that would enable "secessionists . . . to get back by fraud what they failed to get by fighting."[15] In his last public address, he carefully refrained from taking a stand on "whether the seceded States, so called, are in the Union or out of it." Also unlike Johnson and the Democrats, Lincoln indicated no aversion to the use of constitutional amendment to change the historic division of powers between state and federal government. Nor had he objected, as would they, that Congress had no authority to impose a provision in respect to suffrage upon the unreconstructed states. With enfranchisement, as with slavery, it is reasonable to view Lincoln's pressure for state action not as devotion to a narrow concept of state rights federalism but as a practical first step toward an ultimate solution. Given the differences in principle and prejudice between Lincoln and Johnson, Reconstruction history would have followed a different path both at the nation's capital and in the secession states of the South had Lincoln lived out his second term of office. Of that there can be no doubt.

At the nation's capital there would have been no war between president and Congress. Stubborn differences as to "mode, manner, and means of reconstruction" (to use Lincoln's characterization) would, of course, have persisted among Republicans and could not have been resolved easily, for unprecedented constitutional and practical problems were involved. Yet differences cut across congressional leadership and at some point surely would have been amenable to the legislative process. They would not have created a chasm between executive and legislature. With Lincoln as president, whenever a Republican consensus or compromise developed, executive agreement could be expected short of legislation that would force him to repudiate the Louisiana experiment while there was still hope of "hatching the egg." There is good reason to believe that president and congressional majority would have joined in an effort to insure that freedmen obtain at the very least equal standing before the law, schools, the right to bear arms, a measure of present and a more general prospective enfranchisement, plus governmental assistance in acquiring access to land. An eloquent passage in Lincoln's last address pointed to the general direction in which he intended to exert presidential pressure. He would not have the nation say to Louisiana blacks, and by implication to all others who had been slaves, "This cup of liberty . . . we will dash from you, and leave you to the chances of gathering the spilled and scattered contents in some vague and undefined when, where, and how."[16]

If in early 1865 there was a possibility of presidential conflict with Congress, it was not over ends. Nor was it over jurisdiction, for Lincoln had made clear his recognition of the right of Congress to a role in Reconstruction. Possibility for conflict lay in the use of military authority as means. Sending General Banks back to Louisiana indicated Lincoln's readiness to use, though not to acknowledge as such, what the general called "force" in order to obtain "consent" to the Reconstruction of states on a basis the president considered acceptable. It is difficult to believe that the issue would have been fateful in view of the reversal of roles on this question between Congress and President Johnson, and Lincoln's rationale that the military's function in establishing the Louisiana government was only one of "cooperation."[17] One of the unrecognized ironies of Reconstruction history is that Congress, by assigning primacy to the military in the legislation of 1867, in fact capitulated to the stand Lincoln had taken in Louisiana, one that helped bring down upon him in mid-1864 the denunciations of the Wade-Davis Manifesto.

War between Congress and President Johnson was precipitated by two issues: first, continuance and strengthening of the Freedmen's Bureau; and second, establishment of citizenship and basic rights for ex-slaves by national authority. There was a Republican consensus for both measures, and with Lincoln as president, there could only have been cooperation and concurrence. In the case of the civil rights legislation, should Lincoln have considered its constitutional validity questionable, presidential influence could have been expected on behalf of a covering constitutional amendment rather than against one, as with Johnson. As for the Freedmen's Bureau, Lincoln was not at all likely to have turned his back upon the recommendations of O. O. Howard, his choice to head the bureau. It is also worth noting that of the many reasons modern scholars have advanced to explain Johnson's break with Congress, none would have been operative with Lincoln—not the substance of the Freedmen's Bureau and civil rights bills, not state rights principles, not ambition, not identity with the South or misconception of Republican attitudes, certainly not susceptibility to flattery or the personalization of political differences.[18]

The fear that Johnson's policy aroused for the future of the Republican party, as well as for the security of freedmen and of the Union, could not have arisen under Lincoln. Lincoln might have continued into the postwar years the wartime coalition that joined Republicans and some Democrats under the Union party label, but such a development would have stirred few apprehensions of a Democratic take-over. Lincoln's identification with the party's past and his continuing role as party leader precluded suspicion of disloyalty; and he was not one to be taken in by professions of personal political support. As his handling of Bullitt, Cottman, and Kennedy in Louisiana makes unmistakable, Lincoln was adroit at using, rather than being used, by such allies. Johnson was less skillful at manipulating men; he also had less reason to be wary. As a Tennessee slaveholder and Democrat, he perceived neither a proslavery past nor a staunch Democratic party allegiance as signal for caution in matters of postwar political power.

Without the vetoes of the Freedmen's Bureau and civil rights bills, erase from history the events that followed. Erase the bitter contest of 1866 between president and the party that placed him in office; erase the clash over the Fourteenth Amendment and the overturn of presidential restoration by the legislation of 1867 with its reestablishment of primacy for military authority and its grant of suffrage to all blacks in the unreconstructed states; erase the subsequent presidential obstruction of congressional intent which stirred the passion and apprehension that culminated in the impeachment of a president. Erase the

[153]

whole dramatic sequence of events, but with what effect upon the future of the freedmen? Could Lincoln and the Republican Congress working together have secured for the ex-slave a substantial freedom, one reflected in his economic as well as his legal status? Could they have established in the 1860s so firm a basis for equal citizenship that there would have been no turning back—no counterrevolutionary white "redemption," no "nadir" for blacks by the turn of the century?

Without conflict between president and Congress, whatever change Republicans agreed to impose upon the South would have enjoyed better odds for success than the settlement of 1867-1869. Both contemporaries and historians have noted the mood of acquiescence in the South that followed immediately upon the end of hostilities. Although it is unlikely that a pattern for Reconstruction would have emerged in time to capitalize on that mood, definitive requirements would certainly not have been delayed the two years that intervened between war's end and the Reconstruction legislation of 1867.

Even more important than the foreshortening of uncertainty would have been the minimizing of the false hopes, the confusion, and the resultant bitterness that arose from the president's course and its subsequent repudiation. Most white southerners believed from Johnson's conduct of the presidency that they would not have to make more than minimal concessions on the status of the ex-slave—none on suffrage and not even recognition of an absolute equality of traditional rights before the law. Although imposition of black civil and political rights finally was recognized as inescapable, delay fed a widespread reaction that to defeat was being added "dishonor." Had there been from the beginning a consistent southern policy that satisfied majority Republican opinion, it is reasonable to assume that compliance would have been greater and opposition less widespread and ruthless. Resistance had been encouraged by Johnson's stand and strengthened by a sense of injustice at the progressively severe and apparently open-ended peace terms demanded. The conflict between president and Congress fragmented a potential core of state leaders willing to cooperate in implementing the requirements of the victors. Some original supporters of the president became allied with the Conservative Democrats. Others looked to Congress and joined the Republican party. And under the rigidities of congressional Reconstruction even firm Unionists could find themselves ineffectual, barred from voting and officeholding because they had held minor office during the Confederacy. By 1868 southern white recruits to Republican ranks were discredited as traitors to section and to race. To this was added the opprobrium conveyed by the term "scalawag," which came into general use only with congressional Reconstruction. Otto Olsen has pointed out that the opponents of the Republican party in the South did not consider it a legitimate political entity with which to contest state elections, but an alien force to be destroyed.[19] In short, no stable political "nucleus" to implement national policy, such as Lincoln had tried to encourage, could cohere and expand while Johnson held presidential power. With Lincoln in office, odds for success would have been greater, but by no means assured. Nor would there have been any certainty that the white South's acceptance of Republican peace terms would enable blacks to gain a stake in the economy and a participation in the political process sufficiently large to realize the goals of the freedmen and their advocates.[20]

The victory for equal civil and political rights inaugurated by national legislation and the southern state conventions of 1868 was tragically temporary, but it should not be deprecated. Opportunities were opened to former slaves and antebellum free blacks for participation in political power, opportunities they pursued with vigor. However brief and episodic their role in political decision-making and their enjoyment of public facilities formerly denied them, free blacks had defied old taboos and left an imprint upon the institutions of the South—political, social, and economic—which the resurgence of white supremacy never completely annihilated.[21] Some native white southerners not only had supported them out of expediency or loyalty to the Union but had come to accept as valid concepts of racial equity alien to their own past. Yet there can be no question but that the equality of citizenship embodied in national and state law during the 1860s lay shattered and apparently unmendable as the South entered the twentieth century. Most former slaves and their children still lived in agrarian dependence and poverty, poorly educated, increasingly disfranchised and segregated, with little protection against a new surge of white violence.

All accounts of Reconstruction recognize the intensity of white southern resistance to the new status of blacks imposed by Republicans upon the defeated South. Curiously, in explaining the outcome, generally characterized by modern historians as the failure of Reconstruction (though with qualification and some dissent), they tend to place major responsibility not upon the South but upon "the North." By "the North" they usually mean the Republican party, which held national political power, and sometimes say as much. Their explanation is not free of moral stricture, often patently implicit when not expressly stated. Since the mid-1960s there has seldom been missing from accounts of the "First Reconstruction" the pejorative term "betrayal." Present-day scholars do not indulge in "moral discourse" on black slavery, for as David Donald observed "in the middle of the twentieth century there are some things that do not need to be said."[22] Even less likely is an echo of antebellum abolitionist strictures upon slaveholders as "sinners," though there has been lively debate as to whether or not planters harbored a sense of guilt about their peculiar institution. In terms of the moral judgment of history, the vanquished hold an advantage over the victors. Little restraint or understanding has been extended to the latter. Yet few historians would question the statement that those who won the military contest lost the peace. They have not considered the implications. To lose a battle is not to betray a cause; to retreat in the face of a seemingly weak but relentless and resourceful foe is not the equivalent of treachery; to put an end to a bruising fight that has been lost is not without a certain moral justification of its own. In a self-governing nation the will to persevere indefinitely in a just cause, subordinating all else both of interest and conviction, is beyond the realm of reasonable expectation. If Republican politicians and their constituencies of the 1860s and '70s have received little charity, the one professionally acceptable defense of the opprobrium cast upon them is that the political leaders had viable alternatives—viable in the sense that other policies would have changed the outcome, viable also in the sense that such measures could have been perceived and implemented.

An explicit and sweeping statement reflecting that assumption was made by the most distinguished and influential historian of the postbellum South, C. Vann Woodward, in a burst of eloquence that concluded a pathbreaking paper on comparative emancipations and reconstructions. When revised and republished, he did not allow the passage to stand unmodified. However, the original version is quoted at length because it reveals a premise quite generally held, though seldom openly stated or scrutinized. In the paper C. Vann Woodward had argued that postemancipation failure characterized all plantation America, the excesses of brutality, exploitation, and discrimination in the Caribbean and Brazil paralleling and even exceeding those in the South. Then he passed judgment:

But failure, like most human experience, is a relative matter. It depends on expectations and promises, on *commitments and capabilities*. One man's failure is another man's success. And in a way *the American failure was the greatest of all*. For in 1865 the democratic colossus of the New World stood triumphant, flushed with the terrible victories of Gettysburg, Vicksburg, Cold Harbor, and Appomattox. Its crusade for freedom had vindicated the blood shed by its sons, and in the full flush of power and victory and righteousness its leaders solemnly pledged the nation to fulfill its promises, not only of freedom but the full measure of democracy and racial equality. *The powers of fulfillment, sealed by the sacrifices of a victorious war, were unlimited.* And the federal government was no remote trans-Atlantic metropolitan parliament on the banks of the Thames or the Seine. It sat on the Potomac, with General Lee's Arlington Mansion in full view of the White House windows across the river, and its armies garrisoned the defeated states.

In the revision, the key sentence was changed to: "The powers of fulfillment, sealed by the sacrifices of a victorious war, were *seemingly* unlimited, *though of course they were not.*"[23]

A final paragraph, identical in both versions, introduces a note of ambiguity:

Yet we know that, although the North won its four-year war against a fully armed, mobilized, and determined South when the issue was slavery, it very quickly lost its crusade against a disarmed, defeated, and impoverished South when the issue was equality. For on this issue the South was united as it

[157]

had not been on slavery. And the North was even more divided on the issue of equality than it had been on slavery. In fact, when the chips were down, the overwhelmingly preponderant views of the North on that issue were in no important respect different from those of the South—and never had been.

The passage perhaps was meant to open the door, gingerly, to a shared culpability—or even a shared exculpation. Yet the two paragraphs in their final form render an unmistakably censorious verdict upon righteous leaders of a victorious North making pledges on the banks of the Potomac that they were unwilling to enforce against a defenseless South.

The verdict arises from the premise, qualified in the revision but still operative, that Republican leaders had power to force upon the white South equality between the races, a most questionable assumption. And the rhetoric in which it is stated blurs the factual record. With victory at hand, Congress had adjourned deadlocked over Reconstruction. The only leader who could and did speak with a measure of authority for the federal government was Abraham Lincoln. He did so from an upstairs window of the White House two days after Lee's surrender. Cautiously he revealed his hope for Louisiana and the other states awaiting Reconstruction, a hope "to ripen" the changes already under way into "a complete success." Lincoln's statement was significant, potentially momentous had he lived, but it constituted no pledge on behalf of the nation to a "full measure of democracy and racial equality." The Republican commitment even at its peak never pledged "racial equality," a concept resting upon the conviction that there is no inequality in the innate endowment of races and carrying logical imperatives for personal and social conduct. The more limited commitment of the 1860s, and the demand against which the South proved far from "disarmed," was equality of civil and political rights irrespective of any inequality of race that might be thought to exist. There was also a promise, not legally binding but considered implicit in civil and political equality, that former slaves would not be held to an economic status of dependency and disguised servitude.[24] These were issues over which the postwar struggle was joined. And on these issues the preponderant view in the North did in fact differ from that in the South, even

[158]

though its predominance there was far from overwhelming and had crystallized only under the pressure of sectional conflict.

The comparative approach to emancipation and Reconstruction might have led C. Vann Woodward to a charitable conclusion. What was attempted in the United States was of a magnitude and difficulty, and a daring, without equal in other emancipations, and in the body of his paper he made an impressive case for such a generalization. He pointed out the much greater number of slaves affected by emancipation in the South than in all the rest of the Americas, four million of an approximate six million. Despite their great number, blacks in the South, unlike those in most other areas of plantation America, were a minority who as free men faced a white non-slaveholding majority. As nowhere else, their freedom came as the result of a terrible war between whites, and came suddenly, without the transitional period characteristic of most emancipations. In comparative perspective, the situation in the United States was overwhelming. Yet to these elements of magnitude was added, as Woodward clearly states, an effort on an unparalleled scale to force upon white men the sharing of political power and office with blacks. Woodward even argues that the U.S. Congress, despite the constitutional restraints under which it functioned, was more tenacious in its effort to accompany freedom with radical reform than was the English Parliament in abolishing slavery in the West Indies. Similarly, in a comparative study of the response to emancipation, George Fredrickson characterizes the attempt to reconstruct the South as "the most radical departure from white supremacy attempted anywhere in the nineteenth century." And Peyton McCrary holds that until the twentieth century only the French Revolution "rivaled the magnitude of social transformation involved in the abolition of slavery in the United States."[25] In view of the dimensions of the undertaking it would seem fitting for historians of southern Reconstruction to mitigate judgment on the offense of failure.

A comparative approach to Reconstruction also suggests that there is an inherently stubborn difficulty to providing a road out of poverty for a dependent, subservient agrarian people, most especially for nonwhite laborers of a plantation economy. Even in Europe where race and plantation did not block advance, emancipation from the old servile order of the eighteenth century brought peasants escape from poverty and from social-political disadvantage only slowly, and then with major exceptions. In eastern Europe, where industrialization and urbanization lagged, the economic lot of most remained harsh far into the twentieth century. "The freeing of the [European] peasantry from the bonds of their servility" could be characterized by a responsible historian as late as the 1970s as a "still unfinished social revolution."[26]

In regions of plantation dominance, one searches with little success for examples of transformation that have raised the standard of living, except for the few, above a minimum essential for existence. A study of the economy of plantation areas published in 1972 appeared under the suggestive title *Persistent Poverty*. The author holds that plantation societies by their very nature perpetuate underdevelopment.

Rigid patterns of social stratification associated with race and color inhibit social mobility and severely restrict the participation of large goups of people in economic and political affairs. Plural societies pregnant with race conflict exhibit instability which is inimical to development. And the concentration of economic, social, and political power within the society prevents the emergence of a highly motivated population.

With some emancipations, black workers largely escaped the plantation system, as in Jamaica and British Guiana. Their economic gains seldom proved sustained or substantial, even where change brought noneconomic satisfactions, crop innovations, and a lessening of the inequality of income distribution. In grappling with the problem of rural poverty, John Kenneth Galbraith in 1979 reminded his readers that "an end to injustice . . . is not necessarily or even usually an end to poverty."[27] And it is doubtful that any former slave society has completely eradicated economic or racial injustice.

One plantation area that might be expected to have offered the emancipated slave the economic substance of freedom is the São Paulo region of Brazil, a country with little overt or blatant race discrimination.[28] Coffee production there in contrast to that of sugar and cotton elsewhere was a dynamic, expanding, and profitable agriculture in the 1880s at the time of emancipation, and continued to thrive with only a few short interludes of falling prices in the late nineteenth and early twentieth century. Profits from coffee remained largely in the region, helping to fuel urbanization and industrialization. The benefits of a remarkable economic development went not to the upper classes alone, but also to the propertyless men at the bottom. Yet few blacks gained a better livelihood. The jobs open to them remained the least remunerative and the most menial, and many were displaced even on the coffee plantations. Their role in the new order became more marginal than in the old. It was the white immigrants from Europe, predominantly Italian but also Portuguese, Spanish, and German, who took their places and then attained the status of landowners or seized the opportunities open to workmen and entrepreneurs in the bustling city of São Paulo. There occurred, as Florestan Fernandes has put it, not a transformation of freedmen into "free labor" but a substitution of white labor for black. Brazil, a nation that takes pride in a perception of its history as free from color prejudice or discrimination, has been found by modern scholars to nurture an illusion that masks the realities of thought and behavior rooted in its slavery past. They have concluded that Brazilian blacks and mulattoes are victimized without willful white intent, but victimized nonetheless. Men and women marked by color bear a disproportionately heavy burden of poverty, unemployment, underemployment, and low levels of schooling. And this failure of reconstruction occurred in a country that, in sharp contrast to the United States, enjoyed an historic tradition of racial tolerance and, to use Carl Degler's phrase, a "mulatto escape hatch" from the color line.[29]

If the success of Republicans in reconstructing the South rested upon the precondition of an absence of race prejudice, the limits of the possible were so narrow as to have foreordained failure. Modern scholarship has recognized and amply documented the pervasiveness and persistence of racial prejudice. In some form it contaminated almost all white Americans. Had mid-nineteenth-century America constituted a society utopian in its freedom from "racism," the obstacles to successful reordering of southern society would have been immensely lessened, though European experience suggests that they would not have been completely removed.[30] It does not follow, however, that race prejudice precluded an equality of civil and political rights. Differences in the quality and priority of prejudice, not only between individuals but between the two major parties, provided a significant opening for political action. By the 1860s many northerners who did not find objectionable discrimination against blacks in private and social relationships had come to view as unacceptable discrimination against blacks in public matters. Most of them were Republicans. Prejudices existed among Republicans, but they did not prevent the party from making equal citizenship the law of the land. To explain the breakdown of that law by pointing to the racial bias of Republicans is unconvincing unless one assumes that a commitment to civil and political equality can be met only by men who accept and seek to realize the more far-reaching twentieth-century concept of racial equality, a highly questionable premise.

Neither can it be taken for granted that a racism so strong as to reject an equality of basic rights is impervious to change. There is no question but that racial attitudes affect behavior, but it is also recognized that behavior affects racial attitudes, though more slowly. Furthermore, a belief in racial inferiority or an emotional revulsion against accepting one of a different race as an equal does not necessarily result in discriminatory action. That may be held in check by a whole range of countervailing forces—by self-interest or a common goal, by institutions such as law with courts that enforce the law, by a perception of discrimination as unwarranted because it conflicts with other norms of societal behavior. And the experience gained by foregoing discrimination can result in changed views and changed emotional responses.[31] Even when it does not, nondiscriminatory practices may continue. Logically, equality may be indivisible; in practice, it has never been a seamless web.

Failure to enforce black civil and political rights in the South is often attributed to a lack of will on the part of Republican leaders and their constituencies due to their racial views. The explanation may not be susceptible of definite disproof, but it has not been proven and probably cannot be. Many factors entered into the abandonment of the cause of the black man in the South, and Republicans gave up neither quickly or easily. The voting record of regular Republicans in Congress through 1891 remained remarkably consistent and cohesive behind efforts to strengthen federal enforcement of Reconstruction legislation. Democratic party obstruction was equally consistent and created a major roadblock. Republicans enacted a drastic enforcement law in 1870 and another in 1871. For most of the twenty years after the elections of 1870 they did not have the power in Congress to pass additional legislation supportive of black rights but they kept the issue alive. It is true that as early as 1872 some Republicans, notably those who joined the Liberal Republican movement, broke with the policy of national action in support of black rights. But race prejudice was neither a conscious nor a major determinant of their new attitude toward federal intervention in the South. Indeed, the Liberal Republican platform of 1872 tried to reconcile a policy of national retreat with loyalty to the Reconstruction amendments. When Republicans regained control of both houses of Congress in 1890–1891 by only a narrow margin, they passed in the House an enforcement bill to protect black voters but narrowly lost it in the Senate by the perfidy of a few who broke ranks to gain support for silver legislation.[32] On the local front in the northern states, in keeping with party tradition, the Republican record on black rights remained better than that of their opponents.

In 1877 when President Hayes withdrew federal troops and acquiesced to "home rule" for the South, racism was not the key to presidential decision. No critical causal connection has been established between the "betrayal" and race attitudes.[33] There is no doubt but that Hayes' action was related to a general lessening of northern support for intervention in the South. The erosion had been going on for several years, and for that there were a number of reasons. The will to continue the battle was undermined by growing doubt of the wisdom of immediate universal black enfranchisement, increasingly seen as the source of corruption. There was revulsion against the turmoil of disputed elections and the force used to settle them. Many Republicans were discouraged as state after state came under "Redeemer" control, or distracted by the pressure of problems closer at home. There was a general desire in the North for the peace and national reconciliation that

Grant had invoked but could not attain as president. Whatever part race prejudice played in weakening Republican support for continuing military intervention, its role was peripheral rather than central.

In the face of persistent and successful resistance by the white South, President Hayes found a fragile hope. The southern conservative leadership that had returned to power appeared to be pledging its honor that "home rule" would protect black southerners in their civil and political rights. Republicans had not succeeded in forcing the South to accept blacks as equal citizens. Perhaps more could be secured by entrusting their rights to the section's own leaders. The agreement of 1877 has been characterized by C. Vann Woodward as a "honeyfugling" of the North. When Hayes recognized the deception, he tried to change course with means short of military force. They proved ineffectual.[34]

Race prejudice played a larger role in the obstructionist tactics of northern Democrats than in weakening the will of Republicans. During and after the Civil War, appeal to the race prejudice of their constituencies was a standard procedure in election battles. Yet when it failed to yield decisive political profit, northern Democratic leaders changed tactics. By the mid-1870s they had retreated from public avowals to overturn Reconstruction. By the 1880s in northern states they were wooing black voters by helping to enact local civil rights laws and by giving blacks recognition in patronage appointments. Prejudice had bowed to political advantage. Within little more than a decade, an equal right to the ballot was accepted and institutionalized in both northern parties. Continuing support by northern Democrats in Congress for their southern colleagues in opposing federal enforcement of the right to vote rested upon party advantage in maintaining solidarity with the Democratic South.[35]

Racism linked to southern resistance was more politically formidable. As events developed after Congress repudiated Johnsonian Reconstruction and prescribed its own plan, the appeal to white prejudice was critically important. It enabled Democrats to recapture political ascendancy and to cripple the projected operational arm of congressional policy, the Republican party in the South, as an effective contestant for political power. To attain victory the "Redeemers" mobilized a racism whose many faces were evident about them—conviction that white superiority and black incapacity were nature's law, revulsion against accepting the black man on an equal basis in any capacity as both distasteful and insulting, umbrage at being confronted with violations of the race etiquette to which whites had been conditioned by slavery. Racial hostility was used to organize and to justify terror, intimidation, and fraud, particularly in election contests but also in more mundane activities when freedom led blacks beyond "their place."

Even so, racism alone does not explain southern intransigence. It was strongly reinforced by other factors—by the psychological need of white southerners to avoid "dishonor" in defeat, by fears of economic chaos and race warfare, by shock and outrage at the congressional peace terms of 1867, by a perception of Republican demand for black civil and political equality as punitive. Increased taxation at a time of economic stress helped inflame emotions. The result was resistance, sometimes open and sometimes covert, often violent but also subtle. A guerrilla warfare outmaneuvered and overwhelmed Republican forces in the South and gave way before federal military force only to regroup and strike again.[36] It was a resistance strengthened by a sense of right in safeguarding a social order in which blacks were subordinate to whites. If racism was a critical element in the failure to establish securely black civil and political rights, it was not because racial prejudice permeated both sections, both parties, and all classes. It was because prejudice in the South was deeply rooted, intrinsic to the social and economic structure, and effectively mobilized for political combat. To induce a change in southern white racial behavior to the extent of accepting the black man as an equal in the courts and at the ballot box and as a free laborer entitled to choose, to move about, to better his condition—that task was not in theory beyond the power of Congress and president but it was an uncertain undertaking that would have tested the political skill of any party and president. Fortuitous circumstances, both political and economic, may well have precluded success. Lincoln's assassination changed the direction of presidential policy, and the downward slide of the postbellum cotton economy of the South reinforced white resistance to change.

A critical question needs to be addressed. Could a greater use of force have brought white southerners to accept civil and political rights for blacks? Neither history nor theory can answer this question with certainty. A number of historians have implied that direct coercion could have effected a fundamental change, that Reconstruction was the nation's great missed opportunity. Few would go so far as Eugene Genovese, who has written that there was no prospect of a better future for blacks unless several thousand leaders of the Lost Cause had been summarily killed. Michael Perman would have had the political and economic power of the southern elite eliminated by means less Draconian and more nearly representative of recent historiographic opinion. He suggests an immediate "edict of the conqueror" enforced by occupying troops to exclude the elite from political power, give suffrage to blacks, confiscate plantations, and divide their lands among the freedmen. Far too good an historian to argue that such an edict had been a practical postwar possibility, he nonetheless believes that had it been possible, it would have worked. William Gillette has taken a more historically realistic approach to the problem. Recognizing that Republicans were not in a position to enforce their Reconstruction program until 1869 when they obtained control of the presidency as well as of Congress, he examines closely the southern record of the Grant years. While he comes to the conclusion that Republicans might have succeeded, or at least achieved a great deal, his analysis of the requirements for success is not reassuring. The skill he sees lacking but needed by Grant might have overtaxed even a Lincoln. According to Gillette, Grant should have been cautious where he was bold, bold where he was timid. He had to be both master politician and resolute soldier. The situation required his effective direction of an expert bureaucracy and an overwhelming military muscle, neither of which was at his disposal. Grant should have overpowered militarily southern white resistance yet come to terms with the fact that "in the long run coercion could not replace a sanctioned consensus." Given the nation's traditional commitment to civilian control and majority rule, "the use of force was self-defeating."[37]

Force *and* consent, how to achieve the one by use of the other, posed a dilemma which by the 1870s strained the bounds of the possible. The outcome would have been only a little less problematic had Reconstruction been formulated in early 1865 and backed by force, i.e., by force alone. Particularly vulnerable is the assumption that by eliminating the power of the landed aristocracy, resistance would have been broken and a new order of equal rights for blacks securely established. There would still have remained for the South as a whole a white majority with prejudices and interests inimical to the advancement of blacks. A stunned acceptance in the despondency of defeat of such peace terms as Perman has outlined would have been no guarantee of their permanent observance by white southerners. Here theory is of some help to speculation. It lends support to Gillette's perception of the need to reconcile the seemingly irreconcilable. Historians have tended to approach the concepts of coercion/consent, or conflict/consensus, as coercion vs. consent or conflict vs. consensus, and not without precedent in political and sociological thought. There exist, however, theoretical analyses that see coercion and consensus as compatible, even complementary. They suggest that the problem, both in theory and practice, is one of interrelationship. Even theorists identified with the view that conflict and coercion are essential to the creation of a new and better social order seldom argue that force alone is sufficient to bring about the change desired. Nor do they overlook the danger that coercion can be self-defeating. The more consensus oriented see force as unable to operate alone over any length of time. The concern to identify "authority," to examine the sources of its "legitimacy," to distinguish authority from "power," to establish the noncoercive forms of power and the nonphysical forms of coercion—these continuing efforts indicate the importance attached to means other than direct force in effecting and maintaining social change. And there is a long tradition of political thought that admonishes caution in trying to force change contrary to traditional convictions lest it provoke deep and bitter reaction.[38] From an approach either through theory or history, it would seem reasonable to conclude that a policy of force *plus* some form and degree of consent—even if the consent, to borrow from P. H. Partridge, were only "a patchwork of divergent and loosely adjusted values, norms, and objectives"—would have had a better chance of success in reordering the South than force alone. Lincoln was capable of a "patchwork"design in implementing policy.

Certainly by the mid-1870s the use of coercion had intensified a deep and bitter reaction. Instead of passive resignation, coercion led to a "negative consensus" that rejected the legitimacy of national authority over the status of blacks, fed resistance and united white southerners to an unprecedented degree. It is well to be reminded that the coercion used had been considerable. Whatever the formality of consent in the ratification of the Fourteenth Amendment, Congress had left the recalcitrant secession states no effective choice. In the initial enfranchisement of blacks, white southerners were allowed not even the formality of consenting; enfranchisement was mandated by Congress and implemented by military authority and presence. The military also intervened in the reorganization of the South's labor system and in the operation of its local courts. The presence of an occupying army preceded the interim period of military rule set up by Congress in 1867 and did not disappear with the restoration of state authority. Violent resistance to the new order was answered not only by the passage of drastic congressional legislation in 1870 and 1871 but also by the use under these laws of federal armed forces, notably in Mississippi, South Carolina, North Carolina, and Alabama. Troops helped make arrests, guarded prisoners, protected court proceedings, and maintained order at the polls. Over a thousand military arrests were made in three counties of South Carolina in 1871-1872. Federal attorneys obtained 540 criminal convictions in Mississippi in 1872-1873 and 263 in North Carolina in 1873. The district attorney for the northern and middle districts of Alabama obtained indictments of more than 350 persons from two grand juries, one in the fall of 1871 and the other in the spring of 1872. From 1870, when the first enforcement law was passed, through 1874, 3,382 cases under the acts were adjudicated in federal courts in the southern states. In addition, under Grant's direction federal troops in effect decided disputes over who rightfully held elective office in Louisiana, Arkansas, and Mississippi.[39]

The force employed in the 1870s was grossly insufficient for the task at hand. Too often local officials and courts sidestepped justice for blacks without interference. Troops stationed in the South were woefully inadequate in number to contain violent resistance wherever it erupted. Relatively few of the men arrested in South Carolina were brought to trial. In general, indictments were difficult to obtain and even in the federal courts many cases were dismissed. By the end of 1874 little vitality was left in the federal enforcement program. Southern resistance turned increasingly to intimidation and more subtle, less legally vulnerable means than the earlier violence. Democratic power in Congress deprived the executive of resources needed to enforce the laws and prevented legislative action to strengthen them.

Nonetheless, the direct coercion mobilized by the national government in the 1860s and 1870s was substantial, far greater than any similar action in support of desegregation and black voting in the 1950s and '60s. It was large enough to give strong support to the contention that a century ago the amount of force necessary to realize equal civil and political rights in the South was impossible to sustain in a nation whose democratic tradition and constitutional structure limited the use of power, exalted the rule of law, and embodied the concept of government by the consent of the governed. Neither national institutions nor public opinion could be expected to have sustained a military intervention of indefinite length and of sufficient strength to crush all local resistance. And by the mid-1870s, the issue at stake no longer appeared clear-cut, even to northern Republicans. Popular government at the South seemed to have become "nothing but a sham."[40]

Assumptions regarding the potency of national power to effect social change, largely valid for the "Second Reconstruction," may inadvertently have biased historical judgment concerning the earlier period. By the 1950s the capacity for resistance in the South, although still strong, was markedly less than in the post–Civil War decades. Race prejudice remained formidable, but in the wake of Hitler's holocaust and advances in the social sciences, psychology, and biology, prejudice could no longer command arguments of scientific or moral respectability. Despite shocking episodes of violence, white terror never reached the epidemic proportions of the 1860s and '70s. Apparently it was no longer condoned by majority white opinion in the South. Moreover, in the 1950s and '60s not Congress but the judiciary took the initiative in forcing change and remained a vital mechanism for implementing it. The aura of legitimacy created by supportive judicial decisions, lacking in the earlier period, greatly lessened the necessity for direct physical coercion. With a few exceptions, notably at Little Rock in 1957, federal enforcement of court decisions and civil rights legislation proceeded without a show of force. Nor were federal criminal prosecutions numerous. A total of only 323 criminal cases were filed by the newly established civil rights division of the Justice Department from 1958 through mid-1972, only a tenth of the number that had been brought by the attorney general's office in the first five years of the 1870s. Other methods of coercion were available, both more effective and more consonant with the traditional primacy of civil over military authority, of persuasion over force. Civil cases initiated or assisted by the Justice Department far outnumbered criminal ones, and the department was active in negotiating voluntary agreements of compliance and in community counseling. With the great increase in the functions undertaken by the federal government to meet the needs of a mature industrial society, there were at hand powerful monetary and administrative sanctions, and a bureaucracy to use them.

In contrast to the 1870s, during the "Second Reconstruction" votes and time were available to pass a whole array of acts, progressively more comprehensive in scope and more resourceful in their enforcement provisions. What made this achievement possible, according to authorities in the field, was the existence of a national consensus. Although it did not encompass majority white opinion in the South, elsewhere it found support in both major parties, quite unlike the situation in the Civil War era when consensus, on a much more limited program of black rights, existed only within the Republican party. Presidential leadership by the second President Johnson, in contrast to that of the first, was exerted to expand civil rights. In the creation of the national consensus of the 1950s blacks themselves played a key role beyond that open to them a century earlier. Their political influence in the North was considerable because of the numbers who had moved out of the South to fill northern labor needs. The distance from slavery allowed their leaders, South as well as North, to operate with formidable resources, skills, and organization and to present a case that could no longer be evaded by a show of scientific or social justification. They made inescapably visible to white America the injustices piled high during the postemancipation decades.[41]

In short, the "Second Reconstruction" is a false model from which to project in retrospect the limits of the possible a century earlier. As an analogy, however, it suggests the need for far more than direct force to attain success. Its loss of momentum by the 1970s also indicates the difficulty of sustaining a national moral purpose, even with a task recognized as unfinished. In November 1971, the United States Commission on Civil Rights wrote "that the American people have grown somewhat weary, that the national sense of injustice, which was the foundation on which the legislative victories of the 1960s were built, has dimmed." And a few years later other informed analysts agreed. They attributed the fuel for the engine of change during the two previous decades in part to the deceptive clarity of the problems seen through the lens of the New Frontier and the New Society. There had been a naive public faith that new programs of government intervention would quickly bear fruit. Results failed to meet expectations. Advance slowed as injustices were reduced to ones less shockingly visible, as moral issues became clouded by the complexity of problems, as economic conditions turned less favorable, and as conflicts of interest intensified. Analysts concluded that the future was not sanguine. The circumstances of the 1960s had been unusually conducive to change and were not apt to be duplicated.[42]

If the contention is correct that unlike the situation during the "Second Rconstruction," the maximum level of federal force sustainable in the 1870s (conceivably *any* amount of direct coercion) could not have broken southern white resistance, there still remains a space open for the possibility of a happier outcome of Reconstruction in the nineteenth century had Lincoln lived to extend the Louisiana policy of "consent *and* force." Unlike Congress, or Grant as president, Lincoln was usually adept at persuasion and skillful in using those sanctions available to him. He had demonstrated his ability to wield the power of patronage and of military appointment. He could have been expected to exercise with equal skill the extraordinary power he held by virtue of office and of legislation to grant pardons to those subject to penalty under the Confiscation Act of 1862. In the process of reconstructing state governments Lincoln could have been counted on to safeguard presidential authority from the kind of erosion that occurred under his successor. Although at war's end he might have remained for some time "the Confederates' chief villain,"[43] and never acquired the popularity Andrew Johnson established in the South, Lincoln could scarcely have become for white southerners, as did "Radical" Republicans, the symbol of the alien, the fanatic, the self-righteous, and the vindictive. And Lincoln would have enjoyed the advantage of timing lost to Republicans by the 1870s.

Lincoln's presidential style, at odds with that forthrightness which stands high in twentieth-century criteria for presidential leadership, was not inappropriate to the situation he faced. The manner in which he unveiled the crucial, controversial element of his Reconstruction policy—some measure of suffrage for blacks—was designed to crystallize support and minimize opposition. At the time only the most minimal suffrage proposal could command an intraparty consensus; this was all that he asked, actually less than his supporters had sought in Louisiana. Yet he managed to open the door to future enfranchisement for more blacks than the relatively few, Union soldiers and the "very intelligent," whose qualifications he commended. In phrasing that avoided a definite formulation of either means or goal he suggested the desirability of a fuller franchise, one that would meet what "the colored man" "desires." In the same address he stated that "the sole object of the government" was to get the secession states back into "their proper practical relation with the Union" and asked that "all join in doing the acts necessary" to restore them. He refrained from defining the "acts necessary." To counter criticism that he had set up the reconstructed state government, Lincoln minimized his role in Louisiana, but he did not disavow his authority as commander in chief to shape the Reconstruction process.[44] By virtue of that power he had just sent General Banks back to New Orleans with military authority to perform an essentially civil mission—to promote the kind of Unionist government and racial policy the administration desired.

Although his statements could be otherwise interpreted, Lincoln's purpose, like that of his party, went beyond the readmission of the secession states. In early 1865 he was in an excellent position to implement a larger purpose by combining a minimum of direct force with a maximum use of other means of asserting the power and influence of the presidency. Lincoln's election victory the previous November had greatly strengthened his hand with Congress and with the northern public. Final military victory could only have increased the public esteem and congressional respect he had won. In the summer and fall that followed, Lincoln would have found additional support in a mounting sense of indignation in the North as reports from the South confirmed warnings that the freedom of blacks would be in peril if left in the hands of southern whites. A widespread perception of injustice can be a powerful political force, as indeed it became in 1866.[45]

It would have been uncharacteristic of Lincoln not to have recognized the opportunity. In his pragmatic fashion, advancing step by step as events permitted, with caution but when necessary with great boldness, it is just possible that Lincoln might have succeeded in making a policy of basic citizenship rights for blacks "acceptable to those who must support it, tolerable to those who must put up with it."[46] The challenge to presidential leadership was formidable. If any man could have met the challenge, that man was Lincoln.

Had Lincoln in the course of a second term succeeded in obtaining a far broader consent from the white South to terms that would satisfy northern Republican opinion than did Congress in 1867–1869, ultimate victory in the battle over the ex-slave's status as free man would not necessarily have followed. There would still have been the need to build institutions that could safeguard and expand what had been won—laws that the courts would uphold, an economy offering escape from poverty and dependency, a Union-Republican party in the South recognized by its opponents as a legitimate contestant for political power. The opportunities open to Lincoln for institutionalizing gains made toward equal citizenship irrespective of color were limited.

A fatal weakness of Reconstruction, constitutional historians have argued, arose from the constitutional conservatism of Republican lawmakers, particularly their deference to the traditional federal structure embodied in the Constitution. This led them to preserve the primacy of state responsibility for the rights of citizens, thereby denying to the national government effective power to protect the rights of blacks. It has been contended that Reconstruction required "a major constitutional upheaval," that it "could have been effected only by a revolutionary destruction of the states and the substitution of a unitary constitutional system."[47] Part of the argument is unassailable. The new scholarship has demolished the old stereotype of Republican leaders as constitutional revolutionaries. They had, indeed, been waging a war for constitution as well as for nation with every intent of maintaining both. And the concern of Republicans for state and local government was no superficial adulation of the constitution; it was deeply rooted in their commitment to self-government. Yet unlike Democrats who denounced as unconstitutional any amendment to the constitution that enlarged federal authority at the expense of the states, Republicans did not uphold state rights federalism without qualification. They believed that they had found a way to protect freedmen in their new citizenship status by modifying, rather than destroying, the traditional federal structure.

What is questionable in the case against "respect for federalism" as fatally compromising Reconstruction is the assumption that the state rights federalist approach to the problem made a solution impossible. Not all scholars would agree. Some believe that the Reconstruction amendments needed only to have been more carefully framed. Others hold that as written they were adequate to the task. The Supreme Court, of course, seemed to disagree, overturning much of the legislation Congress passed under the amendments. Beginning with the Slaughterhouse decision of 1873, which did not directly affect blacks but carried ominous implications for them, a Republican Court handed down a series of constrictive decisions described in retrospect as "vacuous" and as "a major triumph for the South." Concern to preserve the functions of the states strongly influenced those decisions. Some authorities hold that without destroying federalism the Court could have devised a workable new division of authority between state and nation which would have enabled the latter to protect the rights of blacks against violation by either states or individuals. The Court did not foreclose all avenues of congressional action to protect black rights. However, by 1875 when it rendered the first adverse decision directly relating to the national enforcement effort, further legislation to meet the Court's criteria of adequacy was politically impossible because of the strength in Congress of the Democratic political opposition.[48]

The Supreme Court seemed to have denied to congressional Reconstruction much needed legitimacy and legal sanctions. Without them, it is questionable that the Reconstruction effort could have been successfully defended during the postemancipation decades. The Court's narrow interpretation of which civil rights pertained to national as distinct from state citizenship added to the difficulties the Court had raised for the exercise of power to protect rights recognized as subject to the nation's authority. The decisions presented monumental obstacles to the enforcement of black rights. Better drafted amendments, laws, and indictments, more resourceful judicial reasoning, or less concern in the early decisions for technicalities might have avoided or remedied them.[49] Lincoln's presence was unlikely to have increased those possibilities directly. Yet had he been president in the immediate post-Appomattox period he might have succeeded in dissipating southern resistance, in unifying Republicans on the preconditions for restoration, and in inducing reconstructed state governments to accept those conditions—a tall order. The resulting climate of opinion could have led the Court to play a positive role in the nineteenth-century Reconstruction effort. A possibility, but a very tenuous possibility.

Similarly circumscribed was any potential role for Lincoln in helping shape economic developments to assure freedmen an escape from poverty and dependence. No explanation for the tragic outcome of the postwar decades for black America has been more generally accepted in modern scholarship than that Reconstruction failed because the national government did not provide land for the freedman. The thesis has been sharply challenged, and the challenge has not been met. The work of historians and economists in exploring afresh the roots of poverty, particularly of black poverty, in the postbellum South afford some relevant perspectives. Between 1974 and 1979 six book-length studies appeared with significant bearing on the problem of black poverty, and others were in progress; conference papers and published articles also reflected the vigor of scholarly interest in the question.[50]

No consensus has developed either as explanation for the continuing dependence and poverty of southern blacks or as an analysis of the potential economic effect of land distribution. However, four of five econometricians who addressed the latter question concluded that grants of land, while desirable and beneficial, would not have solved the predicament of the freedmen and their children. Robert Higgs has written that "historians have no doubt exaggerated the economic impact of such a grant." Gavin Wright holds that "the tenancy systems of the South cannot be assigned primary blame for Southern poverty," that a more equitable distribution of land "would not have produced dramatic improvements in living standards" or "generated sustained progress." In their book, *One Kind of Freedom*, Roger Ransom and Richard Sutch appear to accept what Heman Belz has characterized as the "new orthodoxy" of the historians, but they dramatically qualified that position in a subsequent paper. They argued that confiscation and redistribution would have resulted in little improvement in the postbellum situation, which they characterize as one of economic stagnation and exploitation, unless accompanied by federally funded compensation for landowners thereby providing liquid capital for reinvigorating agriculture and possibly developing manufactures.[51] This retrospective prescription is restrained as compared to the requirements outlined by twentieth-century experts who seek land distribution as an avenue out of rural poverty. They see successful land reform as requiring supplementary government programs providing credit, seed and fertilizer distribution, marketing facilities, rural and feeder transportation, pricing mechanisms affecting both what the farmer buys and what he sells, technical research, and agricultural education.[52]

More than a land program was needed to insure the freedman's economic future. Although areas of land with high fertility prospered, it seems doubtful that income from cotton between the close of the war and the turn of the century, even if equitably distributed, could have sustained much beyond a marginal level of existence for those who worked the cotton fields whether as wage earner, cropper, tenant, or small owner. And the lower South because of its soils and climate, as Julius Rubin has convincingly shown, had no viable alternative to cotton as a commercial crop until the scientific and technological advances of the twentieth century.[53] Nor could nonmarket subsistence farming offer much by way of material reward. The "more" that was needed can be envisaged in retrospect, and was glimpsed by contemporaries, but it is not clear how it could have been achieved. Gavin Wright has concluded that the postbellum South "required either a massive migration away from the region or a massive Southern industrial revolution." Both in the North and the South there was enthusiasm for promoting southern industry, but only the future could reveal how elusive would be that "New South" of ever-renewed expectations. Despite scholarship, new and old, there is no certain explanation of why the South failed to catch up with the North. If historians and economists should agree upon a diagnosis, it is unlikely that they will uncover a remedy that could have been recognized and implemented a century ago. The heritage of slavery most certainly will be part of the diagnosis. It left behind an underdeveloped, overwhelmingly rural economy tied to the world market and bereft of adequate foundations for rapid economic growth. Recovery and growth had to be attempted in a period of initial crop disasters, of disadvantage for primary products in terms of world trade, and by the mid-1870s of prolonged and recurrent economic crises.[54] There were high hopes for southern industrialization in the 1880s, but the effort substantially failed. With opportunity drastically limited in the South and industry expanding in the North, there was yet no great out-migration of blacks until the twentieth century. The reasons for this also are not altogether clear.

Neither the restraints placed on southern agricultural labor by law and custom nor the discrimination blacks faced in the North is sufficient explanation. The ways in which European immigrants blocked black advance deserve further study, as does the attitude of blacks themselves both toward leaving the South and toward the unskilled, menial labor which alone might have afforded them large-scale entry into the northern labor market.[55]

Lincoln was a man of his age. The concepts and perceptions then dominant, although not unreasonable on the basis of past experience, were inadequate to meet the challenge of transforming the South. Postwar expectations were buoyant. King Cotton was expected to regain his throne with beneficent results for all. Freed from the incubus of slavery, the South would be reshaped after the image of the bustling North, with large landholdings disintegrated by natural forces, village and school house replacing plantation quarters, internal improvements and local industry transforming the economy. The former slave would share the bright future through diligence and thrift, and the forces of the marketplace.[56] There were, of course, dissenters, both radicals like George W. Julian and Thaddeus Stevens who would confiscate the great estates and conservatives such as those cotton manufacturers, by no means all, who would perpetuate the plantation in some form.[57] Neither had sufficient influence at war's end to shape national policy. Republican leaders who did make postwar policy would have reached beyond prevailing concepts of self-help, the law of supply and demand, and the danger of "class legislation" to enact a modest land program had not President Johnson vetoed it with an appeal to all the economic verities of the day.[58]

In the interest of the emancipated, Lincoln could have been expected to approve and encourage such deviations from the doctrinaire. And it would have been completely out of character for Lincoln to have exercised his power of pardon, as did President Johnson, with ruthless disregard for the former slave's interest and justifiable expectations. Indeed, there are intimations that Lincoln considered using that power to obtain from former masters grants of land for former slaves.[59] Whatever support the national government might have given to the freedman's quest for land would have been a psychological boon, more symbol than substance of equal citizenship and independence, but not without some economic advantage. A land program more effective than the southern homestead act was a real possibility, lost due to President Johnson's opposition. With Lincoln, a Whiggish heritage, as well as humanity and a sense of responsibility for the emancipated, reinforced a pragmatic approach to the relationship between government and the future of the freedmen. Nor was he inhibited by the anxiety felt by many, including Thaddeus Stevens, over the unprecedented debt incurred in fighting the war. In early 1865 he calmly contemplated adding to the war's cost by indemnifying southerners for property seized and not restored.[60] Whatever sums Congress might have appropriated to finance land purchase for freedmen could only have helped alleviate the South's postwar paucity of capital and credit. Its economic recovery would also have benefited from the lesser turbulence of the immediate postwar years had there been no war between president and Congress. Limited gains would have been possible and probable, but there existed neither the power nor the perception necessary to forestall the poverty that engulfed so many southerners, black and white, during the last decades of the nineteenth century.

There were limits to the possible. Yet the dismal outcome for southern blacks as the nation entered the twentieth century need not have been as unrelieved as it was in fact. More than a land program, the civil and political rights Republicans established in law, had they been secured in practice, could have mitigated the discrimination that worsened their condition and constricted whatever opportunities might otherwise have existed for escape from poverty. Moreover, the extraordinary effort black men made to vote—and to vote independently in the face of white cajolery, intimidation, and economic pressure—strongly suggests that for the emancipated to cast a ballot was to affirm the reality of freedom and the dignity of black manhood.[61]

The priority Republicans gave to civil and political rights in their fight to establish a meaningful new status for ex-slaves has been too readily discounted by historians. Small landholdings could not have protected blacks from intimidation, or even from many forms of economic coercion. They would not have brought economic power. In the face of overwhelming white opposition, they could not have safeguarded the new equality of civil and political status. Where blacks voted freely, on the other hand, there was always the potential for sharing political power and using it as a means to protect and advance their interests. There is considerable evidence that this did happen. Local officials elected by black votes during the years of Republican control upheld blacks against planters, state legislators repealed Black Codes, shifted the burden of taxation from the poor, granted agricultural laborers a first lien on crops, increased expenditures for education. Eric Foner has concluded that at least in some areas Republican Reconstruction resulted in subtle but significant changes that protected black labor and prevented planters from using the state to bolster their position. Harold D. Woodman's study of state laws affecting agriculture confirms the generalization that a legislative priority of the Redeemer governments was passage of measures to give landowners greater control over the labor force. By the end of the century legal bonds had been so tightened that as prosperity returned to cotton culture neither cropper nor renter but only their employer was in a position to profit. In a study of rural Edgefield County, South Carolina, Vernon Burton has found that black voting made possible real gains in economic position and social status between 1867 and 1877. Howard Rabinowitz's examination of the urban South discloses that Republican city governments brought blacks a greater share of elected and appointed offices, more jobs in construction work, in fire and police departments.[62] And beyond immediate gains, black votes meant support for educational facilities through which blacks could acquire the literacy and skills essential for advancement.

Security for black civil and political rights required acceptance by white southerners. An acquiescence induced by a judicious combination of force and consent needed for its perpetuation reinforcement by self-interest. The most effective vehicle of self-interest would have been a Union-Republican party able to command substantial continuing support from native whites. The Republican party that gained temporary dominance through the congressional legislation of 1867 enfranchising blacks failed to meet the test of substantial white support.

Despite a strong white following in a few states, its scalawag component from the start was too limited to offset the opposition's attack on it as the party of the black man and the Yankee. And white participation diminished as appeals to race prejudice and sectional animosity intensified.

The potential for a major second party among southern whites existed in the aftermath of Confederate defeat. The Democratic party was in disarray, discredited for having led the South out of the Union and having lost the war. Old Whig loyalties subsumed by the slavery issue had nonetheless endured; southern unionism had survivied in varying degrees from wartime adherence to the Union to reluctant support of the Confederacy. Opposition to Jefferson Davis' leadership and willingness to accept northern peace terms had grown as the hope for southern victory diminished. Such sources of Democratic opposition overlapped with the potential for ready recruits to Union-Republicanism from urban dwellers, from men whose origins had been abroad or in the North, from those whose class or intrasectional interests created hostility to the dominant planter leadership of the Democracy.[63] A "New South" of enterprise and industry presented an attractive vision to many a native son. And there were always those who looked to the loaves and the fishes dispensed from Washington.

Had party recruitment and organization, with full presidential support, begun at the end of hostilities and escaped the period of confusion and bitterness that thinned the ranks of the willing during the conflict between Johnson and Congress, the result could have been promising.[64] Greater white support and the accession of black voters by increments might have eased racial tension and lessened deadly factionalism within the party. Lincoln's political skill and Whig background would certainly have served party-building well, as would the perception of presidential policy as one of moderation and reconciliation. The extent to which southern whites did in fact support the Republican party after 1867 despite its image as Radical, alien, and black-dominated, an image that stigmatized and often ostracized them, suggests the potency of a common goal, or a common enmity, in bridging the chasm between the races.

Even under the guidance of a Lincoln, the building of a permanent biracial major party in the South was by no means assured. A broad enduring coalition of disparate elements would face the necessity of reconciling sharply divergent economic interests. Agricultural workers sought maximum autonomy, more than bare necessities, and an opportunity for land ownership while planter-merchants strove to control labor and maximize profit. The burden of increased taxation to meet essential but unaccustomed social services, particularly for blacks, meant an inescapable clash of class and racial interests.[65] Concessions by the more privileged were especially difficult in a South of limited available resources and credit, impoverished by war and enmeshed in inflated costs, crop disasters, and falling cotton prices. By the mid-1870s a nationwide depression intensified regional problems. Efforts to promote a more varied and vigorous economy by state favor, credit, and appropriation became a political liability as the primary effect appeared to be the proliferation of civic corruption and entrepreneurial plunder.

Outside the South a vigorous Republican party and two-party system managed to endure despite the clash of intraparty economic interests. A similar development in the South faced the additional and more intractable conflict inherent in the new black-white relationship. Within the Republican party that took shape after 1867, factionalism often cut between blacks and carpetbaggers, on the one hand, and scalawags on the other; but there was also a considerable amount of accommodation, not all of it from blacks. A study of the voting record of 87 Republicans, 52 of them native whites, who served in the North Carolina House of Representatives in the 1868 to 1870 session shows scalawags trailing carpetbaggers and blacks in voting on issues of Negro rights and support for public schools, yet compiling a positive overall record, a score of 61.2 and 55.9 respectively. On the few desegregation questions that came to a roll call, however, only a small minority of native whites voted favorably. In Mississippi when the black-carpetbagger faction gained control, they quietly ignored the platform calling for school integration even though black legislators were sufficiently numerous and powerful to have pressed the issue. Black officeholding was a similar matter where fair treatment held danger, and black leaders often showed restraint. Such issues were explosive. They not only threatened the unity of the party but undermined its ability to attract white votes or minimize opposition demagoguery and violence.[66] A Lincolnian approach to building an interracial party would have diminished the racial hazard, but could hardly have eliminated it.

The years of political Reconstruction, to borrow an apt phrase from Thomas B. Alexander's study of Tennessee, offered no "narrowly missed opportunities to leap a century forward in reform."[67] Not even a Lincoln could have wrought such a miracle. To have secured something less, yet something substantially more than blacks had gained by the end of the nineteenth century, did not lie beyond the limits of the possible given a president who at war's end would have joined party in an effort to realize "as nearly as we can" the fullness of freedom for blacks.

Possible is not probable. To the major obstacles must be added the hazards disclosed by the Louisiana story. Lincoln's Louisiana policy had been compromised by Banks' blunders of execution and attacked by Durant and fellow Radicals in part because they distrusted Lincoln's intent. The effective implementation of a president's policy by his surrogates is a problem to plague any administration. Distrust by those otherwise allied in a common goal pertained more distinctively to the man and his style of leadership. Yet Radical distrust of Lincoln may also have reflected dilemmas inherent in presidential leadership—the need for candor and for persuasion, for vision and for practicality, for courage and for flexibility, for heeding while leading a national consensus.[68] Obscured by his characteristic self-effacement, after his own fashion Lincoln as president was both lion and fox. Not all Radicals misjudged him. In 1864 and early 1865, William Lloyd Garrison came to the defense of Lincoln and his Louisiana policy. At a stormy meeting of the Massachusetts Anti-Slavery Society in January 1865 with Banks and the president under harsh attack and black suffrage a central issue, "Mr. Garrison expressed his entire confidence in the integrity of Mr. Lincoln." About two weeks later, and after the passage of the Thirteenth Amendment, Garrison had occasion to write Lincoln.[69] His letter included a like expression of trust:

As an instrument in his hands, you have done a mighty work for the freedom of millions who have so long pined in bondage in our land—nay, for the freedom of all mankind. I have the utmost faith in the benevolence of your heart, the purity of your motives, and the integrity of your spirit. This I do not hesitate to avow at all times. I am sure you will consent to no compromise that will leave a slave in his fetters.

Notes

1. Herman Belz has shown that the language of the Crittenden Resolution, passed by Congress July 22, 1861, while appearing to preclude "Reconstruction" was deliberately phrased to omit any commitment to safeguard the institution; already congressmen recognized that the *result* of war might drastically change southern society. *Reconstructing the Union: Theory and Practice during the Civil War*, pp. 24–28. See also his *A New Birth of Freedom: The Republican Party and Freedmen's Rights, 1861 to 1866* and *Emancipation and Equal Rights: Politics and Constitutionalism in the Civil War Era*.

2. Recent emphasis on the role of blacks includes the impressive unpublished work of Armstead L. Robinson, "Day of Jublio: Civil War and the Demise of Slavery in the Mississippi Valley, 1861–1865," Ph.D. dissertation, University of Rochester, 1976, and Clarence L. Mohr, "Before Sherman: Georgia Blacks and the Union War Effort, 1861–1864," *Journal of Southern History*, XLV (Aug. 1979), 331–52.

3. Striking examples are John S. Rosenberg, "Toward a New Civil War Revisionism," *American Scholar*, XXXVIII (Spring 1969), 250–72, and Daniel A. Novak, *The Wheel of Servitude: Black Forced Labor after Slavery*.

The nature and extent of change, or continuity, following emancipation is a matter of lively concern among scholars dealing with the postemancipation South. For two very different approaches see Leon Litwack, *Been in the Storm So Long: The Aftermath of Slavery;* Roger L. Ransom and Richard Sutch, *One Kind of Freedom: The Economic Consequences of Emancipation*.

4. Two outstanding articles appeared in the 1970s: George M. Fredrickson, "A Man but Not a Brother: Abraham Lincoln and Racial Equality," *Journal of Southern History*, XLI (Feb. 1975), 39–58, and Don E. Fehrenbacher, "Only His Stepchildren: Lincoln and the Negro," *Civil War History*, XX (Dec. 1974), 293–310. In the forefront of older scholarship are the sensitive treatments by Benjamin Quarles, *Lincoln and the Negro* and by Richard N. Current in his "The Friend of Freedom," chapter 9 of *The Lincoln Nobody Knows*, and in his introduction and editor's note, *The Political Thought of Abraham Lin-*

coln. See also his recent characterization of Lincoln's attitude toward blacks in Cullom Davis et al., eds., *The Public and the Private Lincoln: Contemporary Perspectives*, pp. 143–46, and that of Roy P. Basler, pp. 48–52.

On Lincoln's postwar intentions there has been sharp controversy. See Ludwell H. Johnson, "Lincoln's Solution to the Problem of Peace Terms, 1864–1865," *Journal of Southern History*, XXXIV (Nov. 1968), 576–86, and his "Lincoln and Equal Rights: The Authenticity of the Wadsworth Letter," ibid., XXXII (Feb. 1966), 83–87, together with the reply by Harold M. Hyman, "Lincoln and Equal Rights for Negroes: The Irrelevancy of the 'Wadsworth Letter'," *Civil War History*, XII (Sept. 1966), 258–66, and Johnson's rejoinder, "Lincoln and Equal Rights: A Reply," ibid., XIII (Mar. 1967), 66–73. Kenneth Stampp implies that Lincoln was prepared to sacrifice blacks for white political support in the South, *The Era of Reconstruction, 1865–1877*, pp. 48–49. Cf. Stephen B. Oates, "Toward a New Birth of Freedom: Abraham Lincoln and Reconstruction, 1854–1865," *Lincoln Herald* (Spring 1980), pp. 292–96.

The racist charge against Lincoln was pressed by Lerone Bennett, Jr., in "Was Abe Lincoln a White Supremacist?" *Ebony*, XXIII (Feb. 1968), 35–38, and considered by Robert F. Durden in "A. Lincoln: Honkie or Equalitarian?" *South Atlantic Quarterly*, LXXI (Summer 1972), 218–91.

The best approach to the problem of purpose behind Lincoln's Emancipation Proclamation is through Hans L. Trefousse, *Lincoln's Decision for Emancipation* and John Hope Franklin's judicious *The Emancipation Proclamation* supplemented by Mark Krug's sympathetic "The Republican Party and the Emancipation Proclamation," *Journal of Negro History*, XLVIII (Apr. 1963), 98–114. See also James A. Rawley, "The Emancipation Proclamation," in his *Turning Points of the Civil War* and Stephen B. Oates, *Our Fiery Trial: Abraham Lincoln, John Brown, and the Civil War Era*, pp. 61–85.

A convenient documentary history of Lincoln's racial views has been edited by Arthur Zilversmit, *Lincoln on Black and White*. For a perceptive appraisal of Lincoln scholarship through the mid-1960s, see Don E. Fehrenbacher, *The Changing Image of Lincoln in American Historiography*. The changing perspective in respect to Lincoln and the antislavery Radicals initiated by David Donald in *Lincoln Reconsidered* culminated in Hans L. Trefousse, *The Radical Republicans: Lincoln's Vanguard for Racial Justice*.

5. Italics added. Roy P. Basler, ed., *The Collected Works of Abraham Lincoln*, II, 501 (July 10, 1858 at Chicago). Lincoln made substantially the same point in other speeches: "They [the authors of the Declaration of Indepen-

dence] meant simply to declare the *right*, so that the *enforcement* of it might follow as fast as circumstances should permit." "They [the framers of the Constitution] were obliged to bow to the necessity. . . . They did what they could and yielded to the necessity for the rest. I also yield to all which follows from that necessity." Ibid., 406, 520–21 (June 26, 1857, and July 17, 1858, both at Springfield).

6. See Randall's chapter, "The Rule of Law under Lincoln," in *Lincoln the Liberal Statesman*, esp. p. 133, and Harold M. Hyman, *A More Perfect Union: The Impact of the Civil War and Reconstruction on the Constitution*. Hyman's central theme is the success of the Republican effort to reconcile war and law; Kelly's concern was the constitutional dilemma of Reconstruction. The quotations are from Hyman, pp. 544–45.

7. Basler, *Collected Works*, V, 144–46. Behind the scenes Lincoln had been pressing for sometime to get little Delaware to make the first move against slavery by passing legislation for gradual emancipation, contingent upon compensation from the federal government. He had even drafted alternative bills to guide the state legislators. These may have been framed after his annual message of December 3, 1861, rather than before in late November as dated, for the drafts clearly aimed at general emancipation while the ambiguous passage he included in the December message was tied to the limited emancipation provisions of the Confiscation Act of 1861. Ibid., pp. 29–31 cf. p. 48; H. Clay Reed, "Lincoln's Compensated Emancipation Plan and its Relation to Delaware," *Delaware Notes*, 7th series, 1931, pp. 37–45.

As will become clear in the account of Lincoln and Louisiana, the indirection Lincoln used in Delaware to stimulate what would appear a local initiative, was characteristic of his style of leadership.

8. Ibid., including editorial notes no. 1, 13; James M. McPherson, *The Negro's Civil War: How American Negroes Felt and Acted during the War for the Union*, pp. 43–44.

9. Irving H. Bartlett, "New Light on Wendell Phillips: The Community of Reform, 1840–1880," *Perspectives in American History*, XII (1979), 50–51; W. Phillips to Ann Phillips, March 31, 1862, Blagden Papers, Houghton Library, Harvard University, printed in part in ibid.

10. This account is based upon Leonard P. Curry's meticulous study of the Thirty-seventh Congress, *Blueprint for Modern America: Nonmilitary Legislation of the First Civil War Congress*, pp. 44–48.

11. This conclusion is based largely upon an examination of presidential messages cited in Herman V. Ames, *The Proposed Amendments to the Consti-*

tution of the United States during the First Century of its History, American Historical Association, *Annual Report for 1896,* II. For relevant documents, see Basler, *Collected Works,* V, 317–19, 324–25, 527–37.

12. Footnote, ibid., p. 319. The reply by C. A. Wickliffe and nineteen others of July 14, 1862, is available in the Abraham Lincoln Papers, Library of Congress, microfilm [cited hereafter as Lincoln Papers].

13. J. W. Crisfield memorandum, in John G. Nicolay and John Hay, eds., *Complete Works of Abraham Lincoln,* VII, 125; Basler, *Collected Works,* V, 318.

14. Basler, *Collected Works,* V, 537.

15. Ibid., p. 329. For Lincoln's early doubt about presidential power, Lincoln to O. H. Browning, Sept. 22, 1861, ibid., IV, 532.

16. Ibid., V, 388–89, 419–25.

17. Ibid., VII, 49, 282.

18. Attributed to the Washington correspondent of the *Tribune,* reprinted in New York *Times,* Dec. 31, 1862. This interesting report came to my attention through the citation in Roland C. McConnell, "From Preliminary to Final Emancipation Proclamation: The First Hundred Days," *Journal of Negro History,* XLVIII (Oct. 1963), 274.

19. Italics added. Lincoln to Albert G. Hodges, Apr. 4, 1864, Basler, *Collected Works,* VII 281–83; see also Lincoln to James C. Conkling, Aug. 26, 1863, ibid., VI, 408–409.

20. Ibid., V, 336–38, 341–42.

21. Section 1 and 2 of the act of July 17, 1862 provided for the liberation of slaves of persons *convicted* of treason or of aiding rebellion; section 9 declared forever free all slaves of persons thereafter engaging in or aiding rebellion who escaped to Union lines or otherwise came under the control of Union government or forces.

22. Basler, *Collected Works,* VI, 428–29.

23. Ibid., p. 440, VII, 155. David W. Bowen believes that Andrew Johnson shifted to a moral stance against slavery to gain the approbation of Lincoln; see his Ph.D. dissertation, University of Tennessee, 1976, "Andrew Johnson and the Negro," pp. 200–202.

24. *Life and Times of Frederick Douglass,* pp. 357–59.

25. Lincoln to Charles D. Robinson, Aug. 17, 1864, and editorial notes, Interview with Alexander W. Randall and Joseph T. Mills, Aug. 19, 1864, Basler, *Collected Works,* VII, 499–502, 506–8; Earl Schenck Miers, ed., *Lincoln Day by Day: A Chronology, 1809–1865,* III, 278, 279; Quarles, *Lincoln and*

the Negro, pp. 215–16.

26. Basler, *Collected Works,* VI, 429, 440; Chase to Owen, Sept. 6, 1863, Salmon P. Chase Papers, Historical Society of Pennsylvania (hereafter cited HSP); Douglass, *Life and Times,* 360–61.

27. William F. Zornow, *Lincoln and the Party Divided,* pp. 167–68; J. G. Randall and Richard N. Current, *Lincoln the President: Last Full Measure,* pp. 307–10; Annual message, Basler, *Collected Works,* VIII, 149.

28. Ibid., p. 248; for an account of the Seward lobby, see LaWanda Cox and John H. Cox, *Politics, Principle, and Prejudice, 1865–1866: Dilemma of Reconstruction America,* pp. 6–30.

29. Basler, *Collected Works,* VIII, 254–55.

30. Fehrenbacher, "Only His Stepchildren," pp. 300–305.

31. Italics added. Basler, *Collected Works,* II, 255–56, 409, 501, 520.

32. Ibid., III, 16, 145–46, [for Douglass] 177. Italics added.

33. Ibid., p. 399.

34. Douglass, *Life and Times,* pp. 348–50; Mary Frances Berry, *Military Necessity and Civil Rights Policy: Black Citizenship and the Constitution, 1861–1868.* See Also Dudley T. Cornish, *The Sable Arm: Negro Troops in the Union Army, 1861–1865,* pp. 80, 188–95.

35. Mark E. Neely, Jr. has demolished the Butler evidence on the basis of which Lincoln has been portrayed as looking to colonization until his dying day for the solution of the black-white problem in the United States. See his "Abraham Lincoln and Black Colonization: Benjamin Butler's Spurious Testimony," *Civil War History,* XXV (Mar. 1979), 77–83.

36. Basler, *Collected Works,* V, 370–75. In making plans for colonization, Lincoln assured the delegation he "would endeavor to have you made equals, and have the best assurance that you should be the equals of the best."

37. U.S. Department of Justice, *Official Opinions of the Attorneys General,* X, 382–412; Marvin R. Cain, *Lincoln's Attorney General: Edward Bates of Missouri,* pp. 223–25; Don E. Fehrenbacher, *The Dred Scott Case: Its Significance in American Law and Politics,* pp. 575–76.

38. Speech by Douglass at Cooper Union, New York *Times,* Jan. 14, 1864; John Eaton, *Grant, Lincoln and the Freedmen: Reminiscences of the Civil War,* p. 176; Fredrickson, "Man but Not a Brother," pp. 47–48; Basler, *Collected Works,* VII, 483.

39. Ibid., VI, 365.

40. Ibid., IV, 24–25, V, 52; and see G. S. Boritt, *Lincoln and the Economics of the American Dream,* re. blacks, see esp. pp. 172–74.

41. Basler, *Collected Works*, VI, 98–99, 453–59, VII, 98–99; Correspondence of the Direct Tax Commissioners is available in their records, National Archives; for an account of the controversy over the lands, see Willie Lee Rose, *Rehearsal for Reconstruction: The Port Royal Experiment*, pp. 272–96.

42. Louis Gerteis in crediting Chase with the championship of land reform fails to do justice to Lincoln or to examine closely Chase's failure to stand by the December decision in favor of the freedmen, "Salmon P. Chase, Radicalism, and the Politics of Emancipation, 1861–1864," *Journal of American History*, LX (June 1973), 57–60.

43. Chase to W. P. Mellen, Dec. 27, 1863, Letters Received by General Agent from Secretary of Treasury, Record Group 366, National Archives (This document came to my attention through the citation in Louis S. Gerteis, *From Contraband to Freedman: Federal Policy toward Southern Blacks, 1861–1865*, p. 139); George R. Bentley, *A History of the Freedmen's Bureau*, p. 26. For Lincoln's probable postwar land policy, see Chapter Five, esp. note 59.

44. See LaWanda Cox, "The Promise of Land for the Freedmen," *Mississippi Valley Historical Review*, XLV (Dec. 1958), 413–40. Louis Gerteis has objected ("Salmon P. Chase," pp. 61–62) that the "promise" of land was not "real" because the amount and title of land which might be available were uncertain. These uncertainties, disguised neither in the bill nor in my article, are not matters of dispute. As a semantic problem, Gerteis has a point for the term "promise" does not of itself convey the total situation.

Herman Belz has suggested that the intent of the second conference committee which wrote the final version of the bill was only to allow temporary use of rebel estates ("The Freedmen's Bureau Act of 1865 and the Principle of No Discrimination according to Color," *Civil War History*, XXI [Sept. 1975], 212–13). With the Confiscation Act as qualified providing for forfeiture only during the lifetime of the owner, permanent use and title were not available through confiscation without further legislation, which was before Congress and nearly succeeded. The language of the final conference bill—which did not use the term "temporary"—otherwise, as Belz has established, followed the Schenck bill, which did specify temporary usage. While recognizing the uncertainty of government providing fee simple title, the final bill acknowledged it as a possibility. At the time it was not self-evident that the issue of permanent confiscation was settled or that no forfeiture of land during the owner's lifetime, as provided by law, would be effected. Clearly the expectation was for distribution and possession far beyond that which became a postwar reality. The Freedmen's Bureau Act otherwise would not have provided that lessees be protected "in the use and enjoyment of the land" for three years before facing the option of purchase. Moreover, the tracts to be allotted were identified not exclusively as those abandoned or confiscated but included ones to which the United States "shall have acquired title" by "sale, or otherwise." In Mar. 1865 the situation was fluid.

45. Eaton to Lincoln, June 13, 1864, Records of the Bureau of Refugees, Freedmen, and Abandoned Lands, National Archives.

46. Chase to Lincoln, Nov. 25, 1863, copies in Chase Papers, HSP, original in Lincoln Papers.

47. Don Fehrenbacher in his sympathetic assessment of *The Leadership of Abraham Lincoln* (editor's introduction, p. 6) speaks of the president's lack of a postwar racial policy as his "greatest sin of omission," though understandable. See also his "Only His Stepchildren," pp. 308–10.

48. Owen to McKaye, Mar. 19, 1863, American Freedmen's Inquiry Commission Papers, Houghton Library, Harvard University; Chase to McKaye, July 25, 1863, Chase to Owen, Sept. 6, 1863, Chase Papers, HSP; McKaye to Sumner, June 30, 1864, Charles Sumner Papers, Houghton Library, Harvard University; E. D. Townsend to Sumner, June 27, July 23, 1864, Records of the Adjutant General's Office, Letters Sent, vol. 37, RG 94, National Archives. The commission's papers, except those in the Houghton Library, are available on rolls 199–201, Microcopy 619, National Archives. The standard account of the commission is John G. Sproat, "Blueprint for Radical Reconstruction," *Journal of Southern History*, XXIII (Feb. 1957), 25–44.

49. New Orleans *Times*, Feb. 9, 1864. I have sought and been unable to find corroborating evidence, but a number of historians have accepted the newspaper accounts as basis for stating that Lincoln sent McKaye in response to appeals from free men of color. See John Rose Ficklen, *History of Reconstruction in Louisiana*, p. 59; Willie M. Caskey, *Secession and Restoration of Louisiana*, p. 105; Benjamin Quarles, *The Negro in the Civil War*, p. 251.

50. Basler, *Collected Works*, V, 487, VI, 387. Butler's reply is printed in *Private and Official Correspondence of Benjamin F. Butler*, II, 447–50.

51. Lincoln to Alpheus Lewis, Jan. 23, 1864, Basler, *Collected Works*, VII, 145–46.

52. Cornish, *The Sable Arm*, pp. 117, 125–26; Robinson, "Day of Jublio," pp. 488, 496; Roy P. Basler, ed., *The Collected Works of Abraham Lincoln: Supplement, 1832–1865*, pp. 243–44; Basler, "And for His Widow and His Orphan," *Quarterly Journal of the Library of Congress*, XXIV (Oct. 1970), 291–94.

53. Smith Testimony, Freedmen's Inquiry Commission, Microcopy 619, roll 200, file 3, National Archives; Henry Greenleaf Pearson, *James S. Wadsworth of Geneseo*, pp. 130–32, 141, 148, 240–45; *War of the Rebellion: Official Records*, ser. 3, III, 872–73; Wadsworth to Adjutant General, Dec. 16, 1863, Misc. Letters and Papers Received by General Agent, Record Group 366, National Archives; Bentley, *Freedmen's Bureau*, pp. 26–29; Basler, *Collected Works*, VII, 185.

54. Eaton, *Grant, Lincoln and the Freedmen*, pp. 167–76.

55. Basler, *Collected Works*, VIII, 325; see also Lincoln's memorandum of Mar. 22, 1865, ibid., pp. 371–72.

56. Ibid., pp. 394, 399–405.

57. Douglass, *Life and Times*, pp. 488–89.

58. Donald, "The Radicals and Lincoln," *Lincoln Reconsidered*, pp. 103–27; essays by Donald and T. Harry Williams in Grady McWhiney, ed., *Grant, Lee, Lincoln and the Radicals*, pp. 72–115; Trefousse, *The Radical Republicans*; Belz, *Reconstructing the Union*, esp. pp. 252–55, 294–311.

59. Howard K. Beale, ed., *Diary of Gideon Welles*, II, 281; John G. Nicolay and John Hay, *Abraham Lincoln: A History*, X, 283; Basler, *Collected Works*, VII, 56, VIII, 152, 261.

60. Ibid., V, 328–31, VII, 433–34.

61. The explicit contradiction is in section 9 of the bill, which refers back to the enrollment procedures of section 1 and to the voting requirements of section 4. A convenient source for the Wade-Davis bill, Lincoln's response, and the Wade-Davis Manifesto is Harold M. Hyman, ed., *The Radical Republicans and Reconstruction, 1861–1870*, pp. 125–47.

62. *Congressional Globe*, 38 Cong., 1 sess., pp. 1356, 1358 (Ashley, March 30, 1864), 2012 (John Longyear, April 30, 1864) Robert F. Horowitz, *The Great Impeacher: A Political Biography of James M. Ashley*, pp. 95–97.

63. *Congressional Globe*, 38 Cong., 1 sess., pp. 2107–2108 (Davis, May 4, 1864), pp. 3448–51 (Wade, July 1, 1864); Belz, *Reconstructing the Union*, pp. 210–21.

64. Basler, *Collected Works*, VI, 440, VII, 51; Tyler Dennett, ed., *Lincoln and the Civil War in the Diaries and Letters of John Hay*, p. 113.

65. Davis to Wade, June 21, 1864, Benjamin F. Wade Papers, Library of Congress; Basler, *Collected Works*, VII, 433.

CHAPTER TWO: The Creation of a Free State

1. Basler, *Collected Works*, VII, 1–2.

2. Ibid., V, 344–46, 462–63.

3. Ibid., pp. 343, 350; C. Peter Ripley, *Slaves and Freedmen in Civil War Louisiana*, pp. 29–33, 104–5; Gerteis, *From Contraband to Freedman*, pp. 68–72; Cornish, *Sable Arm*, pp. 58–65; Peyton McCrary, *Abraham Lincoln and Reconstruction: The Louisiana Experiment*, pp. 83–84, 88–90.

4. Flanders to Lincoln, Jan. 16, 1864, Lincoln Papers. For Durant, see Joseph G. Tregle, Jr., "Thomas J. Durant, Utopian Socialism, and the Failure of Presidential Reconstruction in Louisiana," *Journal of Southern History*, XLV (Nov. 1979), 485–512.

5. Flanders to Chase, May 9, 1863, Chase Papers, HSP; Hahn to Lincoln, May 9, 1863, Durant to Lincoln, May 9, 1863, Flanders to Chase, May 10, 1863, Lincoln Papers.

6. The Union plan submitted to Governor Shepley, and by him to Washington, together with his letters are printed in *War of the Rebellion: Official Records*, ser. 3, vol. 3, pp. 231–35; the Minute Book of the General Committee of the Union Associations is in the manuscript division, New York Historical Society (hereafter cited NYHS). For the beginnings of the Free State movement, cf. McCrary, *Lincoln and Reconstruction*, pp. 125–31; Caskey, *Secession and Restoration*, 72–74, 77–78; Ficklen, *Reconstruction in Louisiana*, pp. 45–47; Charles H. McCarthy, *Lincoln's Plan of Reconstruction*, pp. 47–48; Fred H. Harrington, *Fighting Politician: Major General N. P. Banks*, p. 142; Ripley, *Slaves and Freedmen*, pp. 161–64. By far the most comprehensive account of the Free State movement and political affairs in Louisiana is that of Peyton McCrary.

7. Italics added. Boutwell to Banks, May 26, 1863, Nathaniel P. Banks Papers, Library of Congress.

8. Basler, *Collected Works*, V, 504–5.

9. Ibid., VI, 287–88; Denison to Chase, Apr. 30, May 9, 24, 1863, *Diary and Correspondence of Salmon P. Chase*, American Historical Association, *Annual Report for* 1902, II, 382–88; Hahn to Lincoln, June 6, 1863, Lincoln Papers, published in part in Basler, *Collected Works*, VI, 288–89.

10. Ibid., p. 288.

11. Extracts from the *True Delta*, July 4, 21, 1863, in Edward H. Durell Papers, NYHS.

12. Denison to Chase, Nov. 29, 1862, May 9, June 13, 26, July 10, 1863, Chase, *Diary and Correspondence*, pp. 333–34, 384–87, 391–94; Chase to Bullitt, July 9, 1863, Chase Papers, HSP.

13. Bullitt to Lincoln, June 14, July 14, Aug. 12, Oct. 2, 1863, Lincoln Papers.

14. Chase to McKaye, July 25, 1863, Chase to Hamilton, Aug. 20, 1863, Chase to Greeley, Oct. 9, 1863, Chase Papers, HSP.

15. *War of the Rebellion: Official Records*, ser. 3, vol. 3, pp. 235, 711–12. Stanton's order to Shepley expressly stated that "the President directs the following instructions to be given to you," and other evidence confirms that the decision was Lincoln's rather than one merely made in his name.

16. Boutwell to Banks, Aug. 5, 1863, Banks Papers.

17. Basler, *Collected Works*, VI, 364–65.

18. Ibid., p. 366; Banks to Lincoln, Sept. 5, 1863, Lincoln Papers.

19. McCrary, *Lincoln and Reconstruction*, pp. 169–71; Minute Book, NYHS, p. 60.

20. Chase to Banks, May 19, 1863, Apr. 13, 1864, Banks Papers. A case could be made that Chase was interested in good relations with Banks in order to further his presidential ambitions, but Chase's interest in the outcome of Reconstruction, which remained constant even after he left the cabinet, seems to me his dominant motivation. Also see below, note 36.

The enmity between Banks and Flanders antedated the split in the Free State ranks. Ripley attributes it to a clash over the home colonies from which Flanders wished to remove the destitute and decrepit while Banks fought to keep control of the plantations for their support. *Slaves and Freedmen*, pp. 54–56.

21. Plumly to Banks, Sept. 18, 24, 1863, Banks Papers; David Donald, ed., *Inside Lincoln's Cabinet: The Civil War Diaries of Salmon P. Chase*, p. 200; Ripley, *Slaves and Freedmen*, pp. 131, 142–45.

22. Boutwell to Banks, May 26, 1863, Banks Papers; Banks to Boutwell, Dec. 27, 1863, printed in George S. Boutwell, *Reminiscences of Sixty Years in Public Affairs*, II, 240–41; Banks to Lincoln, Dec. 6, 30, 1863, Lincoln Papers.

23. Herman Belz, "The Etheridge Conspiracy of 1863: A Projected Conservative Coup," *Journal of Southern History*, XXXVI (Nov. 1970), 549–67; Caskey, *Secession and Restoration*, pp. 80–86; Ficklen, *Reconstruction in Louisiana*, pp. 48–50; Denison to Chase, Nov. 5, 6, 1863, Chase, *Diary and Correspondence*, pp. 413–15, 417–23.

24. Chase to Bullitt, Nov. 6, 1863, Flanders to Chase, Dec. 4, 1863,

Chase Papers, HSP; Bullitt to Lincoln, Nov. 27, 1863 (with enclosures of Chase to Bullitt, Nov. 4 and 6) and Jan. 2, 1864, J. L. Riddell to Lincoln, Dec. 15, 1863, Lincoln Papers; Basler, *Collected Works*, VII, 66–67, 71.

25. Durant to Lincoln, Oct. 1, 1863, enclosed in Durant to Stanton, Oct. 5, 1863, Lincoln Papers.

26. Basler, *Collected Works*, VII, 1–2; Ficklen, *Reconstruction in Louisiana*, p. 51.

27. Basler, *Collected Works*, VII, 53–56, 66–67.

28. Flanders to Lincoln, Dec. 11, 1863, Lincoln Papers and printed in Basler, *Collected Works*, VII, 2; J. S. Whitaker to Chase, Nov. 30, 1863, Durant to Chase, Dec. 4, 1863, John F. Morse to Chase, Dec. 12, 1863, John Hutchins to Chase, Dec. 22, 1863, Salmon P. Chase Papers, Library of Congress; Flanders to Chase, Dec. 4, 12, 1863, Chase Papers, HSP.

29. Basler, *Collected Works*, VII, 6.

30. Boutwell to Banks, Dec. 21, 1863, Banks Papers; Basler, *Collected Works*, VII, 89–90.

31. Banks' letters to Lincoln are available in the Lincoln Papers. Peyton McCrary has tentatively identified a fragment from Banks' copybook as part of the missing letter of Banks to Boutwell, Dec. 11; McCrary, *Lincoln and Reconstruction*, p. 225n30. Banks wrote again to Boutwell Dec. 27, reporting that he had written the president of his plan; see Boutwell, *Reminiscences*, II, 240–41.

32. The unsent letter of Banks to Lincoln, dated Oct. 23, 1863, is in the Banks Papers. Banks' version of what happened in October is confirmed by an account Durant later wrote of his differences with the general. He stated that Banks in October thought things might go faster and had presented to him a proposal "to order an election of a state government under the constitution of 1852," from which Durant had "respectfully dissented." Durant to Dawes, Feb. 8, 1864, Henry L. Dawes Papers, Library of Congress. In the unsent letter to the president Banks had suggested not a direct election of state officers but "a Convention of the people for the organization of a Government" under the old state constitution so far as applicable "to the condition of things now existing, and excepting that part relating to representation."

The verification of Banks' concern in October to speed up reorganization, and his deference at that time to Durant and Shepley, seem to me incompatible with the interpretation that Banks was simply awaiting an opportunity to take over direction of reconstruction and responded to Lincoln's November letter with calculated deception in order to realize his ambition.

33. Banks' sense of grievance over the division of authority was undoubtedly warranted. Flanders had written Chase that the placing of three independent authorities in New Orleans was a great mistake resulting in much evil. Flanders to Chase, Apr. 30, 1863, Chase Papers, HSP. Lincoln's organization and direction of affairs in Louisiana had not been tidy, and he in effect apologized in his Dec. 24 letter, Basler, *Collected Works*, VII, 89.

34. Banks left open the date for election of convention members; it "might take place on the same or a subsequent day with the general election." Banks to Lincoln, Dec. 30, 1863, Lincoln Papers.

35. Basler, *Collected Works*, VII, 89–90, 95, 123–24.

36. McCrary and Tregle attribute the support of Banks' plan by Denison and Plumly to a deal with Banks by which they would obtain delegates to the Republican national convention committed to Chase as presidential nominee. Plumly wrote Chase on the day Denison departed a letter which appears damning. There is no question but that he and Denison were politicing on behalf of Chase and sought to obtain Banks' support or at least his benevolent neutrality. It does not necessarily follow, however, that they would otherwise have opposed Banks' plan. If they were consciously betraying the black cause, Chase must share their culpability. However, as I see it, Banks' plan would appear an attractive alternative to Durant's for men concerned to destroy slavery in Louisiana, quickly and certainly, and troubled by the record of indecision and ineffectiveness under Shepley and Durant. Cf. McCrary, *Lincoln and Reconstruction*, p. 204 and Tregle, "Thomas J. Durant," pp. 508–9. See Plumly to Chase, Jan. 2 [1864, erroneously dated 1863], Frank E. Howe to Chase, Feb. 6, 1864, Chase Papers, LC; Banks to [Howe], Feb. 3, 1864, Chase Papers, HSP; Denison to Chase, Feb. 19, 1864, Mar. 5, 1864, Chase, *Diary and Correspondence*, pp. 432, 434–35.

37. Basler, *Collected Works*, VII, 124.

38. Banks to [Howe], Feb. 3, 1864, Chase to Howe, Feb. 20, 1864, Chase to Plumly, Feb. 26, 1864, Chase to Denison, March 16, 1864, Chase to Banks, draft, Nov. 8, 1864, Chase Papers, HSP. Chase was less explicit in writing Durant, Feb. 6, 1864, ibid. See also Denison to Chase, Feb. 5, 19, 1864, Chase, *Diary and Correspondence*, pp. 430, 431–32; *The Reconstruction of States: Letter of Major General Banks to Senator Lane*, p. 21.

39. James A. Padgett, ed., "Some Letters of George Stanton Denison, 1854–1866: Observations of a Yankee on Conditions in Louisiana and Texas," *Louisiana Historical Quarterly*, XXIII (Oct. 1940), 1210–11.

40. Basler, *Collected Works*, VII, 243; Chase to Banks, Apr. 13, 1864, Banks Papers.

41. Louisiana, *Journal of the House of Representatives*, 1864–65, pp. 173–74; Louisiana, *Journal of the Senate*, 1864–65, p. 153.

CHAPTER THREE: The Struggle for Credibility

1. For Durant, see Tregle, "Thomas J. Durant."

2. Address to Workingmen's Union National League, as reported in New Orleans *Times*, Dec. 4, 1863; Address at meeting of Free State Union Association, ibid., Dec. 20, 1863; for Durant's refusal to register freeborn blacks, see Resolutions passed at Mass Meeting of Natives of Louisiana, ibid., Jan. 6, 1864; *Proceedings of the Convention of the Friends of Freedom, Lyceum Hall, New Orleans*, Dec. 15, 1863 (I am indebted to Peyton McCrary for a copy of this pamphlet); for the correspondence between Durant and Chase, see notes 4, 5, 6, 8, and 9. Cf. McCrary, *Lincoln and Reconstruction*, pp. 182–85.

3. Italics added. *War of the Rebellion, Official Records*, ser. 3, vol. 3, 232, 711; Basler, *Collected Works*, VIII, 400; Chase to Owen, Sept. 6, 1863, Chase Papers, HSP.

4. Chase to Durant, Nov. 19, 1863, Chase Papers, HSP.

5. Durant to Chase, Dec. 4, 1863, Chase Papers, LC; Flanders to Chase, Dec. 12, 1863, Chase Papers, HSP; report of Durant address, *Daily True Delta*, Dec. 4, 1864. At a mass meeting in early November devoted to the suffrage question, reference had been made to the Attorney General's opinion and its implication; New Orleans *Times*, Nov. 6, 1863.

6. Chase to Durant, Dec. 28, 1863, Chase to Stickney, Dec. 29, 1863, Chase Papers, HSP.

7. Lincoln to Banks, Jan. 31, 1864, Memorandum concerning Louisiana Affairs, Basler, *Collected Works*, VII, 71, 161–62; J. L. Riddell to Lincoln, Dec. 15, 1863, Lincoln Papers.

8. Durant to Chase, Jan. 16, 1864, Chase Papers, LC.

9. Durant to Dawes, Feb. 8, 1864, Dawes Papers; Durant to Chase, Jan. 16, 1864, Chase Papers, LC; Durant to Lincoln, Feb. 26, 1864, Lincoln Papers. Banks did not pursue the appointment of senators or the early election of representatives.

10. Banks to Frank E. Howe, Mar. 6, 1864, Chase Papers, LC, also letter-press copy, Banks Papers.

11. McCrary has suggested that the course of Reconstruction in Louisiana might have been different had Shepley acted at once on the request to set an election for January 25, a request made several days before General Banks returned to the city and read Lincoln's November 5 letter. One can further spec-

ulate that Shepley might not have hesitated had he received word of Lincoln's wishes directly from the president or the secretary of war. *Lincoln and Reconstruction*, pp. 199–200.

12. Durant to Dawes, Feb. 8, 1864, Dawes Papers; Flanders to Chase [Jan. 9, 1864], Chase Papers, HSP; Banks to Lincoln, Jan. 11, 1864, Lincoln Papers.

13. Flanders to Lincoln, Jan. 16, 1864, Lincoln Papers; Flanders to Chase, Jan. 14, 23, 1864, Chase Papers, HSP; for the personal animosities, see Plumly to Chase, Dec. 1, 1863, Denison to Chase, Dec. 4, 1863, John Hutchins to Chase, Dec. 12, 1863, Chase Papers, LC.

There had been an understanding that Flanders would resign the Treasury office on becoming president of the new national bank, but he clung to the post.

14. Clipping in Flanders to Chase, Jan. 21, 1864, Chase Papers, HSP; New Orleans *Times*, Jan. 17, 1864.

15. Draft, Banks to State Central Committee, Jan. 29, 1864, Banks Papers; 38 Cong., 2 sess., *Senate Misc. Doc.* No. 9 (Jan. 11, 1865), p. 3; McCrary, *Lincoln and Reconstruction*, pp. 213–14.

During congressional debate in 1867, Boutwell asserted that Lincoln would not have hesitated to intervene with the military if the Louisiana experiment had failed to accomplish his purpose. Banks confirmed that it was a distinct understanding between the military and "those they represented" that had disloyal men been placed in office the whole affair would have been suppressed. 39 Cong., 2 sess., *Congressional Globe*, p. 1208, (Feb. 13, 1867).

16. Scrapbooks, Whitelaw Reid Papers, Library of Congress (The citation in McCrary, *Lincoln and Reconstruction*, p. 233, brought this item to my attention); Bingham Duncan, *Whitelaw Reid: Journalist, Politician, Diplomat*, p. 24.

17. Flanders to Chase, Jan. 23, 1864, Chase Papers, HSP; Emily H. Reed, *Life of A. P. Dostie or the Conflict in New Orleans*, pp. 90–91. For accounts of the nomination and campaign, see Caskey, *Secession and Restoration*, pp. 98–107; Ficklen, *Reconstruction in Louisiana*, pp. 57–63; Joe Gray Taylor, *Louisiana Reconstructed, 1863–1877*, pp. 27–31; McCrary, *Lincoln and Reconstruction*, pp. 216–26, 234–35.

18. New Orleans *Times*, Feb. 6, 1864; Flanders to Lincoln, Jan. 16, 1864, Lincoln Papers; Durant to W. R. Fish, Feb. 5, 1864, Durant Papers; Durant to Chase, Feb. 21, 1864, Hutchins to Chase, Feb. 12, 24, 1864, Chase Papers, LC.

19. Hahn to Lincoln, Nov. 20, 1863, Bullitt to Lincoln, Jan. 2, 1864, to F. W. Seward, Jan. 4, 1864, to O. H. Browning, Feb. 23, 1864, to Simeon Draper, Feb. 23, 1864, to Lincoln, Feb. 23, 1864, to Draper, Feb. 25, 1864, to Lincoln, Feb. 25, Mar. 3, 1864, all in Lincoln Papers.

20. Denison to Chase, Feb. 5, 19, Mar. 5, 1864, Chase, *Diary and Correspondence*, pp. 430–34; New York *Tribune*, Feb. 15, 1864.

21. Hutchins to Chase, Feb. 12, 1864, Chase Papers, LC; Flanders to Chase, Feb. 16, 1864, Chase Papers, HSP. For the race rhetoric of the campaign, see accounts cited above, note 17.

There is need for a careful study of the race attitudes of Durant and Flanders, on the one hand, and on the other of Hahn, Alfred C. Hills (editor of the *Era*), William R. Fish (editor of Hahn's *True Delta*), and A. P. Dostie (the outstanding local Radical allied with Banks). All except Hills were antebellum Louisianians. Their race attitudes, apparently, were not far apart; none were altogether free of prejudice and all were more liberal on racial matters than most whites in Louisiana.

22. Durant to Lincoln, Feb. 26, 1864, Lincoln Papers; Durant to John S. Blatchford, Feb. 5, 1864, Durant Papers; New Orleans *Times*, Feb. 6, 1864.

23. Editorials, New Orleans *Era*, Feb. 9, 10, 14, 16, 19, 20, 21, 1864; *Daily True Delta*, Feb. 23, 1864.

24. New Orleans *Era*, Feb. 9, 12, 14, 1864; Hutchins to Chase, Feb. 12, 1864, Chase Papers, LC; Flanders to Chase, Feb. 26, 1864, Chase Papers, HSP; Caskey, *Secession and Restoration*, p. 104, paraphrasing Flanders.

25. Chase to Flanders, Mar. 7, 1864, Chase to Plumly, Mar. 8, 1864, Chase Papers, HSP; Plumly to Chase, Apr. 30, 1864, Chase Papers, LC.

26. New Orleans *Era*, Feb. 9, 1864; Denison to Chase, Nov. 29, 1862, July 15, 1863, Oct. 8, 1864, Chase, *Diary and Correspondence*, pp. 336, 395, 449–50.

27. Chase to Durant, Dec. 28, 1863, Chase to Denison, Mar. 16, 1864, Chase Papers, HSP; Durant to Chase, Feb. 21, Mar. 5, 1864, Plumly to Chase, Mar. 5, 1864, Chase Papers, LC; Denison to Chase, Mar. 5, 1864, Chase, *Diary and Correspondence*, p. 434; McCrary, *Lincoln and Reconstruction*, p. 239.

28. Chase to Flanders, Mar. 7, 1865, Chase to Denison, Mar. 16, 1864, Chase Papers, HSP.

McCrary and Tregle see the support Denison and Plumly gave Banks as a plot or deal made to secure Louisiana's votes for Chase at the Republican national convention. If this were the case, Chase was a tacit party to the understanding. There is no doubt but that the two Chase men sought and received political assurances from Banks and that Chase himself was concerned to have at least Banks' benevolent neutrality in the presidential contest, but there is no evidence to indicate that Denison, Plumly, and Chase were not convinced that Banks' plan would speedily attain emancipation and reorganization. After the split, Chase claimed that he had expected all Free State men would cooperate with Banks. In assigning blame for the division, his letters are not altogether consistent. The key document suggesting a deal is Plumly's letter to Chase, Jan. 21, [1864, misdated 1863], Chase Papers, LC. See McCrary, *Lincoln and Reconstruction*, p. 204, and Tregle, "Thomas J. Durant," 508–9; also Chapter Two, notes 20 and 32.

29. Durant to Lincoln, Feb. 26, 28, 1864, Lincoln Papers; Durant to Chase, Mar. 5, 1864, Plumly to Chase, Mar. 5, 1864, Chase Papers, LC; Durant's reply to "Avon", Jan. 2, 1865, in *National Anti-Slavery Standard*, Jan. 28, 1865; McCrary, *Lincoln and Reconstruction*, pp. 239–42.

30. Basler, *Collected Works*, VII, 243, 248. For evidence that Lincoln's letter to Hahn was meant and accepted as a directive, see pp. 97–101, 118–19, 129–30.

31. New Orleans *Era*, Mar. 16, 1864; Quarles, *Lincoln and the Negro*, pp. 226–28; Herbert Aptheker, ed., *A Documentary History of the Negro People in the United States*, I, 494–95; F. B. Carpenter, *Six Months at the White House with Abraham Lincoln*, pp. 267–68. Carpenter's account has Lincoln suggesting changes in the petition in order to strengthen it. For comparison with Lincoln's approach to emancipation, see Chapter One.

32. Chase to Durant, Dec. 28, 1863, Chase to L. D. Stickney, Dec. 29, 1863, Chase to Greeley, Dec. 29, 1863, Chase Papers, HSP. Chase later publicly acknowledged that there was a time when he would have been content, "if not satisfied," with suffrage for the intelligent and those who had been soldiers. Chase to Lincoln, Apr. 12, 1865, printed version in Chase Papers, HSP.

For Stickney and Florida, see Jerrell H. Shofner, *Nor Is It Over Yet: Florida in the Era of Reconstruction, 1863–1877*, pp. 4–11.

33. Chase to Lincoln, Nov. 25, 1863, Apr. 12, 1865, printed copy, Chase Papers, HSP; the latter also available in Basler, *Collected Works*, VIII, 399–401, and both originals in Lincoln Papers.

34. Italics added. Banks to Lincoln, Feb. 25, 1864, Lincoln Papers; Banks to McKaye, Mar. 28, 1864, draft, Banks Papers, also available in American Freedmen's Inquiry Commission records, National Archives, Microcopy 619, roll 199.

35. Chase used the phrase "suffrage extended to all equally qualified,"

but it is unlikely that he was suggesting disqualification for illiterate whites. Banks to Durell, Apr. 6, 1864, Durell Papers, NYHS; Thorpe to Banks, Apr. 12, 1864, with Banks' endorsement, Chase to Banks, Apr. 13, 1864, with Banks' endorsement, Banks Papers.

The Banks letter to Durell was something of a discovery. Note that Banks invoked "Washington" in exerting influence behind the scenes. Even before the convention ended, Banks was giving Thorpe support for patronage appointments. Banks to Thorpe, July 19, 1864, Misc. Mss., NYHS.

36. Denison to Chase, Oct. 8, Nov. 25, 1864, Chase, *Diary and Correspondence*, pp. 449–52.

For an outstanding study of the convention's membership and work, both traditional and quantitative, see McCrary, *Lincoln and Reconstruction*, pp. 244–65, and Appendix B and C, pp. 371–80.

37. The constitution of 1864 can be conveniently compared with that of 1852 in Francis N. Thorpe, ed., *Federal and State Constitutions*, vol. 3.

38. Hahn To W. D. Kelley, June 21, 1865, New York *Times*, June 23, 1865, reprinted from the Washington *Chronicle*. This important letter came to my attention through the citation in Amos E. Simpson and Vaughan Baker, "Michael Hahn: Steady Patroit," *Louisiana History*, XIII (Summer 1972), p. 244*n*40.

39. Banks to Lincoln, July 25, 1864, Lincoln Papers.

40. Basler, *Collected Works*, VII, 486; Denison to Lincoln, Sept. 28, 1864, Lincoln Papers. See also Denison to Chase, July 26, Sept. 6, 1864, Chase, *Diary and Correspondence*, pp. 443–45.

41. Rough notes from clippings, XXV, Durell Papers, NYHS; Durant to Davis, July 26, 1864, New York *Evening Post*, Aug. 5, 1864; McCrary, *Lincoln and Reconstruction*, p. 265.

42. Banks to Dostie, Aug. 23, 1864, Dostie to Banks, Aug. 25, 1864, Banks Papers; Caskey, *Secession and Restoration*, pp. 139–40; McCrary, *Lincoln and Reconstruction*, pp. 267–69.

43. The white disfranchisement in the first round of elections specified by the Wade-Davis bill would have been only a little more limiting in practical effect at war's end than Lincoln's required oath taken during wartime. Furthermore, the Banks forces controlled registration until James M. Wells became governor, and there are indications that they contemplated limiting the political rights of returning rebels. See editorial, "Louisiana—The New Constitution," New York *Tribune*, Aug. 4, 1864; and Chapter Four.

44. Differences over Louisiana's readmission, and over Reconstruction in general, doubtless would have remained, but it is highly improbable that they

would have led to a crisis between president and Radical congressional leaders such as that which followed Lincoln's veto of the Wade-Davis bill, or would have prevented the seating of the Louisiana delegation in the final session of the 38th Congress.

45. Although incomplete, the available evidence that documents Durant's arguments and audience is considerable. My view of Durant and his impact is based upon a reading, and then a rereading in chronological sequence, of the following: Durant's letters as preserved in his letterpress at the New York Historical Society library; his letters to Lincoln in Lincoln Papers, those to Chase in the collection of Chase Papers both at the Library of Congress and at the library of the Historical Society of Pennsylvania; Durant to Dawes, Feb. 8, 1864, Dawes Papers, LC; Durant to Sumner, Sept. 29, 1864, Sumner Papers, Houghton Library, Harvard University (cited by Tregle); Durant to H. W. Davis, Mar. 31, 1864, printed in New York *Tribune*, Apr. 23, 1864; Durant to Davis, July 26, 1864, printed in New York *Evening Post*, Aug. 5, 1864; *Letter of Thomas J. Durant to Henry Winter Davis* [Oct. 27, 1864]; "Memorial of Citizens of Louisiana," Nov. 18, 1864, 38 Cong., 2 sess., *Sen. Mis. Doc.* No. 2 (Dec. 7, 1864); "Letter from Thomas J. Durant," Jan. 2, 1865, *National Anti-Slavery Standard*, Jan. 28, 1865, and several speeches reported only in the New Orleans papers. For the controversy over Louisiana in the antislavery movement, and its focus upon Durant's charges, I have used the files of the *National Anti-Slavery Standard*, of Garrison's *Liberator*, and of the Boston *Commonwealth*, Jan. through Mar., 1865.

46. Tregle, "Thomas J. Durant," p. 511.

47. Hyman, ed., *Radical Republicans and Reconstruction*, pp. 137–47.
Herman Belz in *Reconstructing the Union* called attention to the influence of the Louisiana situation upon the Wade-Davis bill and Manifesto. His view was challenged by Michael Les Benedict in *A Compromise of Principle: Congressional Republicans and Reconstruction, 1863–1869* and upheld by McCrary; see his *Lincoln and Reconstruction*, pp. 274–75n8. For the "near-miss" of compromise between president and Congress, see Chapter One, p. , and Belz, *Reconstructing the Union*, Chapter IX.

48. Chase to Durant, Feb. 6, 1864, Chase Papers, HSP; Durant to Chase, Jan. 16, Feb. 21, 1864, Chase Papers, LC.

49. Flanders to Chase, Feb. 26, 1864, Chase to Flanders, Apr. 26, 1864, Chase to Banks, draft, Nov. 8, 1864, Chase Papers, HSP.

50. Chase to Greeley, March 4, 1864, Chase to Howe, July 8, 1864, ibid.;

Donald, ed., *Inside Lincoln's Cabinet*, entry for July 5, 1864, p. 232.

51. Durant had understood that the reorganization movement, in his words, "should appear as little influenced by the military power, as possible," that the "tone" of the reorganization plan was to be "civilian", its execution "carried on without any direct military intereference." Durant to Dawes, Feb. 8, 1864, Dawes Papers; Durant to Lincoln, Feb. 26, 1864, Lincoln Papers; see also above, Chapter Two.

Copies of Banks' proclamations were published in the local press, are available in his papers and in *War of the Rebellion: Official Records*, and are extensively quoted in secondary accounts.

52. Minutebook of the General Committee of Union Associations in New Orleans, p. 127, NYHS; for examples of Durant's logical agility, see Durant to Boutwell, Feb. 25, 1864, Durant Papers, Durant to Lincoln, Feb. 26, 1864, Lincoln Papers.

53. The Davis query is quoted in Durant's reply to Davis, Mar. 31, 1864, New York *Tribune*, Apr. 23, 1864; Denison to Chase, Mar. 5, Oct. 8, 1864, Chase, *Diary and Correspondence*, pp. 433, 448.

54. Durant to Davis, July 26, 1864, New York *Evening Post*, Aug. 5, 1864. The Wade-Davis Manifesto was printed in the same first page column following Durant's letter.

55. Ibid.; *Letter of Thomas J. Durant to Henry Winter Davis* [Oct. 27, 1864], pp. 27–29. This pamphlet was written to demolish a similar one by Banks in defense of the Louisiana government: *The Reconstruction of States: Letter of Major-General Banks to Senator Lane*. On occasion the phrase "equality before the law" was apparently used, particularly by prosuffrage Radicals, as code language to imply equality of political rights [or privileges] as well as civil rights; but such usage was not general.

In the battle for congressional and antislavery support, Banks as well as Durant distorted the facts. For incisive criticism of Banks' defense, see editorial in Boston *Commonwealth*, Mar. 4, 1865, and McCrary, *Lincoln and Reconstruction*, pp. 282–85. Despite Banks' vulnerability, there is more to be said for his general position than his critics have recognized.

56. Boston *Commonwealth*, Feb. 4, 25, Mar. 4, 11, 1865; *National Anti-Slavery Standard*, Dec. 17, 1864, Jan. 21, 28, Feb. 4, 11, 1865; *Liberator*, Jan. 13, Feb. 3, 10, 17, 24, 1865; James M. McPherson, *The Struggle for Equality: Abolitionists and the Negro in the Civil War and Reconstruction*, Chapter XIII; McCrary, *Lincoln and Reconstruction*, p. 297.

CHAPTER FOUR: Defeat before Battle

1. Banks to Preston King, May 6, 1865, Andrew Johnson Papers, Library of Congress; see also Banks to J. W. Forney, May 6, 1865, Banks Papers.

2. Basler, *Collected Works*, VIII, 121, 131, 404.

Just before his assassination Lincoln signaled his intent to use the pressure of patronage to obtain concessions for blacks by appointing to the key patronage post of collector of the customs not an "old resident" of the Bullitt-Cottman persuasion but a northern military man (one who was to become the most hated of the state's carpetbag governors because of his appointment of blacks to state office)—William Pitt Kellogg. Ibid., p. 410; Taylor, *Louisiana Reconstructed*, pp. 253–54.

3. Hahn to Lincoln, Sept. 24, Oct. 29, Nov. 5, 11, Dec. 2, 9, 1864, with enclosures, James T. Tucker to John Hay, Nov. 23, 1864, Lincoln Papers; Basler, *Collected Works*, VIII, 106–7.

Hurlbut had been born and raised in South Carolina, then at the age of thirty moved to Illinois where he practiced law and took an active role in politics. One of many political generals, he volunteered for service and participated in the battle of Shiloh. A special investigating committee in early 1865 recommended that he be arrested for complicity in bribery and corruption. General Canby ordered a court-martial but before it could meet Hurlbut was allowed to resign. The incident apparently was little known and had no adverse consequences for his later career. Lincoln's reprimand seems to have had little effect upon his conduct in Louisiana. At the time of his departure from New Orleans, General Hurlbut was popular with the anti-Banks Conservative forces who succeeded in toppling Banks after Lincoln's death. *National Cyclopaedia*, IV, 218; Final Report, Smith-Brady Commission, Sept. 23, 1865, pp. 124–25, National Archives, Record Group 94.

4. Hurlbut to Lincoln, Nov. 29, 1864, Mar. 15, 1865, Lincoln Papers.

5. Wells to Lincoln, Mar. 6, 1865, original with endorsements in Johnson Papers, copy in Lincoln Papers. Communications in respect to the ominous situation in New Orleans which may have reached Lincoln included T. W. Conway to Banks, Mar. 21, 1865, Banks Papers; Plumly to Lincoln, March 23, 1865, Doolittle to Lincoln, Mar. 25, 1865, Lincoln Papers; see also A. P. Field to Lincoln, Mar. 16, 1865, ibid.

6. Basler, *Collected Works*, VIII, 121, 131, 206–7, 386; Banks to his wife, Dec. 18, 29, 1864, Jan. 7, 8, 10, Feb. 6, 9, 15, 24, 1865, Banks Papers; Harrington, *Fighting Politician*, p. 164.

7. New Orleans *Tribune*, Apr. 23, 1865. The local press featured the meeting and speeches; there are slight variations in the reporting of Banks' address.

8. New Orleans *Tribune*, Apr. 25, 1865.

9. Ibid., May 23, 1865. Three days earlier the *Tribune* had printed a related letter from S.N.T.

10. Hahn to Lincoln, Nov. 11, 1864, Lincoln Papers; Hahn to Kelley, June 21, 1865, printed in New York *Times*, June 23, 1865.

There is evidence that Hahn and Lincoln talked about the constitutional provision for free public schools for all children. Lincoln had made it clear that he did not approve of a proposal to levy a tax on colored persons for colored schools, a provision approved and later deleted by the convention. On his return to New Orleans, Hahn was pleased to reassure Lincoln that this limitation on the principle of public support for education had been stricken from the constitution. Hahn to Lincoln, Aug. 13, 31, 1864, Lincoln Papers.

11. *Daily True Delta*, Dec. 10, 1864; a news story sent from Washington a month later reported that Banks would not leave until the Louisiana question was settled, ibid., Jan. 21, 1865. Denison reported that the governor had not had his way in the election of senators, Chase, *Diary and Correspondence*, p. 453. See also Plumly to Banks, Oct. 20, 1864, Banks Papers; Tucker to Hay, Nov. 23, 1864, Lincoln Papers.

12. Dennett, ed., *Lincoln and the Civil War*, pp. 244–45. Compare the treatment of the incident by Belz, *Reconstructing the Union*, pp. 252–54; Benedict, *Compromise of Principle*, p. 90; McCrary, *Lincoln and Reconstruction*,. pp. 287–92; and Horowitz, *Great Impeacher*, pp. 106–9. Belz uncovered Lincoln's willingness to accept the Wade-Davis procedure except for Louisiana.

13. *Liberator*, Jan. 13, 1865; Banks to wife, Jan. 7 [1865 misdated 1864], Banks Papers.

Public and congressional hesitancy on the suffrage issue, even in Dec. and Jan., is suggested by the enthusiastic response of the Phillips wing of the antislavery movement to the positions taken by B. Gratz Brown and William D. Kelley, two recognized Radical champions of black enfranchisement, even though neither were arguing for immediate suffrage for all blacks. Boston *Commonwealth*, Jan. 21, 28, 1865.

14. Chase to Lincoln, Apr. 11, 12, 1865, Lincoln Papers. Printed versions of the two letters, with a few subtle revisions and Chase's marginal annotations are in the Chase Papers, HSP.

Chase looked to state action on black suffrage despite his awareness of the insistence of the Durant-Flanders-New Orleans *Tribune* faction that no concession could be obtained from the state legislature. For example, see Flanders to Chase, Jan. 10, 1865, Chase Papers, HSP.

15. Chase, *Diary and Correspondence*, p. 455; clipping of address at Tremont Temple, Boston, in Banks Papers; *Liberator*, Nov. 11, 1864; letter to Garrison, Jan. 30, 1865, ibid., Feb. 24, 1865; editorial, Boston *Commonwealth*, Mar. 4, 1865.

16. *Liberator*, Nov. 11, 1864, Feb. 24, Mar. 31, 1865; James Bowen to Garrison, Feb. 11, 1865, *Daily True Delta*, Mar. 19, 1865.

17. *Liberator*, Dec. 30, 1864; *Daily True Delta*, Nov. 18, 20, 1864, Jan. 25, 1865; New Orleans *Times*, Jan. 25, 1865.

18. *Daily True Delta*, Nov. 18, 1864, Jan. 1, 1865.

19. Ibid., Nov. 13, 14, 16, 1864.

20. Ibid., Jan. 15, 18, 1865. Friendly accounts of the dominant sentiment in the Colored Convention can be found in McCrary, *Lincoln and Reconstruction*, pp. 295–96; Charles Vincent, *Black Legislators in Louisiana during Reconstruction*, pp. 31–34; Ripley, *Slaves and Freedmen*, pp. 178–80.

21. *Daily True Delta*, Jan. 25, 1865.

22. Ibid., Feb. 18, 19, 1865.

23. *Black Republican*, Apr. 15, May 20, 1865.

24. Conway to Banks, Mar. 21, 1865, Banks Papers; Plumly to Lincoln, Mar. 23, 1865, Lincoln Papers. Plumly did not yet realize that Governor Wells, who had taken over from Hahn, was also behind the displacements.

On the *Black Republican* and its origin, cf. Vincent, *Black Legislators*, pp. 35–36, esp. *n*39, and Ripley, *Slaves and Freedmen*, p. 85.

25. Plumly to Tucker, Nov. 18, 1864, Tucker to Hay, Nov. 18, 1864, Lincoln Papers; Plumly to Banks, Aug. 9, 1864, Banks Papers; Louisiana, *Journal of the House of Representatives*, Feb. 27, 1865, p. 186; cf. Caskey, *Secession and Restoration*, pp. 147–48.

Hahn had recommended Tucker to Lincoln to replace Flanders. Hahn to Lincoln, Nov. 5, 1864, Lincoln Papers.

26. Brown to editor of *Missouri Democrat* in Boston *Commonwealth*, Jan. 21, 1865; Hahn to Kelley, June 21, 1865, New York *Times*, June 23, 1865. The citation in Belz, *Reconstructing the Union*, pp. 256–57*n*22, brought the Brown letter to my attention.

27. *Congressional Globe*, 38 Cong., 2 sess., p. 300 (Jan. 17, 1865). The citation in Benedict, *Compromise of Principle*, p. 406*n*21, brought this evidence to my attention. See his account, p. 89.

28. There is no indication that the Banks-Hahn forces mounted a major suffrage offensive during his absence. For the record of the legislature on black issues, see Taylor, *Louisiana Reconstructed*, pp. 56–57, Caskey, *Secession and Restoration*, pp. 146–47, and Ficklen, *Reconstruction in Louisiana*, pp. 88–89. All accounts are brief and inadequate.

29. For Lincoln's attitude, see Chapter One, pp. 26–30. William F. Messner in *Freedmen and the Ideology of Free Labor: Louisiana, 1862–1865*, pp. 186–87, holds that the prevalent free-labor ideology foreclosed economic advancement for freedmen. His argument rests upon the assumption that the only possible road to economic emancipation was through publicly financed black communal enterprise.

30. Varying evaluations can be found in Messner, *Freedmen and the Ideology of Free Labor*, McCrary, *Lincoln and Reconstruction*, Ripley, *Slaves and Freedmen*, Gerteis, *From Contraband to Freedman*, John W. Blassingame, *Black New Orleans: 1860–1880*, and J. Thomas May, "Continuity and Change in the Labor Program of the Union Army and the Freedmen's Bureau," *Civil War History*, XVII (Sept. 1971), 245–54.

31. Address at Tremont Temple, Boston, Nov. 4, 1864, as printed in *Daily True Delta*, Nov. 14, 1864; Banks to Garrison, Jan. 30, 1865 in *Liberator*, Feb. 24, 1865; [Banks], *Emancipated Labor in Louisiana*, substantially an address delivered at Boston Oct. 30, 1864, and at Charlestown, Mass., Nov. 1, 1864; Thomas W. Conway, Final Report for Year ending Feb. 1, 1865, *War of the Rebellion: Official Records*, ser. 1, XLVIII, pt. 1, 703–10.

32. *Daily True Delta*, Feb. 11, 21, 23, 1865; *Black Republican*, Apr. 15, May 13, 1865; N. P. Banks, *Address at the Customhouse, New Orleans, Fourth of July, 1865*, p. 7.

33. Hahn's address in *Daily True Delta*, Mar. 7, 1865; clipping of November speech in Hahn to Lincoln, Nov. 20, 1863, Lincoln Papers; Louisiana, *Journal of the House of Representatives*, 1864–65, pp. 12–13, 129, 201; *Debates of the House of Representatives*, 1864–65, pp. 141, 144, 270–72.

34. Banks, *Address on the Fourth of July, 1865*, pp. 10, 14; Mrs. N. P. Banks to Banks, July 30, 1865, Banks to his wife, Aug. 12, 16, 24, 1865, Banks Papers; Banks, Address at Lawrence, Mass., Oct. 2, 1865, as printed in Boston *Daily Journal*, Oct. 3, 1865; Simpson and Baker, "Michael Hahn," pp. 231–32; Taylor, *Louisiana Reconstructed*, p. 29.

McCrary has established the overwhelmingly middle-class character of the constitutional convention, which represented the Banks-Hahn influence; there was almost no representation from the planter class. *Lincoln and Recon-*

struction, pp. 245–53. In his Lawrence address Banks criticized as absurd and insane the entrusting of political power to those who had formerly exercised it and spoke vaguely of giving political power to the laboring class of the South.

35. J. V. C. Smith to Banks, Mar. 18, 1865, Samuel W. Behrman to Banks, Apr. 23, 1865, Banks Papers; New Orleans *Times*, Mar. 22, 1865; *Daily True Delta*, Mar. 22, 24, 30, 1865.

36. New Orleans *Times*, Apr. 28, May 6, 1865; *Daily True Delta*, May 3, 6, 10, 11, 12, 1865; *Black Republican*, May 20, 1865; New Orleans *Tribune*, Apr. 25, May 6, 14, 1865.

The *Tribune* ran only a one sentence announcement of Kennedy's removal. Except for comments on Banks lack of power to settle any question in favor of colored people, the paper ignored Banks return as a matter of "very limited interest." As late as Apr. 13, Durant apparently was less concerned with Governor Wells' reactionary course than with continuing his attack upon the way in which Banks had established the Free State government in 1864. See Durant to New Orleans *Tribune*, reprinted in New Orleans *Times*, Apr. 15, 1865.

37. Extensive reports of the May 17 meeting were published in the *Daily True Delta*, May 18, 1865, New Orleans *Times*, May 18, 19, 1865, and *Black Republican*, May 20, 1865.

38. Banks to Preston King, May 6, 1865, Johnson Papers.

39. Denison to McCullouch, May 6, 1865, in Padgett, ed., "Some Letters of George Stanton Denison, 1854–1866," pp. 1221–23. Denison still held the collector's office, awaiting his successor, William P. Kellogg, whose commission Lincoln had signed Apr. 13.

40. New Orleans *Times*, May 25, 1865; Kennedy to Canby, Feb. 1, 1866, Johnson Papers; Wells to wife, May 23, 1865, Emily E. Weems Collection, Louisiana State Museum (hereafter LSM).

41. New Orleans *Times*, June 18, 1865.

CHAPTER FIVE: Reflections on the Limits of the Possible

1. Beale, ed., *Diary of Gideon Welles*, II, 281; Gideon Welles, *Civil War and Reconstruction: Selected Essays*, compiled by Albert Mordell, pp. 192–93; McCarthy, *Lincoln's Plan of Reconstruction*, p. 426; "Impeachment of the President: Testimony," 40 Cong., 1 sess., *House Report*, No. 7, pp. 401, 403–4; Basler, *Collected Works*, VIII, 404.

2. LeRoy P. Graf and Ralph W. Haskins, eds., *The Papers of Andrew*

Johnson, V, 18 (Oct. 4, 1861), 229 (Mar. 22, 1862), 536 (July 4, 1862).

3. Albert Castel, *The Presidency of Andrew Johnson*, pp. 28–29; Sarah W. Wiggins, *The Scalawag in Alabama Politics, 1865–1881*, pp. 5–17; Francis B. Simkins and Robert H. Woody, *South Carolina during Reconstruction*, pp. 39–42.

Historians have not as yet undertaken the laborious work in the manuscript census to determine with certainty the antebellum wealth and slave ownership of members of the constitutional conventions and legislatures and of officeholders during 1865 and 1866.

4. Beale, ed., *Diary of Gideon Welles*, II, 305, 307.

5. My analysis of Stanton's Reconstruction proposals and subsequent changes is based upon a comparative study of two versions of the May 9, 1865, Executive Order for Virginia and four versions of what evolved into the May 29, 1865, proclamation for North Carolina available in the microfilmed Johnson Papers; various accounts by Gideon Welles—his original diary entries, the revised diary, his letter to Andrew Johnson of July 27, 1869 (Beale, ed., *Diary of Gideon Welles*, II, 281–82, 291, 294, 301–3, 304, 393–95, III, 714–24), his essay on "Lincoln and Johnson" originally published in *The Galaxy*, Apr. and May 1872 (Welles, *Civil War and Reconstruction*, pp. 190–213); the testimony of Stanton and of Grant in 1867 before the House Judiciary Committee considering impeachment ("Impeachment of the President: Testimony," pp. 400–406, 828–36); and the exhaustively researched biographies of Stanton by Benjamin P. Thomas and Harold M. Hyman (*Stanton: The Life and Times of Lincoln's Secretary of War*, pp. 306, 357–58, 402–4, 438–39, 444–46) and of Welles by John Niven (*Gideon Welles: Lincoln's Secretary of the Navy*, pp. 491–92, 497–99, 501–5, 508–512).

I have been unable to locate the original Stanton proposal that combined Virginia and North Carolina nor his revised Executive Order for North Carolina except for its heading. To the printed heading has been pasted three separate sheets of handwritten manuscript, followed by a printed sheet that itself is three pieces pasted together, and lastly a final sheet of handwritten manuscript. I am indebted to Paul T. Heffron, acting chief, Manuscript Division, Library of Congress, for the careful inspection of the document to determine its composition.

Without the two missing documents it is not possible to determine with certainty whether the change from military to civilian governor was made at the May 9 cabinet meeting or earlier, but it would appear to have been made subsequent to Lincoln's death. Similarly there is some uncertainty about the suffrage provision, or rather the lack of one, in the paper Stanton prepared for Lincoln. Stanton testified that he left the matter blank, a statement Welles contested but on the basis of Stanton's second proposal, the one of May 9. Welles was not certain as to the content of the first which he had only heard read. Welles had a copy of the printed proposal dated May 9 for an executive order covering North Carolina only, but it cannot be found in any collection of his papers and was probably destroyed in a fire. The earlier paper which Lincoln saw is apparently still extant although not available to scholars.

The official Executive Order for Virginia differed from Stanton's version in omitting the provision in respect to volunteers for occupation duty in the South but retained the preceding part of the sentence which read: "That the Secretary of War assign such Assistant Provost Marshal General, and such Provost Marshals in each district of said State as he may deem necessary." A like statement was not included, however, in the North Carolina and subsequent proclamations. Another difference worth noting is that Johnson's proclamations dropped all reference to the secretary of war but enjoined every other member of the cabinet by specific reference to proceed to reestablish the functions and laws under his jurisdiction. What seems to have happened is that Johnson transformed a temporary framework, within which Lincoln intended to develop the substance of Reconstruction, into a "plan" which Johnson treated as itself the substantive settlement between North and South. This has been obscured by loose usage of the term "plan" and by a necessarily heavy reliance upon Welles' accounts, which were biased by his own extreme state rights views, his strong aversion to military control, and his defense of President Johnson.

Niven has suggested that Welles' influence may have been decisive in Johnson's decision to make no concession on suffrage, that had Welles spoken for limited black suffrage the outcome might have been different. Hyman sees the question of centralized control of the provost marshal corps as a matter of army organization and command authority rather than one of presidential policy.

I am indebted to both Professor Niven and Professor Hyman for help in my fruitless attempt to locate the missing documents, and also to the staff of the Huntington Library, the Connecticut Historical Society, the manuscript division of the University of Rochester Library, the manuscript division of the Library of Congress, and the Military Archives Division of the National Archives.

6. Cuthbert Bullitt to Johnson, May 5, 1865, Wells to Johnson, May 22,

1865, July 3, 1865, Cottman to Johnson, June 5, 1865, Johnson Papers; Wells to his wife, May 23, 1865, Weems Collection, LSM.

For Johnson's ambition, see introductions to each volume of *Papers of Andrew Johnson*; Cox and Cox, *Politics, Principle and Prejudice*, pp. 95–106; Castel, *Presidency of Andrew Johnson*, passim, esp. pp. 29, 227; James E. Sefton, *Andrew Johnson and the Uses of Constitutional Power*, pp. 52, 59, 71–72, 74, 114, 124.

7. For Johnson's race attitudes, see Cox and Cox, *Politics, Principle and Prejudice*, pp. 151–71; Hans L. Trefousse, *Impeachment of a President: Andrew Johnson, the Blacks, and Reconstruction* pp. 3–16; David W. Bowen, "Andrew Johnson and the Negro," East Tennessee Historical Society *Publications*, XL (1968), 28–49, and his dissertation of the same title.

8. I am indebted to James Gutmann and Ernest Nagel for reassurance on this point and for the following citations: Sidney Hook, *Reason, Social Myths, and Democracy*, pp. 216–20; Paul Edwards, ed., *The Encyclopedia of Philosophy*, II, 392–93 (H. B. Acton); Frederick Engels, *Dialectics of Nature*, pp. 83–91; *Hegel's Science of Logic*, trans. by W. H. Johnston and L. G. Struthers, I, 386–90.

9. *Papers of Andrew Johnson*, I, 135, II, 355, 477, III, 62, 162–65, 277, 336–38, 495–96, V, 535.

10. Ibid., V, 231, 233. See also his address of Apr. 23, 1862, ibid., p. 328.

11. Wendell Phillips to Ann Phillips, Mar. 31, 1862, Blagden Papers, Houghton Library, Harvard University, printed in part in Bartlett, "New Light on Wendell Phillips."

12. *Papers of Andrew Johnson*, I, 136, II, 477, III, 319–20, 328–28.

13. Ibid., V, 4. William T. M. Riches, "The Commoners: Andrew Johnson and Abraham Lincoln to 1861," Ph.D. dissertation, University of Tennessee, 1976; Bowen, "Andrew Johnson and the Negro," and his forthcoming "Andrew Johnson, Governor of Tennessee," in the governors of Tennessee series; Cox and Cox, *Politics, Principle and Prejudice*, pp. 153, 162–63. Cf. Sefton, *Andrew Johnson*, pp. 126–27, who accepts the arguments advanced in Johnson's Freedmen's Bureau veto message as evidence that Johnson held an "equality of expectations" for black advancement by honest effort.

14. For Johnson's impact especially upon the Freedmen's Bureau and the army, see John and LaWanda Cox, "General O. O. Howard and the 'Misrepresented Bureau'," *Journal of Southern History*, XIX (Nov. 1953), 435–39; William S. McFeely, *Yankee Stepfather: General O. O. Howard and the Freedmen*, pp. 241, 246–55; Donald G. Nieman, *To Set the Law in Motion: The*

Freedmen's Bureau and the Legal Rights of Blacks, 1865–1868, pp. 4–8, 18–20, 119–21 and his "Andrew Johnson, the Freedmen's Bureau, and the Problem of Equal Rights, 1865–1866," *Journal of Southern History*, XLIV (Aug. 1978), 399–420; Michael Perman, *Reunion Without Compromise: The South and Reconstruction, 1865–1868*, pp. 98–102; Otto H. Olsen, ed., *Reconstruction and Redemption in the South*, pp. 17–19.

15. Phillip S. Paludan, *A Covenant with Death: The Constitution, Law, and Equality in the Civil War Era*, p. 42, including *n*33.

16. Basler, *Collected Works*, VIII, 404.

17. Ibid., pp. 207, 402.

18. Basic revisionist studies of the break between President Johnson and Congress are Eric L. McKitrick, *Andrew Johnson and Reconstruction*, Cox and Cox, *Politics, Principle, and Prejudice*, W. R. Brock, *An American Crisis: Congress and Reconstruction, 1865–1867*, and Trefousse, *Impeachment*. For recent summations, see Patrick W. Riddleberger, *1866: The Critical Year Revisited*, and Castel, *Presidency of Andrew Johnson*. The latter includes a critique of revisionism and hails a new "conservative revisionist" trend in Reconstruction scholarship (pp. 222–30).

19. Olsen, ed., *Reconstruction and Redemption*, pp. 5, 168. For southern reaction and strategy, Perman, *Reunion Without Compromise*; for Unionist disfranchisement and "scalawag" usage, Wiggins, *Scalawag in Alabama Politics*, pp. 19–21, 28–34, 37; for excellent accounts of confusion, division, and realignment at the state level, William C. Harris, *Presidential Reconstruction in Mississippi*, esp. pp. 228–45, 248, and Carl H. Moneyhon, *Republicanism in Reconstruction Texas*, esp. pp. 24–41, 44–55. See also Gordon B. McKinney, *Southern Mountain Republicans, 1865–1900: Politics and the Appalachian Community*, p. 30.

20. An amendment at least as strong as the Fourteenth in its protection for blacks would probably have been hammered out and ratified with the cooperation of the president. Indeed, section two, which sought to resolve the problems created by the demise of the three-fifths compromise and the controversy over black enfranchisement, in all likelihood would have been strengthened by a more direct provision for black suffrage. Cf. Fehrenbacher in Cullom Davis et al., eds., *The Public and the Private Lincoln: Contemporary Perspectives*, p. 124; Stampp, *Era of Reconstruction*, p. 215; Castel, *Presidency of Andrew Johnson*, p. 228.

21. Some measure of black political influence survived Redemption and the compromise of 1877 until the turn of the century. Eric Anderson, *Race and*

Politics in North Carolina, 1872–1901: The Black Second; Robert F. Engs, *Freedom's First Generation: Black Hampton, Virginia, 1861–1890*; Thomas Holt, *Black over White: Negro Political Leadership in South Carolina during Reconstruction*; Arnold H. Taylor, *Travail and Triumph: Black Life and Culture in the South Since the Civil War*, Chapter One; Charles Vincent, *Black Legislators in Louisiana During Reconstuction*; John W. Blassingame, *Black New Orleans, 1860–1880*; Peter Kolchin, *First Freedom: The Responses of Alabama's Blacks to Emancipation and Reconstruction*; Joe M. Richardson, *The Negro in the Reconstruction of Florida, 1865–1877*; Joel Williamson, *After Slavery: The Negro in South Carolina During Reconstruction, 1861–1877*; Vernon L. Wharton, *The Negro in Mississippi, 1865–1890*; Alrutheus A. Taylor, *The Negro in Tennessee, 1865–1880*.

22. David Donald, *Charles Sumner and the Coming of the Civil War*, p. x.

23. Italics added. The original version was presented at the XIII International Congress of Historical Sciences held in Moscow in Aug. 1970 and first printed as a pamphlet for participants and then reprinted in 1973 as part of a volume of the collected papers of the Congress. The revised version was delivered at the Symposium on Southern History at the University of Mississippi, Sept. 1976 and printed under the title "The Price of Freedom" in David G. Sansing, ed., *What Was Freedom's Price?*, pp. 93–113.

24. For a graphic description of the setting of Lincoln's April 11 address, and the response to it, see Stephen B. Oates, *With Malice Toward None: The Life of Abraham Lincoln*, pp. 460–62.

A commitment comparable to that of the mid-twentieth century was not altogether lacking in the 1860s for a number of abolitionists attacked the concept of racial inequality on the basis of biblical authority and logic. See McPherson, *Struggle for Equality*, pp. 136–53.

The economic implications of the civil-political equalitarianism of the mid-nineteenth century differed from those of the equalitarianism of the late twentieth century, particularly as to the obligations of government, but neither have embraced the goal of a complete equality of condition. For a stimulating examination of the nature and history of the concept of equality in the United States, see J. R. Pole, *The Pursuit of Equality in American History*.

25. George M. Fredrickson, "After Emancipation: a Comparative Study of the White Responses to the New Order of Race Relations in the American South, Jamaica, and the Cape Colony of South Africa," in Sansing, ed., *What Was Freedom's Price*, pp. 71–92; Peyton McCrary, "After the Revolution:

American Reconstruction in Comparative Perspective," paper presented at the annual meeting of the American Historical Association, New York, Dec. 28, 1979.

For other comparative studies relevant to postemancipation, George M. Fredrickson, *White Supremacy: A Comparative Study in American and South African History*, esp. pp. 179–238, and his "Comparative History," in Michael Kammen, ed., *The Past Before Us: Contemporary Historical Writing in the United States*, pp. 465–70. Work in progress by Peter Kolchin on Russia and by Stanley Engerman on the West Indies will yield further comparative insights. See the latter's comments in Engerman and Eugene D. Genovese, eds., *Race and Slavery in the Western Hemisphere*, pp. 495–526, and Kolchin's "In Defense of Servitude: American Proslavery and Russian Proserfdom Arguments, 1760–1860, *American Historical Review*, LXXXV (Oct. 1980), 809–27.

26. Jerome Blum, *The End of the Old Order in Rural Europe*, pp. 429–41; see also Daniel Chirot, *Social Change in a Peripheral Society*, and his "The Growth of the Market and Servile Labor Systems in Agriculture," *Journal of Social History* (Winter 1975), pp. 67–80.

27. George Beckford, *Persistent Poverty: Underdevelopment in Plantation Economies of the Third World*, xxvi, and his "Toward an Appropriate Theoretical Framework for Agricultural Development Planning and Policy," *Social and Economic Studies*, XVII (Sept. 1968), 233–42. For Jamaica, Gisela Eisner, *Jamaica, 1830–1930: A Study in Economic History*; Philip D. Curtin, *Two Jamaicas: The Role of Ideas in a Tropical Colony, 1830–1865*. For Guiana, Alan H. Adamson, *Sugar without Slaves: The Political Economy of British Guiana, 1838–1904*; Jay R. Mandle, *The Plantation Economy: Population and Economic Change in Guyana, 1838–1960*; Michael Moohr, "The Economic Impact of Slave Emancipation in British Guiana, 1832–1852," *Economic History Review*, 2d. ser., XXV (Nov. 1972), 588–607. See also Sidney Mintz, *Caribbean Transformations*; Woodville K. Marshall, "Notes on Peasant Development in the West Indies Since 1838," *Social and Economic Studies*, XVII (Sept. 1968), 252–63; W. F. Wertheim, "Asian Society: Southeast Asia," and "Economy, Dual" in *International Encyclopedia of the Social Sciences*, I, 423–38, IV, 495–500. The Galbraith quotation is from *The Nature of Mass Poverty*, p. 133.

28. For calling the São Paulo comparison to my attention, I am indebted to Patricia Mulvey, fellow member of the Political History Group of the Institute for Research in History.

29. Florestan Fernandes, *The Negro in Brazilian Society*, his "Immigra-

tion and Race Relations in São Paulo," in Magnus Mörner, ed., *Race and Class in Latin America*, pp. 122–42, and his "Beyond Poverty: The Negro and the Mulatto in Brazil" in Robert Brent Toplin, ed., *Slavery and Race Relations in Latin America*, pp. 277–97; Toplin, introduction and "Abolition and the Issue of the Black Freedman's Future in Brazil," ibid., pp. 253–76; Arthur F. Corwin, "Afro-Brazilians: Myths and Realities," ibid., esp. pp. 385–400; Donald Coes, "Brazil," in W. Arthur Lewis, ed., *Tropical Development, 1880–1913*, pp. 100–113; Charles Wagley, *An Introduction to Brazil*, pp. 74–79; Carl N. Degler, *Neither Black Nor White: Slavery and Race Relations in Brazil and the United States*. Thomas H. Holloway's recent study, *Immigrants on the Land: Coffee and Society in São Paulo, 1886–1934*, provides an effective analysis of how the coffee plantation economy in its heyday made possible viable family farm ownership for many immigrants who started life in Brazil as penniless farm workers.

30. For a perceptive review of the literature on prewar racism in the North, particularly among Republicans, see Kenneth M. Stampp, "Race, Slavery, and the Republican Party of the 1850s" in his *The Imperiled Union: Essays on the Background of the Civil War*, pp. 105–35. For the distinction between the race attitudes of President Johnson's supporters and opponents, Cox and Cox, *Politics, Principle, and Prejudice*, pp. 211–28.

Daniel Chicot argues that an ideology equivalent to racism, one that insists laborers are culturally inferior to masters, has been used to justify enduring peasant poverty where masters and serfs are of common ethnic origin and color, "Growth of the Market and Servile Labor Systems in Agriculture," p. 75.

31. A helpful introduction to these concepts can be found in the articles of the *International Encyclopedia of the Social Sciences* on "Prejudice: The Concept," by Otto Klineberg, "Prejudice: Social Discrimination," by J. Milton Yinger, and "Race Relations: Social Psychological Aspects," by Thomas F. Pettigrew.

32. For a selection of relevant documents, 1869–1891, and interpretive comment, LaWanda Cox and John H. Cox, eds., *Reconstruction, the Negro, and the New South*, pp. 105–207. On the Liberal Republicans, Richard A. Gerber, "Liberal Republicanism, Reconstruction, and Social Order: Samuel Bowles as a Test Case," *New England Quarterly*, XLV (Sept. 1972), 393–407; Patrick W. Riddleberger, "The Break in the Radical Ranks: Liberals vs. Stalwarts in the Election of 1872," *Journal of Negro History*, XLIV (Apr. 1959), 136–57; John G. Sproat, *"The Best Man": Liberal Reformers in the Guilded Age*, pp. 29–44. For antislavery men who embraced the "let-alone" policy to-

ward the South, James M. McPherson, "The Antislavery Legacy: From Reconstruction to the NAACP," in Barton J. Bernstein, ed., *Towards a New Past: Dissenting Essays in American History*, pp. 131–45, and his *The Abolitionist Legacy: From Reconstruction to the NAACP*, pp. 24–34, 81–94. For the effort to enact an enforcement bill in the 51st Congress, Richard E. Welch, Jr., "The Federal Elections Bill of 1890: Postscript and Prelude," *Journal of American History*, LII (Dec. 1965), 511–26. See also J. Morgan Kousser, *The Shaping of Southern Politics: Suffrage Restriction and the Establishment of the One-Party South, 1880–1910*, pp. 18–33, in which the view of the national Republican record is compatible with that expressed here, and William Gillette, *Retreat from Reconstruction, 1869–1879*, which passes a much harsher judgment upon northern Republican leadership. Further light on the reasons for Republican retreat can be expected in a forthcoming study by Michael Les Benedict. A thoughtful overview of Reconstruction as an aborted revolution can be found in James M. McPherson, "Reconstruction: A Revolution Manqué," reprinted in Allen F. Davis and Harold D. Woodman, *Conflict and Consensus in Early American History*, pp. 413–25.

33. William Gillette makes a strong case for the desegregation Civil Rights Bill as a factor in the overwhelming Republican defeat of 1874, but does not claim that it was the only cause. *Retreat from Reconstruction*, pp. 246–58.

34. C. Vann Woodward, "Yes, There was a Compromise of 1877," *Journal of American History*, LX (June 1973), 221–22; Stanley P. Hirshson, *Farewell to the Bloody Shirt: Northern Republicans & the Southern Negro, 1877–1893*, pp. 45–59; Vincent P. DeSantis, *Republicans Face the Southern Question: The New Departure Years, 1877–1897*, pp. 99–101; Gillette, *Retreat from Reconstruction*, pp. 333–34.

35. Lawrence Grossman, *The Democratic Party and the Negro: Northern and National Politics, 1868–92*; Joel H. Silbey, *A Respectable Minority: The Democratic Party in the Civil War Era, 1860–1868*, pp. 27–28, 80–83, 190–93, 199–203, 209, 232, 241–42.

36. For the use of violence, Allen W. Trelease, *White Terror: The Ku Klux Klan Conspiracy and Southern Reconstruction*. Many state and more general studies have recounted the various techniques of white southern resistance. A recent noteworthy effort to examine the potential for success or failure of Republicanism in the post–Civil War South is Olsen, ed., *Reconstruction and Redemption*. The editor's introduction is perceptive, informed and provocative.

37. Eugene Genovese, "Re-examining Reconstruction," *New York Times*

Book Review Section, May 4, 1980, pp. 9, 40; Perman, *Reunion Without Compromise*, esp. p. 14; Gillette, *Retreat from Reconstruction*, pp. 76–185 (the quotations are from pp. 171–72).

38. I have found particularly helpful P. H. Partridge, *Consent and Consensus*. See also Carl Joachim Friedrich, *Man and His Government: An Empirical Theory of Politics*, pp. 159–79, and his *Tradition and Authority*; David Lockwood, "Some Remarks on 'The Social System'," *British Journal of Sociology*, VII (1956), 134–46; Samuel Du Bois Cook, "Coercion and Social Change," in J. Roland Pennock and John W. Chapman, eds., *Coercion*, pp. 107–143, and Robert Paul Wolff "Is Coercion 'ethically neutral'?" ibid, pp. 144–47; Hannah Arendt, "Authority" in *Between Past and Present*, pp. 99–141; and articles in the *International Encyclopedia of the Social Sciences* on "Consensus: the Concept of Consensus," by Edward Shils, "Power," by Robert A. Dahl, and "Sanctions," by A. L. Epstein.

Ralf Dahrendorf in developing a conflict-coercion theory first affirmed and then repudiated the compatability of consensus and conflict. In this *Eassays in the Theory of Society*, cf, pp. 127–28 with 149–50.

39. Everette Swinney, "Suppressing the Ku Klux Klan: The Enforcement of the Reconstruction Amendments, 1870–1874," (Ph, D. dissertation, University of Texas, 1966), esp. pp. 233–35, 300–301, 317; Gillette, *Retreat from Reconstruction*, pp. 25–55, 104–65.

40. The quotation is from Gillette, ibid., p. 102. Swinney puts the number of troops occupying the South at from 12,000 to 13,000 in 1867–68 and about 5,000 in 1870–72, "Suppressing the Ku Klux Klan," p. 190.

41. *Annual Reports of the Attorney General of the United States, 1957–1972*; U.S. Commission on Civil Rights, *The Federal Civil Rights Enforcement Effort: A Report* and their *The Voting Rights Act: Ten Years After: A Report*; Sar A. Levitan, William B. Johnston, Robert Taggart, *Still a Dream: The Changing Status of Blacks since 1960*, esp. pp. 267–92, 331–55; Neil R. McMillen, "Black Enfranchisement in Mississippi: Federal Enforcement and Black Protest in the 1960s," *Journal of Southern History*, XLIII (Aug. 1977), 351–72.

42. U.S. Commission on Civil Rights, *The Federal Civil Rights Enforcement Effort: One Year Later*, p. xii; Levitan, *Still a Dream*, pp. 349–55. See also *The Unfinished Business: Twenty Years Later: A Report Submitted to the U.S. Commission on Civil Rights by its Fifty-one State Advisory Committee*, Sept. 1977, pp. 4–5.

43. The characterization is from Michael Davis, *The Image of Lincoln in*

the South, p. 63.

44. Basler, *Collected Works*, VIII, 401-4.

Lincoln's remarks in reference to black suffrage have been interpreted as a commitment to leave the decision to the states, as a matter of right. In fact, he avoided the issue of authority. Gideon Welles was very influential, but clearly in error, in identifying Lincoln's views with those of Andrew Johnson and his own.

45. The practical impact of an aroused sense of injustice, the conditions that evoke it and those that restrain it, deserve more attention than they have received from historians. For suggestive discussions of the sense of justice and injustice directed primarily to the concerns of political and legal theorists, see Edmond N. Cahn, *The Sense of Injustice: An Anthropocentric View of Law*, esp. pp. 13-27, and his article "Justice" in the *International Encyclopedia of the Social Sciences*, VIII, 346-47; Giorgio del Vecchio, *Justice, An Historical and Philosphical Essay*, pp. 77-81; Carl J. Friedrich and John W. Chapman, eds., *Justice*, p. 30 (Friedrich), 191-97 (Iredell Jenkins).

Circumstances in the post–Civil War period suggest that a sense of injustice to have an important political impact requires the arousing of public attention and indignation and a general perception that something can be done to remedy the injustice. Also important would seem to be reinforcement by linkage to other concerns of party and nation, and a minimum of conflict with such interests.

46. The quotation was a general statement, not one used in the context of Lincoln's leadership. Richard E. Neustadt, *Presidential Power: The Politics of Leadership from FDR to Carter*, p. 135.

James MacGregor Burns faults Lincoln as opportunistic, expedient, cautious and orthodox to a degree that blocked the federal action necessary to carry out the nation's moral commitment to the freedmen. Though Lincoln was skillful in using those "transactional" aspects of leadership Burns demeans, he also exemplified the "transforming" leadership Burns most admires. *Leadership*, pp. 391-92, 429-30. Otto H. Olsen presents Lincoln as leader of revolution, "Abraham Lincoln as Revolutionary." *Civil War History*, XXIV (Sept. 1978), 213-24.

47. Alfred H. Kelly, in Harold M. Hyman, ed., *New Frontiers of the American Reconstruction*, pp. 52-56; Hyman, *A More Perfect Union*, pp. 414-553 (esp. 438-41, 447-48, 477, 490); Michael Les Benedict, "Preserving the Constitution: The Conservative Basis of Radical Reconstruction," *Journal of American History*, LXI (June 1974), 65-90; Paludan, *Covenant with*

Death, pp. 1–60, 274–82. The first part of the quotation is from Paludan, the second from Kelly.

48. Robert J. Harris, *The Quest for Equality: The Constitution, Congress and the Supreme Court*, 24–56, 82–108; Laurent B. Frantz, "Congressional Power to Enforce the Fourteenth Amendment against Private Acts," *Yale Law Journal*, LXXIII, part 2 (July 1964), 1353–84; Mark DeWolfe Howe, "Federalism and Civil Rights," Massachusetts Historical Society, *Proceedings*, LXXVII (1965), 15–27; Alfred Avins, "The Ku Klux Klan Act of 1871: Some Reflected Light on State Action and the Fourteenth Amendment," *Saint Louis University Law Journal*, XI (Winter 1967), 331–81; John Anthony Scott, "Justice Bradley's Evolving Concept of the Fourtenth Amendment from the Slaughterhouse Cases to the Civil Rights Cases," *Rutgers Law Review*, XXV (Spring 1971), 552–69; Charles Fairman, *Reconstruction and Reunion, 1864–88*, Part I, pp. 1354, 1359, 1387–88; Robert J. Kaczorowski, "Searching for the Intent of the Framers of the Fourteenth Amendment," *Connecticut Law Review*, V (Winter 1973), 368–98, and his two papers on civil rights during Reconstruction presented at the annual meetings of the Southern Historical Association, 1973, and the Organization of American Historians, 1975; Charles W. McCurdy, "Legal Institutions, Constitutional Theory, and the Tragedy of Reconstruction," *Reviews in American History*, IV (June 1976), 210–11; Belz, *Emancipation and Equal Rights*, pp. 120–25, 129–39.

The characterization as "vacuous" is from Fairman, that of "a major triumph for the South" from Harris.

49. Michael Les Benedict has made a persuasive case for the Supreme Court under Chief Justice Morrison R. Waite (1873–1888) as having gone a long distance in its obiter dicta toward reconciling federalism with broad congressional power to protect and extend black rights. "Preserving Federalism: Reconstruction and the Waite Court," *Supreme Court Review*, 1978, pp. 39–79.

50. The challenge to the land thesis was made by Herman Belz in "The New Orthodoxy in Reconstruction Historiography," *Reviews in American History*, I (Mar. 1973), 106–13.

The six books referred to are Stephen J. DeCanio, *Agriculture in the Postbellum South: The Economics of Production and Supply*, Robert Higgs, *Competition and Coercion: Blacks in the American Economy, 1865–1914*, Ransom and Sutch, *One Kind of Freedom*, Jay R. Mandle, *The Roots of Black Poverty: The Southern Plantation Economy After the Civil War*, Jonathan M. Wiener, *Social Origins of the New South: Alabama, 1860–1885*, and Gavin Wright,

The Political Economy of the Cotton South: Households, Markets, and Wealth in the Nineteenth Century. See also Edward Magdol, *A Right to the Land: Essays on the Freedmen's Community*, Claude F. Oubre, *Forty Acres and a Mule: The Freedmen's Bureau and Black Land Ownership*, Daniel A. Novak, *The Wheel of Servitude*, and Dwight B. Billings, Jr., *Planters and the Making of a "New South": Class, Politics, and Development in North Carolina, 1865–1900.*

Agricultural History devoted two entire issues to the southern economy, those of Apr. 1975 (XLIX, No. 2) and Jan. 1979 (LIII, No. 1) and *Explorations in Economic History* used its Jan. 1979 issue (XVI, No. 1) for publication of papers from a symposium at Duke University on issues raised by Ransom and Sutch, *One Kind of Freedom.* Sansing, ed., *What was Freedom's Price?* is a collection based upon a symposium held in 1976 at the University of Mississippi. A number of relevant papers were presented at the St. Louis Conference on The First and Second Reconstructions, Feb. 1978, organized by members of the Department of History, University of Missouri-St. Louis. Major articles have been published by *Journal of Southern History*, XLII (Nov. 1977), 523–54, Harold D. Woodman, "Sequel to Slavery: The New History Views the Postbellum South," and by *American Historical Review*, LXXXIV (Oct. 1979), 970–1006, Jonathan M. Wiener, "Class Structure and Economic Development in the American South, 1865–1955," with comments by Higgs and Woodman.

There are sharp differences in approach and analysis in the recent scholarship. Ransom and Sutch emphasize merchant monopoly; Wright, the world demand for cotton; Mandle, a continuing plantation economy; Wiener, the persistence of large landholdings and the political power of planters; Higgs, black economic advances and the limitations attributable to racial coercion; DeCanio, agricultural labor as not technically "exploited" but disadvantaged by lack of land and capital; Woodman, the emergence of a peculiarly southern type of working class in agriculture.

51. Higgs, *Competition and Coercion*, pp. 77–80, 93; Wright, *Political Economy of the Cotton South*, pp. 177–80, and his "Freedom and the Southern Economy," *Explorations in Economic History*, XVI (Jan. 1979), 106; Ransom and Sutch, *One Kind of Freedom*, p. 80, and their "The Economic Reorganization of the Post-Emancipation South," paper presented at the conference on The First and Second Reconstructions. Cf. DeCanio, *Agriculture in the Postbellum South*, pp. 223, 239–40, and his "Accumulation and Discrimination in the Postbellum South," *Explorations in Economic History*, XVI

(Apr. 1979), 202–4.

There is also a growing doubt as to whether having obtained landownership blacks could have maintained it. See Willie Lee Rose in *What Was Freedom's Price?* pp. 12–14, Manning Marable, "The Politics of Black Land Tenure, 1877–1915," *Agricultural History*, LIII (Jan. 1979), 142–52; Leo McGee and Robert Boone, eds., *The Black Rural Landowner; Endangered Species.* For studies with somewhat more positive implications for the success of black landownership, see Carol K. R. Bleser, *The Promised Land: the History of the South Carolina Land Commission, 1869–1890*, pp. 140–56 and James T. Currie, *Enclave: Vicksburg and Her Plantations, 1863–1870*, pp. 83–145; but cf. Norman L. Crockett, *The Black Towns.* See also Janet Sharp Hermann, *The Pursuit of a Dream*, esp. pp. 195–245. My own misgivings about the adequacy of a land program to solve the problem of black poverty go back many decades when a comparative study of tenure, 1870–1900, in selected antebellum plantation counties disclosed the atypically high black landownership in Beaufort County, South Carolina, yet the area was one of marked poverty. See my Ph.D. dissertation, University of California, 1941, "Agricultural Labor in the United States, 1865–1900, with Special Reference to the South."

52. Beckford, *Persistent Poverty*, pp. 224–27; Doreen Warriner, *The Economics of Peasant Farming*, p. xxxii, and her *Land Reform in Principle and Practice*, pp. vi, 427–36; Michael P. Todaro, *Economic Development in the Third World: An Introduction to Problems and Policies in a Global Perspective*, pp. 227–28.

53. Julius Rubin, "The Limits of Agricultural Progress in the Nineteenth Century South," *Agricultural History*, XLIX (Apr. 1975), 362–73. The cotton South was, of course, only one of several southern economies but the focus upon it is reasonable in view of the concentration of blacks in cotton production.

The classic study of cotton production in the South is M. B. Hammond, *The Cotton Industry: An Essay in American Economic History.* See also Harold D. Woodman, *King Cotton and His Retainers: Financing and Marketing the Cotton Crop of the South, 1800–1925*, pp. 334–59; Fred A. Shannon, *The Farmer's Last Frontier: Agriculture, 1860–1897*, pp. 110–17, 415; Ransom and Sutch, *One Kind of Freedom*, pp. 188–92; Wright, *Political Economy of the Cotton South*, pp. 158–84, and his "Cotton Competition and the Post-Bellum Recovery of the American South," *Journal of Economic History*, XXXIV (Sept. 1974), 610–35; Robert L. Brandfon, *Cotton Kingdom of the*

New South: A History of the Yazoo Mississippi Delta from Reconstruction to the Twentieth Century, esp. pp. 21, 114–39.

The immediate postwar years were disastrous for cotton growers and had far-reaching consequences. See Lawrence N. Powell, *New Masters: Northern Planters During the Civil War and Reconstruction*, pp. 145–50; Currie, *Enclave*, pp. 156–63; Cox and Cox, eds., *Reconstruction, the Negro, and the New South*, pp. 331–36.

54. The quotation is from Gavin Wright, "One Kind of Freedom," *The Civil Liberties Review*, May/June 1978, p. 49. He has called attention to the high fertility rates of the rural population which transformed the region from one of labor scarcity to one of labor surplus. "Freedom and the Southern Economy," p. 106, and *Political Economy of the Cotton South*, p. 160. For his view of the relationship between the slave plantation economy and that of the post-bellum South, ibid., pp. 43–126; see also Douglass C. North, *The Economic Growth of the United States, 1790–1860*, pp. 4–7, 122–33, 153–55.

C. Vann Woodward's attribution of the South's industrial backwardness to a colonial status in relation to the Northeast long dominated historical interpretation, *Origins of the New South, 1877–1913*, pp. 291–320. For a summation of challenges to this view prior to the 1970s, Sheldon Hackney, "Origins of the New South in Retrospect," *Journal of Southern History*, XXXVIII (May 1972), 208–13.

For radical approaches to underdevelopment as an aspect of a capitalist world order, E. J. Hobsbawm, *The Age of Capital, 1848–1875*, pp. 27–71, 189–211; Immanuel Wallerstein, *The Modern World System: Capitalist Agriculture and the Origins of the European World Economy in the Sixteenth Century*, pp. 229–39, his "Dependence in an Interdependent World: The Limited Possibilities of Transformation within the Capitalist World Economy," *African Studies Review*, XVII (Apr. 1974), 1–26, and his "The Rise and Future Demise of the World Capitalist System: Concepts for Comparative Analysis," *Comparative Studies in Society and History*, XVI (Sept. 1974), 387–415; James D. Cockcroft, André Gunder Frank, and Dale L. Johnson, *Dependence and Underdevelopment: Latin America's Political Economy*.

The starkest explanation for the plight of the cotton South, particularly that of its black workers, was made in passing by the distinguished economist W. Arthur Lewis in discussing the factoral terms of trade. He argues that the disadvantage of tropical countries in the yield per acre of foodstuffs resulted in a standard of living that made available in the second half of the nineteenth century a vast reservoir of Indian and Chinese labor "willing to travel anywhere to work on plantations for a shilling a day." Since cotton as a commercial staple could be grown in the tropics, the American South, even with its higher yields per acre, could not have competed with tropical cotton except by exploiting black labor: "American blacks earned so little because of the large amount of cotton that would have flowed out of Asia and Africa and Latin America at a higher cotton price." *The Evolution of the International Economic Order*, pp. 14–20.

55. The study of black migration underway by William Cohen should fill an important gap in our understanding of the lack of a sizable out-migration. He has kindly confirmed the implication of his published article that physical coercion or involuntary servitude do not go very far in accounting for the lack of a black movement to the North. Cohen to Cox, Apr. 11, 1980; William Cohen, "Negro Involuntary Servitude in the South, 1865–1940: A Preliminary Analysis," *Journal of Southern History*, XLII (Feb. 1976), 31–60. See also Harold D. Woodman, "Post–Civil War Southern Agriculture and the Law," *Agricultural History*, LIII (Jan. 1979), 319–37; Mandle, *Roots of Black Poverty*, pp. 71–83; cf. the extreme interpretation presented by Novak, *Wheel of Servitude*. I found suggestive the accounts of black employment opportunities in Elizabeth H. Pleck, *Black Migration and Poverty: Boston, 1865–1900*; and in David A. Gerber, *Black Ohio and the Color Line, 1860–1915*, and also references to black reluctance to migrate in Engs, *Freedom's First Generation*, pp. 116–17, and in Vernon Burton, "Ungrateful Servants? Edgefield's Black Reconstruction: Part I of the Total History of Edgefield County, South Carolina" (Ph.D. diss., Princeton, 1976), pp. 131–57. See also two recent studies, Stanley Lieberson, *A Piece of the Pie: Blacks and White Immigrants Since 1800*, esp. pp. 30–47, 298–325, 328–38; and David M. Johnson and Rex R. Campbell, *Black Migration in America: A Social Demographic History*, pp. 43–70, 86.

Why blacks did not leave the South for public lands in the North is a special aspect of the problem. Geographically, Kansas was the most obvious and available destination. Robert G. Athearn believes that the consequence of the great unplanned millenarian black exodus to that state in 1879–1880 was to block further migrations which might have been assimilated if made gradually on a more limited scale. No intensive study has been made of how those blacks fared who obtained a foothold on the public lands of the Great Plains, a harsh environment for homesteaders, black or white. Athearn, *In Search of Canaan: Black Migration to Kansas, 1879–80*; Nell Irvin Painter, *Exodusters: Black Migration to Kansas after Reconstruction*. For black settlements in Kansas and Oklahoma, see Crockett, *Black Towns*.

56. Willie Lee Rose has limned these attitudes with understanding and tolerance, *Rehearsal for Reconstruction*, pp. 211–16, 228–29. See also Eric Foner, *Politics and Ideology in the Age of the Civil War*, pp. 100–112 and his *Free Soil, Free Labor, Free Men: The Ideology of the Republican Party Before the Civil War*, pp. 11–18, 29–34; Carl R. Osthaus, *Freedmen, Philanthropy, and Fraud: A History of the Freedman's Savings Bank*, pp. 1–20, 221–25; Nieman, *To Set the Law in Motion*, pp. 53–59; Daniel T. Rodgers, *The Work Ethic in Industrial America, 1850–1920*, pp. 14–22.

The break-up of the large landed estates was generally assumed to be a natural and inevitable process. General James Wadsworth told the Freedmen's Inquiry Commission that confiscation and redistribution of southern land was unnecessary because "natural causes would bring it about." American Freedmen's Inquiry Commission, Testimony, National Archives. See also Lawrence N. Powell, "The American Land Company and Agency: John A. Andrew and the Northernization of the South," *Civil War History*, XXI (Dec. 1975), 305–6, and his *New Masters*, pp. 43–44.

Two studies suggest to me that had economic conditions in the postwar South developed as anticipated, and with the new civil-political status of blacks sustained, the expectations for black advancement at least in urban areas would not have been unrealistic. Engs, *Freedom's First Generation*; Frank J. Huffman, "Old South, New South: Continuity and Change in a Georgia County, 1850–1880" (Ph.D. diss., Yale, 1974). Also suggestive is the study by Donald L. Winters, *Farmers Without Farms: Agricultural Tenancy in Nineteenth-Century Iowa*, which finds that despite the difficulties northern farmers faced in the last decades of the nineteenth century, tenancy remained a stepping-stone to land ownership for a significant number. Cf. LaWanda Cox, "Tenancy in the United States, 1865–1900: A Consideration of the Validity of the Agricultural Ladder Hypothesis," *Agricultural History*, XVIII (July 1944), 97–105.

57. George W. Julian, not Thaddeus Stevens, took the lead in trying to obtain homesteads for blacks. Edward Atkinson, the most articulate spokesman for the northern cotton industry, championed small farms. For a recent study of Stevens' role, see Eric Foner, "Thaddeus Stevens, Confiscation, and Reconstruction," reprinted in *Politics and Ideology*, pp. 128–49.

58. The significance of the land provisions of the vetoed Freedmen's Bureau bill, first pointed out in my 1941 dissertation and subsequently in McFeely, *Yankee Stepfather*, pp. 228–31, have not generally been recognized by historians with the recent exception of Eric Foner, *Politics and Ideology*, p.

140. For relevant documents and comments, Cox and Cox, eds., *Reconstruction, the Negro and the New South*, pp. xxviii–xxx, 31–47, 315–26.

59. See above, p. 28n43. General James Wadsworth, after his conference with Lincoln on returning from the Valley inspection tour, testified that he did not think confiscation was the policy of the government "unless it becomes necessary to do it to carry out the policy of emancipation." American Freedmen's Inquiry Commission, Testimony, National Archives.

In 1864 Lincoln indicated a willingness to sign a bill providing for permanent forfeiture of real property, although in 1862 he had forced Congress on threat of a veto to limit forfeiture under the second Confiscation Act to the lifetime of the owner. The circumstances surrounding this major reversal of policy suggest that it was prompted by consideration for the freedmen. I hope elsewhere to examine the episode in some detail. Also of potential significance for the freedmen's future was an exception to restoration of property rights in Lincoln's amnesty proclamation (but not in Johnson's) "where rights of third parties shall have intervened." Similarly, Lincoln's support of John Eaton's effort at Davis Bend to promote the development of an independent black yeomanry is especially suggestive in view of the analysis of Eaton's purpose by Stephen Joseph Ross in "Freed Soil, Freed Labor, Freed Men: John Eaton and the Davis Bend Experiment," *Journal of Southern History*, XLIV (May 1978), 213–30; Lincoln to Eaton, Feb. 10, 1865, Basler, *Collected Works*, VIII, 274.

60. Nicolay and Hay, *Abraham Lincoln*, X, 123.

61. The recollection of former slaves confirm that black voting was "an act of defiance to the local white community," i.e., a rejection of white norms for black subordination. Paul D. Escott, *Slavery Remembered: A Record of Twentieth-Century Slave Narratives*, pp. 153–54.

62. Foner, *Politics and Ideology*, pp. 114–20, 123–24; Woodman, "Post–Civil War Southern Agriculture and the Law," pp. 329, 333–34, 336–37; Burton, "Ungrateful Servants?" and his "Race and Reconstruction: Edgefield County, South Carolina," *Journal of Social History*, XII (Fall 1978), 31–56; Howard N. Rabinowitz, *Race Relations in the Urban South, 1865–1890*, pp. 264–66, 279–81; see also Kousser, *Shaping of Southern Politics*, pp. 14, 37, his "Progressivism—For Middle-Class Whites Only: North Carolina Education, 1880–1910," *Journal of Southern History*, XLVI (May 1980), 179–85, 191–92, and Anderson, *Race and Politics in North Carolina*, 315–30, 335. In contrast, Holt in *Black over White*, pp. 148–79, sees black political leaders as failing black labor because of bias arising from their class, color, and origins.

63. For southern Whigs, Confederate dissidents, and scalawags see

Charles Grier Sellers, Jr., "Who Were the Southern Whigs," *American Historical Review*, LIX (Jan. 1954), 335–46; Thomas B. Alexander, "Persistent Whiggery in the Confederate South, 1860–1877," *Journal of Southern History*, XXVII (Aug. 1961), 305–29; John V. Mering, "Persistent Whiggery in the Confederate South: A Reconsideration," *South Atlantic Quarterly*, LXIX (Winter 1970), 124–43; Wilfred B. Yearns, *The Confederate Congress*, pp. 218–35; Thomas B. Alexander and Richard E. Beringer, *The Anatomy of the Confederate Congress*, esp. pp. 337–44; David Donald, "The Scalawag in Mississippi Reconstruction," *Journal of Southern History*, X (Nov. 1944), 447–60; Allen W. Trelease, "Who Were the Scalawags," ibid., XXIX (Nov. 1963), 445–68; "Communications" from Donald and Trelease, ibid., XXX (May 1964), 253–57; Warren A. Ellem, "Who Were the Mississippi Scalawags," ibid., XXXVIII (May 1972), 217–40; "Communication" from Trelease and Ellem, ibid. (Nov. 1972), 703–706; Otto H. Olsen, "Reconsidering the Scalawags," *Civil War History*, XII (Dec. 1966), 304–20; Richard O. Curry, "The Civil War and Reconstruction, 1861–1877: A Critical Overview of Recent Trends and Interpretations," ibid. XX (Sept. 1974), 230–33; Elizabeth S. Nathans, *Losing the Peace: Georgia Republicans and Reconstruction, 1865–1871*, esp. pp. vi–vii, 225–27; Wiggins, *Scalawag in Alabama Politics*, esp. pp. 128–35; Gordon B. McKinney, "Southern Mountain Republicans and the Negro, 1865–1900," *Journal of Southern History*, XLI (Nov. 1975), 493–516, and his *Southern Mountain Republicans*, esp. pp. 3–61; James Alex Baggett, "Origins of Scalawag Leadership in the Upper South," paper presented at the annual meeting of the Southern Historical Association, Atlanta, 1979, and his "Origins of Early Texas Republican Party Leadership," *Journal of Southern History*, XL (Aug. 1974), 441–54; Moneyhon, *Republicanism in Reconstruction Texas*.

64. See above, p. 154–55. Peter Kolchin in a study of southern congressmen, 1868–1872, has concluded that carpetbaggers were the driving element within reconstruction governments and that a predominantly scalawag delegation was a sign of Republican weakness. "Scalawags, Carpetbaggers, and Reconstruction: A Quantitative Look at Southern Congressional Politics, 1868–1872," *Journal of Southern History*, XLV (Feb. 1979), 63–76.

65. William C. Harris has argued that despite the exaggeration of Redeemers and their apologists, the tax burden imposed by Republicans was heavy given the hard times and led to a genuine taxpayer revolt that helped topple the Republican regime in Mississippi. *The Day of the Carpetbagger:*

Republican Reconstruction in Mississippi, pp. 626–33, and in Olsen, ed., *Reconstruction and Redemption*, pp. 93–97.

66. Allen W. Trelease, "Republican Reconstruction in North Carolina: A Roll-Call Analysis of the State House of Representatives, 1868–70," *Journal of Southern History*, XLII (Aug. 1976), 319–44; Olsen, ed., *Reconstruction and Redemption*, pp. 28, 35–36, 38–43 (Jerrel H. Shofner on Florida), 59–60 (Wiggins on Alabama), 85–86 (Harris on Mississippi), 120–25 (Jack P. Maddex on Virginia), 173–75, 189 (Olsen on North Carolina); Gillette, *Retreat from Reconstruction*, pp. 190–258; McKinney, *Southern Mountain Republicans*, pp. 41, 43–44, 49–50, 54–56, 60, 131–41; Moneyhon, *Republicanism in Reconstruction Texas*, pp. 71–72, 98, 118–19, 138, 155–58, 168–70, 178–79, 182, 195–96.

For a fresh perspective on segregation as an advance over exclusion, see Rabinowitz, *Race Relations in the Urban South*, Part II. No less principled a Radical than Albion W. Tourgée considered Charles Sumner's Civil Rights bill with its provision for desegregated schools a "blister-plaster. . . . It will be like the firebrands between the tails of Samson's foxes." Cox and Cox, eds., *Reconstruction, the Negro, and the New South*, pp. 125–26.

67. Thomas B. Alexander, "Political Reconstruction in Tennessee, 1865–1870," in Richard O. Curry, ed., *Radicalism, Racism, and Party Realignment: The Border States during Reconstruction*, p. 77.

68. On Louisiana, see above, Part II; on leadership dilemmas, Ross Clayton and William Lammers, "Presidential Leadership Reconsidered: Contemporary Views of Top Federal Officials," *Presidential Studies Quarterly*, VIII (Summer 1978), 239–40, 242–43, 244.

Had Banks returned to New Orleans from Washington when Lincoln first asked him to do so, there would have been little likelihood of a "counter-revolution" in Louisiana during Lincoln's lifetime whether or not Michael Hahn would then have sought escape from the governorship by election as senator. This was the act which, in Banks' absence, opened the gates of power for the Kennedy-Cottman-Wells men. The opposition to the Free State government, which Durant had done so much to arouse and continued to nurture, was, of course, an important factor both in Hahn's discomfiture as governor and in Banks' protracted stay in Washington.

69. *Liberator*, Feb. 3, 1865, p. 18; McPherson, *Struggle for Equality*, pp. 298–99; Walter M. Merrill, ed., *Let the Oppressed Go Free, 1861–1867: The Letters of William Lloyd Garrison*, V, 258.

Bibliography

This bibliography includes only materials cited in the Notes.

Adamson, Alan H. *Sugar without Slaves: The Political Economy of British Guiana, 1838–1904*. New Haven, 1972.

Alexander, Thomas B. "Persistent Whiggery in the Confederate South, 1860–1877," *Journal of Southern History*, XXVII (Aug. 1961), 305–29.

———and Richard E. Beringer. *The Anatomy of the Confederate Congress.* Nashville, Tenn., 1972.

Ames, Herman V. *The Proposed Amendments to the Constitution of the United States during the First Century of its History*, American Historical Association, *Annual Report for 1896*, II. Washington, D.C., 1897.

Anderson, Eric. *Race and Politics in North Carolina, 1872–1901: The Black Second*. Baton Rouge and London, 1981.

Aptheker, Herbert, ed. *A Documentary History of the Negro People in the United States*. 2 vols. New York, 1968.

Arendt, Hannah. *Between Past and Present*. New York, 1977.

Athearn, Robert G. *In Search of Canaan: Black Migration to Kansas, 1879–80*. Lawrence, Kans., 1978.

Avins, Alfred. "The Ku Klux Klan Act of 1871: Some Reflected Light on State Action and the Fourteenth Amendment," *Saint Louis University Law Journal* XI (Winter 1967), 331–81.

Baggett, James Alex. "Origins of Early Texas Republican Party Leadership," *Journal of Southern History*, XL (Aug. 1974), 441–54.

———."Origins of Scalawag Leadership in the Upper South." Paper presented at the annual meeting of the Southern Historical Association, Atlanta, 1979.

Banks, Nathaniel P. *Address at the Customhouse, New Orleans, Fourth of July, 1865*. Pamphlet, n.p., n.d.

———.*Emancipated Labor in Louisiana*. Pamphlet, n.p., n.d.

———.*The Reconstruction of States: Letter to Senator Lane*. Pamphlet, New Orleans, 1864.

———."Suggestions Presented to the Judiciary Committee of the Senate of the United States," *Senate Misc. Doc.* No. 9, 38 Cong., 2 sess.

Bartlett, Irving H. "New Light on Wendell Phillips: The Community of Reform, 1840–1880," *Perspectives in American History*, XII (1979), 1–232.

Basler, Roy P. "And for His Widow and His Orphan," *Quarterly Journal of the Library of Congress*, XXIV (Oct. 1970), 291–94.

———, ed. *The Collected Works of Abraham Lincoln*. 9 vols. New Brunswick, N.J., 1953–55.

———, ed. *The Collected Works of Abraham Lincoln: Supplement, 1832–1865*. Westport, Conn., 1974.

Beale, Howard K., ed. *Diary of Gideon Welles*. 3 vols. New York, 1960.

Beckford, George. *Persistent Poverty: Underdevelopment in Plantation Economies of the Third World*. New York, 1972.

———."Toward an Appropriate Theoretical Framework for Agricultural Development Planning and Policy," *Social and Economic Studies*, XVII (Sept. 1968), 233–42.

Belz, Herman. *Emancipation and Equal Rights: Politics and Constitutionalism in the Civil War Era*. New York, 1978.

———."The Etheridge Conspiracy of 1863: A Projected Conservative Coup," *Journal of Southern History*, XXXVI (Nov. 1970), 549–67.

———."The Freedmen's Bureau Act of 1865 and the Principle of No Discrimination according to Color," *Civil War History*, XXI (Sept. 1975), 207–30.

———.*A New Birth of Freedom: The Republican Party and Freedmen's Rights, 1861 to 1866*. Westport, Conn., 1976.

———."The New Orthodoxy in Reconstruction Historiography," *Reviews in American History*, I (Mar. 1973), 106–13.

———.*Reconstructing the Union: Theory and Practice during the Civil War*. Ithaca, N.Y., 1969.

Benedict, Michael Les. *A Compromise of Principle: Congressional Republicans and Reconstruction, 1863–1869*. New York, 1974.

———."Preserving the Constitution: The Conservative Basis of Radical Reconstruction," *Journal of American History*, LXI (June 1974), 65–90.

———."Preserving Federalism: Reconstruction and the Waite Court," *Supreme Court Review*, 1978, pp. 39–79.

Bennett, Lerone, Jr. "Was Abe Lincoln a White Supremacist?" *Ebony*, XXIII (Feb. 1968), 35–38.

Bentley, George R. *A History of the Freedmen's Bureau*. Philadelphia, 1955.

Bernstein, Barton J. *Towards a New Past: Dissenting Essays in American History*. New York, 1969.

Berry, Mary Frances. *Military Necessity and Civil Rights Policy: Black Citizenship and the Constitution, 1861–1868.* Port Washington, N.Y., 1977.

Billings, Dwight B., Jr. *Planters and the Making of a "New South": Class, Politics, and Development in North Carolina, 1865–1900.* Chapel Hill, N.C., 1979.

Blassingame, John W. *Black New Orleans: 1860–1880.* Chicago and London, 1973.

Bleser, Carol K. R. *The Promised Land: The History of the South Carolina Land Commission, 1869–1890.* Columbia, S.C., 1969.

Blum, Jerome. *The End of the Old Order in Rural Europe.* Princeton, 1978.

Boritt, G. S. *Lincoln and the Economics of the American Dream.* Memphis, Tenn., 1978.

Boutwell, George S. *Reminiscences of Sixty Years in Public Affairs.* 2 vols. New York, 1902.

Bowen, David W. "Andrew Johnson and the Negro," East Tennessee Historical Society *Publications*, XL (1968), 28–49.

———. "Andrew Johnson and the Negro," Ph.D. dissertation, University of Tennessee, 1976.

Brandfon, Robert L. *Cotton Kingdom of the New South: A History of the Yazoo Mississippi Delta from Reconstruction to the Twentieth Century.* Cambridge, Mass., 1967.

Brock, W. R. *An American Crisis: Congress and Reconstruction, 1865–1867.* London, 1963.

Burns, James MacGregor. *Leadership.* New York, 1978.

Burton, Vernon. "Race and Reconstruction: Edgefield County, South Carolina," *Journal of Social History*, XII (Fall 1978), 31–56.

———. "Ungrateful Servants? Edgefield's Black Reconstruction: Part I of the Total History of Edgefield County, South Carolina," Ph.D. dissertation, Princeton, 1976.

Butler, Benjamin F. *Private and Official Correspondence during the Period of the Civil War.* 5 vols. Norwood, Mass., 1917.

Cahn, Edmond N. *The Sense of Injustice: An Anthropocentric View of Law.* New York and London, 1949.

Cain, Marvin R. *Lincoln's Attorney General: Edward Bates of Missouri.* Columbia, Mo., 1965.

Carpenter, F. B. *Six Months at the White House with Abraham Lincoln.* New York, New York, 1866.

Caskey, Willie M. *Secession and Restoration of Louisiana*. University, La. 1938, reprint New York, 1970.

Castel, Albert. *The Presidency of Andrew Johnson*. Lawrence, Kans., 1979.

Chase, Salmon P. *Diary and Correspondence*, American Historical Association, *Annual Report for* 1902, II.

Chirot, Daniel. "The Growth of the Market and Servile Labor Systems in Agriculture," *Journal of Social History* (Winter 1975), pp. 67–80.

———.*Social Change in a Peripheral Society*. New York, 1976.

Clayton, Ross, and William Lammers, "Presidential Leadership Reconsidered: Contemporary Views of Top Federal Officials," *Presidential Studies Quarterly*, VIII (Summer 1978), 237–45.

Crockcroft, James D., André Gunder Frank, and Dale L. Johnson. *Dependence and Underdevelopment: Latin America's Political Economy*. New York, 1972.

Cohen, William. "Negro Involuntary Servitude in the South, 1865–1940: A Preliminary Analysis," *Journal of Southern History*, XLII (Feb. 1976), 31–60.

Congressional Globe.

Cornish, Dudley T. *The Sable Arm: Negro Troops in the Union Army, 1861–1865*. New York, 1966.

Cox, LaWanda. "Agricultural Labor in the United States, 1865–1900, with Special Reference to the South," Ph.D. dissertation, University of California, 1941.

———."The Promise of Land for the Freedmen," *Mississippi Valley Historical Review*, XLV (Dec. 1958), 413–40.

———."Tenancy in the United States, 1865–1900: A Consideration of the Validity of the Agricultural Ladder Hypothesis," *Agricultural History*, XVIII (July 1944), 97–105.

——— and John H. Cox. "General O. O. Howard and the 'Misrepresented Bureau'," *Journal of Southern History*, XIX (Nov. 1953), 427–56.

———.*Politics, Principle, and Prejudice, 1865–1866: Dilemma of Reconstruction America*. New York, 1963.

Cox, LaWanda, and John H. Cox, eds. *Reconstruction, the Negro, and the New South*. Columbia, S.C., 1973.

Crockett, Norman L. *The Black Towns*. Lawrence, Kans., 1979.

Current, Richard N. *The Lincoln Nobody Knows*. New York, 1958.

———,ed. *The Political Thought of Abraham Lincoln*. Indianapolis and New York, 1967.

Currie, James T. *Enclave: Vicksburg and Her Plantations, 1863–1870.* Jackson, Miss., 1980.

Curry, Leonard P. *Blueprint for Modern America: Nonmilitary Legislation of the First Civil War Congress.* Nashville, Tenn., 1968.

Curry, Richard O. "The Civil War and Reconstruction, 1861–1877: A Critical Overview of Recent Trends and Interpretations," *Civil War History,* XX (Sept. 1974), 215–38.

————,ed. *Radicalism, Racism and Party Realignment: The Border States during Reconstruction.* Baltimore, Md., 1969.

Curtin, Philip D. *Two Jamaicas: The Role of Ideas in a Tropical Colony, 1830–1865.* Greenwood, N.Y., 1968.

Dahrendorf, Ralf. *Essays in the Theory of Society.* Palo Alto, Calif., 1968.

Davis, Allen F., and Harold D. Woodman. *Conflict and Consensus in Early American History.* Lexington, Mass., 1976.

Davis, Cullom et al., eds. *The Public and the Private Lincoln: Contemporary Perspectives.* Carbondale, Ill., 1979.

Davis, Michael. *The Image of Lincoln in the South.* Knoxville, Tenn., 1971.

DeCanio, Stephen J. "Accumulation and Discrimination in the Postbellum South," *Explorations in Economic History,* XVI (Apr. 1979), 182–206.

————.*Agriculture in the Postbellum South: The Economics of Production and Supply.* Cambridge, Mass., 1974.

Degler, Carl N. *Neither Black Nor White: Slavery and Race Relations in Brazil and the United States.* New York, 1971.

Dennett, Tyler, ed. *Lincoln and the Civil War in the Diaries and Letters of John Hay.* New York, 1939.

DeSantis, Vincent P. *Republicans Face the Southern Question: The New Departure Years, 1877–1897.* Baltimore, Md., 1959.

Donald, David. *Charles Sumner and the Coming of the Civil War.* New York, 1960.

————,ed. *Inside Lincoln's Cabinet: The Civil War Diaries of Salmon P. Chase.* New York, 1954.

————. *Lincoln Reconsidered.* New York, 1956.

————."The Scalawag in Mississippi Reconstruction," *Journal of Southern History,* X (Nov. 1944), 447–60.

Douglass, Frederick. *Life and Times.* Reprinted from revised edition of 1892, New York, 1967.

Duncan, Bingham. *Whitelaw Reid: Journalist, Politician, Diplomat.* Athens, Ga., 1975.

Durant, Thomas J. *Letter to Henry Winter Davis.* Pamphlet, New Orleans, 1864.

Durden, Robert F. "A. Lincoln: Honkie or Equalitarian?" *South Atlantic Quarterly,* LXXI (Summer 1972), 218–91.

Eaton, John. *Grant, Lincoln and the Freedmen: Reminiscences of the Civil War.* New York, 1907.

Eisner, Gisela. *Jamaica, 1830–1930: A Study in Economic Growth.* Manchester, 1961.

Ellem, Warren A. "Who Were the Mississippi Scalawags," *Journal of Southern History,*XXXVIII (May 1972), 217–40.

The Encyclopedia of Philosophy. 8 vols. New York, 1967.

Engels, Frederick. *Dialectics of Nature.* Moscow, 1954.

Engerman, Stanley L., and Eugene D. Genovese, eds. *Race and Slavery in the Western Hemisphere.* Princeton, N.J., 1975.

Engs, Robert F. *Freedom's First Generation: Black Hampton, Virginia, 1861–1890.* Philadelphia, Pa., 1979.

Escott, Paul D. *Slavery Remembered: A Record of Twentieth-Century Slave Narratives.* Chapel Hill, N.C., 1979.

Fairman, Charles. *Reconstruction and Reunion, 1864–88, Part I.* New York, 1971.

Fehrenbacher, Don E. *The Changing Image of Lincoln in American Historiography.* Oxford, Eng., 1968.

———.*The Dred Scott Case: Its Significance in American Law and Politics.* New York, 1978.

———,ed. *The Leadership of Abraham Lincoln.* New York, 1970.

———."Only His Stepchildren: Lincoln and the Negro," *Civil War History,* XX (Dec. 1974), 293–310.

Fernandes, Florestan. *The Negro in Brazilian Society.* English translation, New York and London, 1969.

Ficklen, John Rose.*History of Reconstruction in Louisiana.* 1910. Reprint, Gloucester, Mass., 1966.

Foner, Eric. *Free Soil, Free Labor, Free Men: The Ideology of the Republican Party Before the Civil War.* New York, 1970.

———. *Politics and Ideology in the Age of the Civil War.* New York, 1980.

Franklin, John Hope. *The Emancipation Proclamation.* Garden City, N.Y., 1963.

Frantz, Laurent B. "Congressional Power to Enforce the Fourteenth Amendment against Private Acts," *Yale Law Journal,* LXXIII, part 2 (July 1964), 1353–84.

Fredrickson, George M. "A Man but Not a Brother: Abraham Lincoln and Racial Equality," *Journal of Southern History*, XLI (Feb. 1975), 39–58.

———.*White Supremacy: A Comparative Study in American and South African History*. New York and Oxford, 1981.

Friedrich, Carl Joachim. *Man and His Government: An Empirical Theory of Politics*. New York, 1963.

———. *Tradition and Authority*. New York and London, 1972.

——— and John W. Chapman, eds. *Justice*. New York, 1963.

Galbraith, John Kenneth. *The Nature of Mass Poverty*. Cambridge, Mass., and London, 1979.

Gerber, David A. *Black Ohio and the Color Line, 1860–1915*. Urbana, Ill., 1976.

Gerber, Richard A. "Liberal Republicanism, Reconstruction, and Social Order: Samuel Bowles as a Test Case," *New England Quarterly*, XLV (Sept. 1972), 393–407.

Gerteis, Louis S. *From Contraband to Freedman: Federal Policy toward Southern Blacks, 1861–1865*. Westport, Conn., 1973.

———."Salmon P. Chase, Radicalism, and the Politics of Emancipation, 1861–1864," *Journal of American History*, LX (June 1973), 42–62.

Gillette, William. *Retreat from Reconstruction, 1869–1879*. Baton Rouge, La., 1979.

Graf, LeRoy P., and Ralph W. Haskins, eds. *The Papers of Andrew Johnson*. 5 vols. to date. Knoxville, Tenn., 1967–.

Grossman, Lawrence. *The Democratic Party and the Negro: Northern and National Politics, 1868–92*. Urbana, Ill., 1976.

Hackney, Sheldon. "Origins of the New South. in Retrospect," *Journal of Southern History*, XXXVIII (May 1972), 191–216.

Hall, Douglas. *Free Jamaica, 1838–1865: An Economic History*. New Haven, 1959.

Hammond, M. B. *The Cotton Industry: An Essay in American Economic History*. New York, 1897.

Harrington, Fred H. *Fighting Politician: Major General N. P. Banks*. Philadelphia, 1948.

Harris, Robert J. *The Quest for Equality: The Constitution, Congress and the Supreme Court*. Baton Rouge, La., 1960.

Harris, William C. *The Day of the Carpetbagger: Republican Reconstruction in Mississippi*. Baton Rouge, La., 1979.

———. *Presidential Reconstruction in Mississippi*. Baton Rouge, La., 1967.

Hegel's Science of Logic. Translated by W. H. Johnston and L. G. Struthers, 2 vols. London and New York, 1929.

Herman, Janet Sharp. *The Pursuit of a Dream.* New York and Oxford, 1981.

Higgs, Robert. *Competition and Coercion: Blacks in the American Economy, 1865–1914.* Cambridge, London, New York, Melbourne, 1977.

Hirshson, Stanley P. *Farewell to the Bloody Shirt: Northern Republicans & the Southern Negro, 1877–1893.* Bloomington, Ind., 1962.

Hobsbawm, E. J. *The Age of Capital, 1848–1875.* New York, 1975.

Holloway, Thomas H. *Immigrants on the Land: Coffee and Society in São Paulo, 1886–1934.* Chapel Hill, N.C., 1980.

Holt, Thomas. *Black over White: Negro Political Leadership in South Carolina during Reconstruction.* Urbana, Ill., 1977.

Hook, Sidney. *Reason, Social Myths, and Democracy.* New York, 1966..

Horowitz, Robert F. *The Great Impeacher: A Political Biography of James M. Ashley.* New York, 1979.

Howe, Mark DeWolfe. "Federalism and Civil Rights," Massachusetts Historical Society *Proceedings,* LXXVII (1965), 15–27.

Huffman, Frank J. "Old South, New South: Continuity and Change in a Georgia County, 1850–1880," Ph.D. dissertation, Yale, 1974.

Hyman, Harold M. "Lincoln and Equal Rights for Negroes: The Irrelevancy of the 'Wadsworth Letter'," *Civil War History,* XII (Sept. 1966), 258–66.

———. *A More Perfect Union: The Impact of the Civil War and Reconstruction on the Constitution.* New York, 1973.

———, ed. *New Frontiers of the American Reconstruction.* Urbana, Ill., 1966.

———, ed. *The Radical Republicans and Reconstruction, 1861–1870.* Indianapolis, Ind., 1967.

"Impeachment of the President: Testimony," *House Report* No. 7, 40 Cong., 1 sess.

International Encyclopedia of the Social Sciences. 17 vols. New York, 1968.

Johnson, Daniel M., and Rex R. Campbell. *Black Migration in America: A Social Demographic History.* Durham, N.C., 1981.

Johnson, Ludwell H. "Lincoln and Equal Rights: The Authenticity of the Wadsworth Letter," *Journal of Southern History,* XXXII (Feb. 1966), 83–87.

———. "Lincoln's Solution to the Problem of Peace Terms, 1864–1865," *Journal of Southern History,* XXXIV (Nov. 1968), 576–86.

Kaczorowski, Robert J. "Searching for the Intent of the Framers of the Fourteenth Amendment," *Connecticut Law Review,* V (Winter 1973), 368–98.

Kammen, Michael. *The Past Before Us: Contemporary Historical Writing in the United States.* Ithaca, N.Y., and London, 1980.

Kolchin, Peter. *First Freedom: The Responses of Alabama's Blacks to Emancipation and Reconstruction.* Westport, Conn., 1972.

———."In Defense of Servitude: American Proslavery and Russian Proserfdom Arguments, 1760–1860," *American Historical Review,* LXXXV (Oct. 1980), 809–27.

———."Scalawags, Carpetbaggers, and Reconstruction: A Quantitative Look at Southern Congressional Politics, 1868–1872," *Journal of Southern History,* XLV (Feb. 1979), 63–76.

Kousser, J. Morgan. "Progressivism—For Middle-Class Whites Only: North Carolina Education, 1880–1919," *Journal of Southern History,* XLVI (May 1980), 169–94.

———.*The Shaping of Southern Politics: Suffrage Restriction and the Establishment of the One-Party South, 1880–1910.* New Haven, Conn., 1974.

Krug, Mark. "The Republican Party and the Emancipation Proclamation," *Journal of Negro History,* XLVIII (Apr. 1963), 98–114.

Levitan, Sar A., William B. Johnston, Robert Taggart. *Still a Dream: The Changing Status of Blacks since 1960.* Cambridge, Mass., 1978.

Lewis, W. Arthur. *The Evolution of the International Economic Order.* Princeton, N.J., 1978.

———, ed. *Tropical Development, 1880–1913.* Evanston, Ill., 1970.

Lieberson, Stanley. *A Piece of the Pie: Blacks and White Immigrants Since 1880.* Berkeley, Los Angeles, and London, 1980.

Litwack, Leon. *Been in the Storm So Long: The Aftermath of Slavery.* New York, 1979.

Lockwood, David. "Some Remarks on 'The Social System,' " *British Journal of Sociology,* VII (1956), 134–46.

Louisiana. *Debates of the House of Representatives.*

———.*Journal of the House of Representatives.*

———.*Journal of the Senate.*

McCarthy, Charles H. *Lincoln's Plan of Reconstruction.* New York, 1901.

McConnell, Roland C. "From Preliminary to Final Emancipation Proclamation: The First Hundred Days," *Journal of Negro History,* XLVIII (Oct. 1963), 274.

McCrary, Peyton. "After the Revolution: American Reconstruction in Comparative Perspective." Paper presented at the annual meeting of the American Historical Association, New York, Dec. 28, 1979.

————.*Abraham Lincoln and Reconstruction: The Louisiana Experiment.* Princeton, N.J., 1978.

McCurdy, Charles W. "Legal Institutions, Constitutional Theory, and the Tragedy of Reconstruction," *Reviews in American History*, IV (June 1976 203–11.

McFeely, William S. *Yankee Stepfather: General O. O. Howard and the Freedmen.* New Haven, 1968.

McGee, Leo, and Robert Boone, eds. *The Black Rural Landowner: Endangered Species.* Westport, Conn., 1979.

McKinney, Gordon B. "Southern Mountain Republicans and the Negro, 1865–1900," *Journal of Southern History*, XLI (Nov. 1975), 493–516.

————.*Southern Mountain Republicans, 1865–1900: Politics and the Appalachian Community.* Chapel Hill, N.C., 1978.

McKitrick, Eric L. *Andrew Johnson and Reconstruction.* Chicago, 1960.

McMillen, Neil R. "Black Enfranchisement in Mississippi: Federal Enforcement and Black Protest in the 1960s," *Journal of Southern History*, XLIII (Aug. 1977), 351–72.

McPherson, James M. *The Abolitionist Legacy: From Reconstruction to the NAACP.* Princeton, N.J., 1975.

————, ed. *The Negro's Civil War: How American Negroes Felt and Acted during the War for the Union.* New York, 1965.

————.*The Struggle for Equality: Abolitionists and the Negro in the Civil War and Reconstruction.* Princeton, N.J., 1964.

McWhiney, Grady, ed. *Grant, Lee, Lincoln and the Radicals.* Evanston, Ill., 1964.

Magdol, Edward. *A Right to the Land: Essays on the Freedmen's Community.* Westport, Conn., 1977.

Mandle, Jay R. *The Plantation Economy: Population and Economic Change in Guyana, 1838–1960.* Philadelphia, Pa., 1973.

————.*The Roots of Black Poverty: The Southern Plantation Economy After the Civil War.* Durham, N.C., 1978.

Marable, Manning. "The Politics of Black Land Tenure, 1877–1915," *Agricultural History*, LIII (Jan. 1979), 142–52.

Marshall, Woodville K. "Notes on Peasant Development in the West Indies Since 1838," *Social and Economic Studies*, XVII (Sept. 1968), 252–63.

May, J. Thomas. "Continuity and Change in the Labor Program of the Union Army and the Freedmen's Bureau," *Civil War History*, XVII (Sept. 1971), 245–54.

"Memorial of Citizens of Louisiana," Nov. 18, 1864, *Senate Misc. Doc.* No 2, 38 Cong., 2 sess.

Merrill, Walter M., ed. *Let the Oppressed Go Free: 1861–1867, The Letters of William Lloyd Garrison.* Cambridge, Mass., and London, 1979.

Mering, John V. "Persistent Whiggery in the Confederate South: A Reconsideration," *South Atlantic Quarterly,* LXIX (Winter 1970), 124–43.

Messner, William F. *Freedmen and the Ideology of Free Labor: Louisiana, 1862–1865.* Lafayette, La., 1978.

Miers, Earl Schenck, ed. *Lincoln Day by Day: A Chronology, 1809–1865.* 3 vols. Washington, D.C., 1960.

Mintz, Sidney. *Caribbean Transformations.* Chicago, 1974.

Mörner, Magnus, ed. *Race and Class in Latin America.* New York and London, 1970.

Mohr, Clarence L. "Before Sherman: Georgia Blacks and the Union War Effort, 1861–1864," *Journal of Southern History,* XLV (Aug. 1979), 331–52.

Moneyhon, Carl H. *Republicanism in Reconstruction Texas.* Austin, Tex., 1980.

Moohr, Michael. "The Economic Impact of Slave Emancipation in British Guiana, 1832–1852," *Economic History Review,* 2d. ser., XXV (Nov. 1972), 588–607.

Nathans, Elizabeth S. *Losing the Peace: Georgia Republicans and Reconstruction,* Baton Rouge, La., 1968.

Neely, Mark E., Jr. "Abraham Lincoln and Black Colonization: Benjamin Butler's Spurious Testimony," *Civil War History,* XXV (Mar. 1979), 77–83.

Neustadt, Richard E. *Presidential Power: The Politics of Leadership from FDR to Carter.* New York, 1980.

Nicolay, John G., and John Hay. *Abraham Lincoln: A History.* 10 vols. New York, 1890.

———, eds. *Complete Works of Abraham Lincoln.* 12 vols. New York, 1905.

Nieman, Donald G. "Andrew Johnson, the Freedmen's Bureau, and the Problem of Equal Rights, 1865–1866," *Journal of Southern History,* XLIV (Aug. 1978), 399–420.

———. *To Set the Law in Motion: The Freedmen's Bureau and the Legal Rights of Blacks, 1865–1868.* Millwood, N.Y., 1979.

Niven, John. *Gideon Welles: Lincoln's Secretary of the Navy.* New York, 1973.

North, Douglass C. *The Economic Growth of the United States, 1790–1860.* Englewood Cliffs, N.J., 1961.

Novak, Daniel A. *The Wheel of Servitude: Black Forced Labor after Slavery.* Lexington, Ky., 1978.

Oates, Stephen B. *Our Fiery Trial: Abraham Lincoln, John Brown, and the Civil War Era.* Amherst, Mass., 1979.

———."Toward a New Birth of Freedom: Abraham Lincoln and Reconstruction, 1854–1865," *Lincoln Herald* (Spring 1980), pp. 287–96.

———.*With Malice Toward None: The Life of Abraham Lincoln.* New York and Scarborough, Ontario, 1978.

Olsen, Otto H. "Abraham Lincoln as Revolutionary," *Civil War History,* XXIV (Sept. 1978), 213–24.

———."Reconsidering the Scalawags," *Civil War History,* XII (Dec. 1966), 304–20.

———, ed. *Reconstruction and Redemption in the South.* Baton Rouge, La., 1980.

Osthaus, Carl R. *Freedmen, Philanthropy, and Fraud: A History of the Freedman's Savings Bank.* Urbana, Ill., 1976.

Oubre, Claude F. *Forty Acres and a Mule: The Freedmen's Bureau and Black Land Ownership.* Baton Rouge, La., 1978.

Padgett, James A., ed. "Some Letters of George Stanton Denison, 1854–1866: Observations of a Yankee on Conditions in Louisiana and Texas," *Louisiana Historical Quarterly,* XXIII (Oct. 1940), 1132–1240.

Painter, Nell Irvin. *Exodusters: Black Migration to Kansas after Reconstruction.* New York, 1977.

Paludan, Phillip S. *A Covenant with Death: The Constitution, Law, and Equality in the Civil War Era.* Urbana, Ill., 1975.

Partridge, P. H. *Consent and Consensus.* London, 1971.

Pearson, Henry Greenleaf. *James S. Wadsworth of Geneseo.* New York, 1913.

Pennock, J. Roland and John W. Chapman, eds. *Coercion.* Chicago, 1972.

Perman, Michael. *Reunion Without Compromise: The South and Reconstruction, 1865–1868.* Cambridge, Eng., 1973.

Pleck, Elizabeth H. *Black Migration and Poverty: Boston, 1865–1900.* New York, 1979.

Pole, J. R. *The Pursuit of Equality in American History.* Berkeley, Calif., 1978.

Powell, Lawrence N. "The American Land Company and Agency: John A. Andrew and the Northernization of the South," *Civil War History,* XXI (Dec. 1975), 293–308.

———.*New Masters: Northern Planters During the Civil War and Reconstruction.* New Haven, Conn., 1980.

Proceedings of the Convention of the Friends of Freedom, Lyceum Hall, New Orleans, Dec. 15, 1862. Pamphlet, New Orleans, 1863.

Quarles, Benjamin. *Lincoln and the Negro*. New York, 1962.

———. *The Negro in the Civil War*. Boston, 1953.

Rabinowitz, Howard N. *Race Relations in the Urban South, 1865–1890*. New York, 1978.

Randall, J. G. *Lincoln the Liberal Statesmman*. New York, 1947.

——— and Richard N. Current. *Lincoln the President: Last Full Measure*. New York, 1955.

Ransom, Roger L., and Richard Sutch. "The Economic Reorganization of the Post-Emancipation South." Paper presented at the conference on The First and Second Reconstructions, University of Missouri-St. Louis, Feb. 17, 1978.

———. *One Kind of Freedom: The Economic Consequences of Emancipation*. London and New York, 1977.

Rawley, James A. *Turning Points of the Civil War*. Lincoln, Neb., 1966.

Reed, Emily H. *Life of A. P. Dostie or the Conflict in New Orleans*. New York, 1868.

Reed, H. Clay. "Lincoln's Compensated Emancipation Plan and its Relation to Delaware," *Delaware Notes*, 7th series, 1931, pp. 37–45.

Richardson, Joe M. *The Negro in the Reconstruction of Florida, 1865–1877*. Tallahassee, Fla., 1965.

Riches, William T. N. "The Commoners: Andrew Johnson and Abraham Lincoln to 1861," Ph.D. dissertation, University of Tennessee, 1976.

Riddleberger, Patrick W. "The Break in the Radical Ranks: Liberals vs. Stalwarts in the Election of 1872," *Journal of Negro History*, XLIV (Apr. 1959), 136–57.

———. *1866: The Critical Year Revisited*. Carbondale, Ill., 1979.

Ripley, C. Peter. *Slaves and Freedmen in Civil War Louisiana*. Baton Rouge, La., 1976.

Robinson, Armstead L. "Day of Jublio: Civil War and Demise of Slavery in the Mississippi Valley, 1861–1865," Ph.D. dissertation, University of Rochester, 1976.

Rodgers, Daniel T. *The Work Ethic in Industrial America, 1850–1920*. Chicago, 1974.

Rose, Willie Lee. *Rehearsal for Reconstruction: The Port Royal Experiment*. Indianapolis, Ind., 1964.

Rosenberg, John S. "Toward a New Civil War Revisionism," *American Scholar*, XXXVIII (Spring 1969), 250–72.

Ross, Steven Joseph. "Freed Soil, Freed Labor, Freed Men: John Eaton and the

Davis Bend Experiment," *Journal of Southern History*, XLIV (May 1978), 213–32.

Rubin, Julius. "The Limits of Agricultural Progress in the Nineteenth Century South," *Agricultural History*, XLIX (Apr. 1975), 362–73.

Sansing, David G., ed. *What Was Freedom's Price?* Jackson, Miss., 1978.

Scott, John Anthony. "Justice Bradley's Evolving Concept of the Fourteenth Amendment from the Slaughterhouse Cases to the Civil Rights Cases," *Rutgers Law Review*, XXV (Spring 1971), 552–69.

Sefton, James E. *Andrew Johnson and the Uses of Constitutional Power*. Boston and Toronto, 1980.

Sellers, Charles Grier, Jr. "Who Were the Southern Whigs," *American Historical Review*, LIX (Jan. 1954), 335–46.

Shannon, Fred A. *The Farmer's Last Frontier: Agriculture, 1860–1897*. New York, 1945.

Shofner, Jerrell H. *Nor Is It Over Yet: Florida in the Era of Reconstruction, 1863–1877*. Gainesville, Fla., 1974.

Silbey, Joel H. *A Respectable Minority: The Democratic Party in the Civil War Era, 1860–1868*. New York, 1977.

Simkins, Francis B., and Robert H. Woody. *South Carolina during Reconstruction*. Chapel Hill, N.C., 1932.

Simpson, Amos E., and Vaughan Baker. "Michael Hahn: Steady Patriot," *Louisiana History*, XIII (Summer 1972), 229–52.

Sproat, John G. *"The Best Men": Liberal Reformers in the Gilded Age*. New York, 1968.

———."Blueprint for Radical Reconstruction," *Journal of Southern History*, XXIII (Feb. 1957), 25–44.

Stampp, Kenneth M. *The Era of Reconstruction, 1865–1877*. New York, 1965.

———.*The Imperiled Union: Essays on the Background of the Civil War*. New York, 1980.

Swinney, Everette. "Suppressing the Ku Klux Klan: The Enforcement of the Reconstruction Amendments, 1870–1874," Ph.D. dissertation, University of Texas, 1966.

Taylor, Alrutheus A. *The Negro in Tennessee, 1865–1880*. Washington, D.C., 1941.

Taylor, Arnold H. *Travail and Triumph: Black Life and Culture in the South Since the Civil War*. Westport, Conn., 1976.

Taylor, Joe Gray. *Louisiana Reconstructed, 1863–1877*. Baton Rouge, La., 1974.

Thomas, Benjamin P., and Harold M. Hyman. *Stanton: The Life and Times of Lincoln's Secretary of War.* New York, 1962.

Thorpe, Francis N., ed. *Federal and State Constitutions.* 7 vols. Washington, D.C., 1909.

Todaro, Michael P. *Economic Development in the Third World: An Introduction to Problems and Policies in a Global Perspective.* London and New York, 1977.

Toplin, Robert Brent, ed. *Slavery and Race Relations in Latin America.* Westport, Conn., 1974.

Trefousse, Hans L. *Impeachment of a President: Andrew Johnson, the Blacks, and Reconstruction.* Knoxville, Tenn., 1975.

———.*Lincoln's Decision for Emancipation.* Philadelphia, New York, and Toronto, 1975.

———.*The Radical Republicans: Lincoln's Vanguard for Racial Justice.* New York, 1969.

Tregle, Joseph G., Jr. "Thomas J. Durant, Utopian Socialism, and the Failure of Presidential Reconstruction in Louisiana," *Journal of Southern History*, XLV (Nov. 1979), 485–512.

Trelease, Allen W. "Republican Reconstruction in North Carolina: A Roll-Call Analysis of the State House of Representatives, 1868–70," *Journal of Southern History*, XLII (Aug. 1976), 319–44.

———.*White Terror: The Ku Klux Klan Conspiracy and Southern Reconstruction.* New York, 1971.

———."Who Were the Scalawags," *Journal of Southern History*, XXIX (Nov. 1963), 445–68.

U.S. Attorney General. *Annual Reports.*

———.*Official Opinions.*

U.S. Commission on Civil Rights. *The Federal Civil Rights Enforcement Effort: A Report.* Washington, D.C., 1970.

———.*The Federal Civil Rights Enforcement Effort: One Year Later.* Washington, D.C., 1971.

———.*The Unfinished Business: Twenty Years Later: A Report Submitted to the U.S. Commission on Civil Rights by its Fifty-one State Advisory Committees,* Sept. 1977.

———.*The Voting Rights Act: Ten Years Later: A Report.* Washington, D.C., 1975.

Vecchio, Giorgio del. *Justice, An Historical and Philosophical Essay.* Edinburgh, 1952.

Vincent, Charles. *Black Legislators in Louisiana during Reconstruction*. Baton Rouge, La., 1976.

Wagley, Charles. *An Introduction to Brazil*. New York and London, 1963.

Wallerstein, Immanuel. "Dependence in an Interdependent World: The Limited Possibilities of Transformation within the Capitalist World Economy," *African Studies Review*, XVII (Apr. 1974), 1–26.

———.*The Modern World System: Capitalist Agriculture and the Origins of the European World Economy in the Sixteenth Century*. New York, 1976.

———."The Rise and Future Demise of the World Capitalist System: Concepts for Comparative Analysis," *Comparative Studies in Society and History*, XVI (Sept. 1974), 387–415.

War of the Rebellion: Official Records of the Union and Confederate Armies. 128 vols. Washington, D.C., 1880–1901.

Warriner, Doreen. *The Economics of Peasant Farming*. New York, 1965.

———.*Land Reform in Principle and Practice*. Oxford, 1969.

Welch, Richard E., Jr. "The Federal Elections Bill of 1890: Postscript and Prelude," *Journal of American History*, LII (Dec. 1965), 511–26.

Welles, Gideon. *Civil War and Reconstruction: Selected Essays*. Compiled by Albert Mordell, New York, 1959.

Wharton, Vernon L. *The Negro in Mississippi, 1865–1890*. Chapel Hill, N.C., 1947.

Wiener, Jonathan M. "Class Structure and Economic Development in the American South, 1865–1955," *American Historical Review*, LXXXIV (Oct. 1979), 970–1006.

———. *Social Origins of the New South: Alabama, 1860–1885*. Baton Rouge, La., 1978.

Wiggins, Sarah W. *The Scalawag in Alabama Politics, 1865–1881*. University, Ala., 1977.

Williamson, Joel. *After Slavery: The Negro in South Carolina During Reconstruction, 1861–1877*. Chapel Hill, N.C., 1965.

Winters, Donald L. *Farmers Without Farms: Agricultural Tenancy in Nineteenth-Century Iowa*. Westport, Conn., 1978.

Woodman, Harold D. *King Cotton and His Retainers: Financing and Marketing the Cotton Crop of the South, 1800–1925*. Lexington, Ky., 1968.

———,"Post-Civil War Southern Agriculture and the Law," *Agricultural History*, LIII (Jan. 1979), 319–37.

——,"Sequel to Slavery: The New History Views the Postbellum South," *Journal of Southern History*, XLII (Nov. 1977), 523–54.

Woodward, C. Vann. *Origins of the New South, 1877–1913*. Baton Rouge, La., 1951.

——."Yes, There was a Compromise of 1877," *Journal of American History*, LX (June 1973), 215–23.

Wright, Gavin. "Cotton Competition and the Post-Bellum Recovery of the American South," *Journal of Economic History*, XXXIV (Sept. 1974), 610–35.

——."Freedom and the Southern Economy," *Explorations in Economic History*, XVI (Jan. 1979), 90–108.

——."One Kind of Freedom," *The Civil Liberties Review*, May/June 1978, pp. 47–50.

——.*The Political Economy of the Cotton South: Households, Markets, and Wealth in the Nineteenth Century*. New York, 1978.

Yearns, Wilfred B. *The Confederate Congress*. Athens, Ga., 1960.

Zilversmit, Arthur. *Lincoln on Black and White*. Belmont, Calif., 1971.

Zornow, William F. *Lincoln and the Party Divided*. Norman, Okla. 1954.

MANUSCRIPTS

American Freedmen's Inquiry Commission Papers. Houghton Library, Harvard University.

American Freedmen's Inquiry Commission Records. Microfilm 619, National Archives.

Nathaniel P. Banks Papers. Library of Congress.

Blagden Papers. Houghton Library, Harvard University.

Bureau of Refugees, Freedmen, and Abandoned Lands. Record Group 105, National Archives.

Salmon P. Chase Papers. Historical Society of Pennsylvania.

Salmon P. Chase Papers. Library of Congress.

Henry L. Dawes Papers. Library of Congress.

Thomas J. Durant Papers. New York Historical Society.

Edward H. Durell Papers. New York Historical Society.

Andrew Johnson Papers. Library of Congress. Originals and Microfilm edition, 1961.

Abraham Lincoln Papers. Library of Congress. Microfilm edition, 1959.
Minute Book of the General Committee of the Union Associations (New Orleans). New York Historical Society.
Whitelaw Reid Papers. Library of Congress.
Smith-Brady Commission Reports. Record Group 94, National Archives.
Charles Sumner Papers. Houghton Library, Harvard University.
U.S. Direct Tax Commission for South Carolina Records. National Archives.
U.S. Treasury Department, Special Agency Records. Record Group 366, National Archives.
Banjamin F. Wade Papers. Library of Congress.
Emily E. Weems Collection. Louisiana State Museum.

NEWSPAPERS

Black Republican (New Orleans)
Boston *Commonwealth*
Boston *Daily Journal*
Daily True Delta (New Orleans)
Liberator
National Anti-Slavery Standard
New Orleans *Era*
New Orleans *Times*
New Orleans *Tribune*
New York *Evening Post*
New York *Times*
New York *Tribune*

Index